I0011585

FORWARD/COMMENTARY

The National Institute of Standards and Technology (NIST) is a measurement standards laboratory, and a non-regulatory agency of the **United States Department of Commerce**. Its mission is to promote innovation and industrial competitiveness. Founded in 1901, as the National Bureau of Standards, NIST was formed with the mandate to provide standard weights and measures, and to serve as the national physical laboratory for the United States. With a world-class measurement and testing laboratory encompassing a wide range of areas of computer science, mathematics, statistics, and systems engineering, NIST's cybersecurity program supports its overall mission to promote U.S. innovation and industrial competitiveness by advancing measurement science, standards, and related technology through research and development in ways that enhance economic security and improve our quality of life.

The need for cybersecurity standards and best practices that address interoperability, usability and privacy has been shown to be critical for the nation. NIST's cybersecurity programs seek to enable greater development and application of practical, innovative security technologies and methodologies that enhance the country's ability to address current and future computer and information security challenges.

The cybersecurity publications produced by NIST cover a wide range of cybersecurity concepts that are carefully designed to work together to produce a holistic approach to cybersecurity primarily for government agencies and constitute the best practices used by industry. This holistic strategy to cybersecurity covers the gamut of security subjects from development of secure encryption standards for communication and storage of information while at rest to how best to recover from a cyber-attack.

Why buy a book you can download for free?

Some are available only in electronic media. Some online docs are missing pages or barely legible.

We at 4th Watch Books are former government employees, so we know how government employees actually use the standards. When a new standard is released, an engineer prints it out, punches holes and puts it in a 3-ring binder. While this is not a big deal for a 5 or 10-page document, many NIST documents are over 100 pages and printing a large document is a time-consuming effort. So, an engineer that's paid $75 an hour is spending hours simply printing out the tools needed to do the job. That's time that could be better spent doing engineering. We publish these documents so engineers can focus on what they were hired to do – engineering. It's much more cost-effective to just order the latest version from Amazon.com

If there is a standard you would like published, let us know. Our web site is Cybah.webplus.net

Please see the Cybersecurity Standards list at the end of this book.

CyberSecurity Standards Library™

Get a Complete Library of Over 300 Cybersecurity Standards on 1 Convenient DVD!

The **4th Watch CyberSecurity Standards Library** is a DVD disc that puts over 300 current and archived cybersecurity standards from NIST, DOD, DHS, CNSS and NERC at your fingertips! Many of these cybersecurity standards are hard to find and we included the current version and a previous version for many of them. The DVD includes four books written by Luis Ayala: **The Cyber Dictionary, Cybersecurity Standards, Cyber-Security Glossary of Building Hacks and Cyber-Attacks**, and **Cyber-Physical Attack Defenses: Preventing Damage to Buildings and Utilities**.

- ✓ DVD includes many Hard-to-find Cybersecurity Standards - some still in Draft.
- ✓ Docs are organized by source and listed numerically so each standard is easy to locate.
- ✓ The listing of standards on the DVD includes an abstract of the subject, and date issued.
- ✓ PDF format for use on PC, Mac, eReaders, or tablets.
- ✓ No need for WiFi / Internet.
- ✓ Save countless hours of searching and downloading.
- ✓ Carry in a briefcase - terrific for travel.

4th Watch Publishing is releasing the CyberSecurity Standards Library DVD to make it easier for you to access the tools you need to ensure the security of your computer networks and SCADA systems. We also publish many of these standards on demand so you don't need to waste valuable time searching for the latest version of a standard, printing hundreds of pages and punching holes so they can go in a three-ring binder. **Order on Amazon.com**

The DVD works on PC and Mac with the standards in PDF format. To view the CyberSecurity Standards Library on the DVD, a computer with a DVD drive is required. The most current version of your internet browser, at least 2GB of RAM, and current version of Adobe Reader is recommended. (Compatible browsers include Internet Explorer 8+, Mozilla Firefox 4+, Apple Safari 5+, Google Chrome 15+)

NISTIR 7628 Revision 1

Guidelines for Smart Grid Cybersecurity

Volume 2 - Privacy and the Smart Grid

**The Smart Grid Interoperability Panel –
Smart Grid Cybersecurity Committee**

http://dx.doi.org/10.6028/NIST.IR.7628r1

National Institute of
Standards and Technology
U.S. Department of Commerce

NISTIR 7628 Revision 1

Guidelines for Smart Grid Cybersecurity

Volume 2 - Privacy and the Smart Grid

The Smart Grid Interoperability Panel–
Smart Grid Cybersecurity Committee

This publication is available free of charge from:
http://dx.doi.org/10.6028/NIST.IR.7628r1

September 2014

U. S. Department of Commerce
Penny Pritzker, Secretary

National Institute of Standards and Technology
Willie May, Acting Under Secretary of Commerce for Standards and Technology and Acting Director

National Institute of Standards and Technology Interagency Report 7628 Rev. 1, Vol. 2
190 pages (September 2014)

Comments on this publication may be submitted to:
National Institute of Standards and Technology
Attn: Computer Security Division, Information Technology Laboratory
100 Bureau Drive (Mail Stop 8930) Gaithersburg, MD 20899-8930
Email: NISTIR.7628.Rev1@nist.gov

Reports on computer systems technology

The Information Technology Laboratory (ITL) at the National Institute of Standards and Technology (NIST) promotes the U.S. economy and public welfare by providing technical leadership for the Nation's measurement and standards infrastructure. ITL develops tests, test methods, reference data, proof of concept implementations, and technical analyses to advance the development and productive use of information technology. ITL's responsibilities include the development of management, administrative, technical, and physical standards and guidelines for the cost-effective security and privacy of other than national security-related information in Federal information systems.

Abstract

This three-volume report, *Guidelines for Smart Grid Cybersecurity*, presents an analytical framework that organizations can use to develop effective cybersecurity strategies tailored to their particular combinations of smart grid-related characteristics, risks, and vulnerabilities. Organizations in the diverse community of smart grid stakeholders—from utilities to providers of energy management services to manufacturers of electric vehicles and charging stations—can use the methods and supporting information presented in this report as guidance for assessing risk and identifying and applying appropriate security requirements. This approach recognizes that the electric grid is changing from a relatively closed system to a complex, highly interconnected environment. Each organization's cybersecurity requirements should evolve as technology advances and as threats to grid security inevitably multiply and diversify.

Keywords

advanced metering infrastructure; architecture; cryptography; cybersecurity; electric grid; privacy; security requirements; smart grid

ACKNOWLEDGMENTS

This privacy volume was developed by members of the Smart Grid Interoperability Panel (SGIP) Smart Grid Cybersecurity Committee (SGCC) (formerly the Cyber Security Working Group (CSWG)) Privacy Subgroup. The members of the SGCC Privacy Subgroup come from a wide range of organizations, including some with energy expertise, some with utilities expertise, some with privacy expertise, and some with government expertise, to name just a few of the primary perspectives represented. Special thanks are extended to some of the long-time group members who made exceptional contributions their time and expertise to the group's work products over the years.

- Rebecca Herold (CEO of the Privacy Professor® and Partner, Compliance Helper) has led the SGIP-CSWG Privacy Group since June, 2009. As part of the group activities Rebecca also led the first ever smart grid privacy impact assessment (PIA) in July and August, 2009. She also was an active member of the sub-teams.
- Tanya Brewer of NIST has been the NIST sponsor of the group during this entire time, in addition to being an integral and highly active member of the group, actively contributing to all the sub-teams, coordinating logistics for group meetings, providing insights for scoping issues, along with being the lead editor of this report.
- Amanda Stallings (Ohio Public Utilities Commission (PUC)), has provided extensive time participating in the group's sub-teams, taking meeting notes, and leading a sub-team.
- Brent Struthers (NeuStar) has provided extensive time participating in the group's sub-teams, hosting face-to-face meetings, and leading multiple sub-teams.
- Christine Hertzog (CEO of the Smart Grid Library) has provided extensive time leading the Privacy Use Cases sub-team for the last 2 ½ years of the group's work.
- Sarah Cortes (President, Inman Technology) has provided extensive time leading the sub-team that created, and then updated, the privacy laws section of the report, in addition to being part of the privacy use cases team for 2 ½ years.
- Various representatives of Southern Company contributed significant time and effort during the revision phase of this document and the final development of the privacy use cases.
- We also had some significant contributions from group members for specific topical discussions we've covered over the past three years, with particularly valuable input from Ken Wacks (GridWise Architecture Council), Timothy Schoechle (Smarthome Laboratories, Ltd.), Megan Hertzler (Xcel Energy), and Chris Villarreal (California Public Utilities Commission).

The dedication and commitment of all these individuals over the past four years is significant. In addition, appreciation is extended to all the other group members and various organizations that have committed resources to supporting this endeavor. Members of the CSWG Privacy Subgroup are listed in Appendix K of this report (with the other members of the SGCC). Finally, appreciation and acknowledgment is extended to all the other individuals who have contributed their time and knowledge to ensure this report addresses the privacy needs of the smart grid.

TABLE OF CONTENTS

LIST OF FIGURES

LIST OF TABLES

CHAPTER 5
PRIVACY AND THE SMART GRID

The smart grid is an evolving construct of new technologies, services, and entities integrating with legacy solutions and organizations. The Smart Grid Cybersecurity Committee (SGCC)[1] Privacy Subgroup views the privacy chapter as a starting point for continuing the work to improve upon privacy practices as the smart grid continues to evolve and as new privacy threats, vulnerabilities and associated risks emerge. Conformance with technical standards does not necessarily result in adequate protections for customer privacy. Privacy is driven by business practices that are supported, but not directed, by technology.

The information in this chapter was developed as a consensus document by a diverse subgroup consisting of representatives from the privacy, electric energy, telecommunications and cyber industry, academia, and government organizations. The chapter does not represent legal opinions, but rather was developed to explore privacy concerns, and provide associated recommendations for addressing them. NISTIR 7628 does not prescribe public policy with respect to privacy issues. It does, however, explain how technology (such as security tools, e.g., encryption, authorization, and authentication) and internal privacy practices can either enhance or lead to compromises of customer privacy, such as a data breach. Technology choices can complement privacy policies. Privacy impacts and implications may change as the smart grid expands and matures. This chapter addresses residential users and their data. The SGCC Privacy Subgroup will continue to deliver updates to existing work to address any new privacy considerations based on the pace of smart grid evolution.

CHAPTER ABSTRACT

The smart grid brings with it many new data collection, communication, and information sharing capabilities related to energy usage that introduce concerns about privacy. *Privacy* relates to individuals. Four dimensions of privacy are considered: (1) *personal information*— any information relating to an individual, who can be identified, directly or indirectly, by that information and in particular by reference to an identification number or to one or more factors specific to his or her physical, physiological, mental, economic, cultural, locational or social identity; (2) *personal privacy*—the right to control the integrity of one's own body; (3) *behavioral privacy*—the right of individuals to make their own choices about what they do and to keep certain personal behaviors from being shared with others; and (4) *personal communications privacy*—the right to communicate without undue surveillance, monitoring, or censorship.

Most smart grid entities directly address the first dimension, because privacy of personal information is what most data protection laws and regulations cover. However, the other three dimensions are important privacy considerations as well and should be considered by smart grid entities.

---

[1] The SGIP transitioned to a member-funded non-profit organization in January 2013 and the CSWG was renamed the Smart Grid Cybersecurity Committee (SGCC). For information on the new SGIP organization, see: http://www.sgip.org.

When considering how existing laws may deal with privacy issues within the smart grid—and likewise the potential influence of other laws that explicitly apply to the smart grid—it is important to note that while smart grid privacy concerns may not be expressly addressed, existing laws and regulations may still be applicable. Nevertheless, the innovative technologies of the smart grid pose new issues for protecting consumers' privacy that will have to be tackled by law or by other means.

The smart grid will greatly expand the amount of data that can be monitored, collected, aggregated, and analyzed. This expanded information, particularly from energy consumers and other individuals, raises added privacy concerns. For example, specific appliances and generators may potentially be identified from the signatures they exhibit in electric information at the meter when collections occur with greater frequency, unlike traditional monthly meter readings or smart meter readings that occur once an hour or less frequently.[2] This more detailed information expands the possibility of intruding on consumers' and other individuals' privacy expectations.

The research behind the material presented in this chapter focused on privacy within personal dwellings and electric vehicles and did not address business premises and the privacy of individuals within such premises. The researchers' conclusions about privacy risks and issues based upon work in these primary areas are as follows:

- Evolving smart grid technologies and associated new types of information related to individuals, groups of individuals, and their behavior within their premises and electric vehicles may pose privacy risks and challenges that have not been tested and may or may not be mitigated by existing laws and regulations.

- New smart grid technologies, particularly smart meters, smart appliances, and similar types of endpoints, create new privacy risks and concerns that may not be addressed adequately by the existing business policies and practices of utilities and smart grid-related Third Parties.

- Utilities and third-parties providing smart grid products and services need to follow standard privacy and information security practices to effectively and consistently safeguard the privacy of personal information.

- Many consumers may not understand their privacy exposures or their options for mitigating those exposures within the smart grid.

- The consequences of a data breach not only affect the customers whose data may fall into the wrong hands, but may also be costly to smart grid entities. These entities may incur costs to restore the data, to provide compensation such as free credit monitoring for affected customers, to pay any court-awarded damages, and to repair a diminished reputation and loss of corporate good will.

- Privacy protection designed into a system is preferable to a privacy patch or "bolted on" in an attempt to remedy a limitation or omission.

Based on research and the details of the associated findings, a high-level summary listing of all recommendations includes the following points for entities that participate within the smart grid:

---

[2] K.C. Armel, A. Gupta, G. Shrimali, G., and A. Albert, "Is Disaggregation The Holy Grail of Energy Efficiency? The Case of Electricity," *Energy Policy* 52, January 2013, pp. 213-234. http://dx.doi.org/10.1016/j.enpol.2012.08.062.

- Conduct pre-installation processes and activities for using smart grid technologies with the most transparency possible.

- Conduct an initial privacy impact assessment to understand the current strategy and baseline of privacy risks and benefits before making the decision to invest in and/or install advanced technologies in support of the smart grid. Additional privacy impact assessments should be conducted following significant organizational, systems, applications, or legal changes—and particularly, following privacy breaches and information security incidents involving personal information, as an alternative, or in addition, to an independent audit.

- Develop and document privacy policies and practices that are drawn from the full set of Organisation for Economic Cooperation and Development (OECD) Privacy Principles and other authorities (see §5.4 "Consumer-to-Utility PIA Basis and Methodology"). This should include establishing responsibilities for personnel for ensuring privacy policies and protections are implemented.

- Provide regular privacy training and ongoing awareness communications and activities to all workers who have access to personal information within the smart grid.

- Develop privacy use cases that track data flows containing personal information to address and mitigate common privacy risks that exist for business processes within the smart grid.

- Establish processes for de-identifying energy usage data when using aggregated data for activities beyond energy operations for individual customers.

- Educate, through various sources and entities, consumers and other individuals about the privacy risks within the smart grid and what they can do to mitigate them.

- Establish privacy protections for Third Party access to customer energy usage data, in addition to privacy protections related to the commissioning, registration, and enrollment of smart devices with Third Parties.

- Establish information security and privacy protection for wireless transmissions.

- Specific solutions or mitigations for potential electric vehicles/plug-in electric vehicles/plug-in hybrid electric vehicles (generalized as PEVs in this report) privacy issues will need to be explored as technology solutions are deployed going forward. System and infrastructure architects and engineers should, in the meantime, stay aware of potential issues.

- Share information with other smart grid market participants concerning solutions to common privacy-related risks.

Additionally, manufacturers and vendors of smart meters, smart appliances, and other types of smart devices, should engineer these devices to collect only the data necessary for the purposes of the smart device operations. The defaults for the collected data should be established to use and share the data only as necessary to allow the device to function as advertised and for the purpose(s) agreed to by smart grid consumers.

5.1. INTRODUCTION

Modernization of the current electric grid through increasing computerization and networking of intelligent components holds the promise of a smart grid infrastructure that can—

- Deliver electricity more efficiently;

- Provide better power quality;

- Link with a wide array of electricity resources in addition to energy produced by power plants (such as renewable energy sources);

- Maintain better reliability in the form of faster and more efficient outage detection and restoration;

- Enable self-healing in cases of disturbance, physical and cyber attack, or natural disaster; and

- Provide customers, and other consumers,[3] with more choices based on how, when, and how much electricity they use.

Communications technology that enables the bidirectional flow of information throughout the infrastructure is at the core of these smart grid improvements, which rely upon energy usage data provided by smart meters, sensors, computer systems, and many other devices to derive understandable and actionable information for consumers and utilities—and it is this same technology that also brings with it an array of privacy challenges. The granularity, or depth and breadth of detail, captured in the information collected and the interconnections created by the smart grid are factors that contribute most to these new privacy concerns.

The SGCC/CSWG has worked since June 2009 to research privacy issues within the existing and planned smart grid environment. Its research to date has focused on privacy concerns related to consumers' personal dwellings and use of electric vehicles.[4] In July and August of 2009, the Privacy Subgroup performed a comprehensive privacy impact assessment (PIA) for the consumer-to-utility portion of the smart grid, and the results of this study, along with subsequent research activities, have enabled the group to make the recommendations found in this chapter for managing the identified privacy risks.

The Privacy Subgroup membership is derived from a wide range of organizations and industries, including utilities, state utility commissions, privacy advocacy groups, academia, smart grid appliance and applications vendors, information technology (IT) engineers, government agency representatives, and information security (IS) practitioners. This diversity of disciplines and areas of interest among the group's participants helps to ensure all viewpoints are considered when looking at privacy issues, and it brought a breadth of expertise both in recognizing inherent

---

[3] Because customers are often thought of as the individuals who actually pay the energy bills, the SGIP-CSWG Privacy Subgroup determined it was important to include reference to all individuals who would be within a particular dwelling or location since their activities could also be determined in the ways described within this chapter. From this point forward, for brevity, only the term "consumers" will be used, but it will mean all consumers applicable to the situation being described.

[4] This document does not address potential privacy concerns for individuals within business premises, such as hotels, hospitals, and office buildings, in addition to privacy concerns for transmitting smart grid data across country borders. This document in some areas addresses small businesses that would only have one meter and a very small number of employees. This group has previously identified additional potential privacy issues at http://collaborate.nist.gov/twiki-sggrid/pub/SmartGrid/CSCTGPrivacy/Smart_Grid_Privacy_Groupings_Nov_10_2010_v6.7.xls.

privacy risk areas and in identifying feasible ways in which those risks might be mitigated while at the same time supporting and maintaining the value and benefits of the smart grid.

Because this chapter will be read by individuals with a wide range of interests, professional fields, and levels of expertise with respect to smart grid privacy issues, careful consideration has been given to the chapter's structure, which is as follows:

1. **Discussion of the concept of privacy**. This establishes our common ground in understanding the notion of "privacy," and defines the notion of privacy, where readers may hold different viewpoints on the subject.

2. **Definitions of privacy terms**. Privacy terms are defined differently among various industries, groups, countries, and even individuals. The privacy terms used in this chapter are defined in Appendix G.

3. **Overview of current data protection laws and regulations with respect to privacy**. Even though numerous laws exist to establish a range of privacy protections, it is important to consider how those privacy protections apply to the smart grid.

4. **Determination of personal activities within the smart grid**. This explains the creation of new data types in the smart grid, as well as new uses for data that has formerly only been in the possession of utilities, with the exception of retail choice states.[5]

5. **Summary of the consumer-to-utility PIA**. Identifies key privacy issues identified by the privacy subgroup in performing its PIA for the consumer-to-utility portion of the smart grid and provides a guide for subsequent research.

6. **In-depth look at privacy issues and concerns**. Addresses follow-on research based on the PIA findings in which the privacy subgroup explored the broader privacy issues that exist within the entire expanse of the smart grid.

7. **Smart grid data accessed by Third Parties**. Provides privacy protections that organizations who deal directly with energy consumers should implement.

8. **Plug-in electric and plug-in hybrid electric vehicles privacy concerns**. Identifies potential privacy issues and risks related to plug-in electric vehicle communications and provides approaches to mitigate risks.

9. **Smart grid privacy awareness and training**. Explains why providing privacy training and awareness communications to employees and energy consumers is important, and provides links to training slides created to provide train-the-trainer education for those who will be providing smart grid privacy training sessions and modules.

10. **Mitigating privacy concerns with the smart grid and privacy use cases**. Provides a discussion and overview of some existing privacy risk mitigation standards and frameworks. Also includes a description of some methods that can be used to mitigate privacy risks, and points to privacy use cases the group created to help smart grid architects and engineers build privacy protections into the smart grid. The privacy use cases were created by expanding the current collection of SGCC use cases to cover all smart grid value chain participants, in addition to regulated and non-regulated utilities,

---

[5] "Retail choice states" refers to those states allowing electricity customers the ability to choose their electricity supplier from a variety of electricity service competitors.

that will offer smart grid-related products and services. Developers of smart grid applications, systems, and operational processes can employ a more comprehensive set of privacy use cases, utilizing these cases as a model, to create architectures that build in privacy protections to mitigate identified privacy risks.

11. **Emerging smart grid privacy risks.** Provides brief discussions of fifteen emerging smart grid privacy risks for which organizations and consumers should stay aware.

12. **Conclusions and recommendations**. This section summarizes the main points and findings on the subject of privacy and collects in one place all of the recommendations found within this Privacy Chapter.

13. **NIST privacy-related work.** Provides an overview of the National Strategy for Trustworthy Identities in Cyberspace (NSTIC) program and discusses the potential privacy impacts to the smart grid. This section also provides an overview of new NIST work in the area of privacy engineering.

14. **Appendices**. References and additional material.

5.2. WHAT IS PRIVACY?

There is not one universal, internationally accepted definition of "privacy;" it can mean many things to different individuals. At its most basic, privacy can be seen as the right to be left alone.[6] Privacy is not a plainly delineated concept and is not simply the specifications provided within laws and regulations. Furthermore, privacy should not be confused, as it often is, with being the same as confidentiality; and personal information[7] is not the same as confidential information. Confidential information[8] is information for which access should be limited to only those with a business need to know and that could result in compromise to a system, data, application, or other business function if inappropriately shared.[9]

Additionally, privacy can often be confused with security. Although there may be significant overlap between the two, they are also distinct concepts. There can be security without having privacy, but there cannot be privacy without security; it is one of the elements of privacy. Security involves ensuring the confidentiality, integrity, and availability of data. However, privacy goes beyond having proper authentication and similar security protections. It also addresses such needs as ensuring data is only used for the purpose for which it was collected and properly disposing of that data once it is no longer needed to fulfill that purpose.[10]

It is important to understand that privacy considerations with respect to the smart grid include examining the rights, values, and interests of *individuals*; it involves the related characteristics, descriptive information and labels, activities, and opinions of individuals, to name just a few

---

[6] S.D. Warren and L.D. Brandeis, "The Right to Privacy," *Harvard Law Review* IV(5), December 15, 1890, http://faculty.uml.edu/sgallagher/Brandeisprivacy.htm [accessed 8/11/2014].

[7] See a full definition and discussion of "personal information" in Appendix G.

[8] The use of the phrase "confidential information" in this document does not refer to National Security/classified information.

[9] For example, market data that does not include customer-specific details is considered confidential. Other chapters within this report address confidentiality in depth.

[10] For more on security protections or high-level security requirements, *see* Vol. 1, Chapter 3.

applicable considerations. Data privacy is impacted by the practices of customers who supply personal data and all entities that gather or handle that data.

For example, some have described privacy as consisting of four dimensions:[11]

1. **Privacy of personal information**. This is the most commonly thought-of dimension. Personal information is any information relating to an individual, who can be identified, directly or indirectly, by that information and in particular by reference to an identification number or to one or more factors specific to his or her physical, physiological, mental, economic, cultural, locational or social identity. Privacy of personal information involves the right to control when, where, how, to whom, and to what extent an individual shares their own personal information, as well as the right to access personal information given to others, to correct it, and to ensure it is safeguarded and disposed of appropriately.
2. **Privacy of the person**. This is the right to control the integrity of one's own body. It covers such things as physical requirements, health problems, and required medical devices.
3. **Privacy of personal behavior**. This is the right of individuals to keep any knowledge of their activities, and their choices, from being shared with others.
4. **Privacy of personal communications**. This is the right to communicate without undue surveillance, monitoring, or censorship.

Most smart grid entities directly address the first dimension, because most data protection laws and regulations cover privacy of personal information. However, the other three dimensions are important privacy considerations as well; thus dimensions 2, 3, and 4 should also be considered in the smart grid context because new types of energy use data may be created and communicated. For instance, unique electric signatures for consumer electronics and appliances could be compared against some common appliance usage profiles to develop detailed, time-stamped activity reports within personal dwellings. Charging station information might reveal the detailed whereabouts of an electric vehicle/plug-in electric vehicle/plug-in hybrid electric vehicle (generalized as PEVs in this report). This data did not exist before the application of smart grid technologies.[12]

The Privacy Subgroup looked at how the smart grid, and the data contained therein, could potentially be used to infringe upon or otherwise negatively impact individuals' privacy in the four identified dimensions and then sought ways to assist smart grid organizations in identifying and protecting the associated information. While many of the types of data items accessible through the smart grid are not new, there is now the possibility that other parties, entities or individuals will have access to those data items; and there are now many new uses for and ways to analyze the collected data, which may raise substantial privacy concerns. The reputation of an energy service provider might also be impacted by lapses in customer data privacy protection.

---

[11] *See* Roger Clarke, "What's Privacy?" (August 7, 2006) at http://www.rogerclarke.com/DV/Privacy.html. Clarke makes a similar set of distinctions between the privacy of the physical person, the privacy of personal behavior, the privacy of personal communications, and the privacy of personal data. Roger Clarke is a well-known privacy expert from Australia who has been providing privacy research papers and guidance for the past couple of decades.

[12] For instance, consider the enhanced ability the smart grid will give to determining a person's behavior within a premise through more granular energy usage data.

New energy usage data collected outside of smart meters, such as from home energy management systems, is also created through applications of smart grid technologies. As those data items become more specific and are made available to additional individuals, the complexity of the associated privacy issues increases as well.

The mission of the Privacy Subgroup is to recognize privacy concerns within the smart grid and to identify opportunities and recommendations for their mitigation. In addition, the group strives to clarify privacy expectations, practices, and rights with regard to the smart grid by—

- Identifying potential privacy problems and encouraging the use of relevant Fair Information Practice Principles;[13]

- Seeking input from representatives of smart grid entities and subject matter experts, and then providing guidance to the public on options for protecting the privacy of—and avoiding misuse of—personal information used within the smart grid. This guidance is included in this chapter; and

- Making suggestions and providing information to organizations, regulatory agencies, and smart grid entities in the process of developing privacy policies and practices that promote and protect the interests of both smart grid consumers and entities.

To meet this mission, this chapter explores the types of data within the smart grid that may place individuals' privacy at risk, and how the privacy risks related to the use, misuse, and abuse of energy usage data may increase as a result of this new, always-connected type of technology network.

Because "privacy" and associated terms mean many different things to different audiences, definitions for the privacy terms used within this chapter are found in Appendix G, and definitions for energy terms are included in Appendix J in Volume 3.

5.3. LEGAL FRAMEWORKS AND CONSIDERATIONS

Since this document was first published in 2010, the legislative frameworks, concepts, and themes have remained generally the same. However, additional smart grid-specific privacy laws and regulations have been passed.[14] Further, an increase[15] during this period in privacy threats

---

[13] Fair Information Practice Principles describe the manner in which entities using automated data systems and networks should collect, use, and safeguard personal information to assure their practice is fair and provides adequate information privacy protection. For more information, see §5.9.

[14] In Appendix C, we review at length an example process in which California and Colorado arrived at a legislative and regulatory outcome that may be of use to others in formulating legal and regulatory privacy approaches.

[15] For example, the threat of government surveillance and privacy considerations:

"Seeking Reporters Telephone Records Without Required Approvals", p. 89; "Inaccurate Statements to the Foreign Intelligence Surveillance Court," p. 122; "FBI Issues 11 Improper Blanket NSLs in May to October 2006," p. 165, et al, *A Review of the FBI's Use of Exigent Letters and Other Informal Requests for Telephone Records*, Oversight and Review Division, U.S. Department of Justice, Office of the Inspector General, January 2010. http://www.justice.gov/oig/special/s1001r.pdf [accessed 8/11/2014].

Department of Justice Statistics and reports to Congress on surveillance requests—http://www.justice.gov/criminal/foia/elect-read-room.html [accessed 8/11/2014].

Congressman Markey's Letters to cellphone carriers and their responses with statistical information—http://web.archive.org/web/20130702231920/http://markey.house.gov/content/letters-mobile-carriers-reagrding-use-cell-phone-tracking-law-enforcement [7/2/2013 web snapshot from the Internet Archive Wayback Machine; accessed 8/11/2014].

and public awareness of those threats adds a few considerations to the discussion of legal frameworks and privacy in the smart grid.

Utilities often store Social Security Numbers (SSNs) and financial account numbers in their payroll or billing systems and have been obligated to follow the associated legal requirements for safeguarding this data for many years. The sharing and storage capabilities that the smart grid network brings to bear creates the need to protect not only the items specifically named within existing laws, but in addition to protect energy usage data and associated personal information in ways that existing laws may or may not address.

Generally, privacy concerns include considerations related to the collection and use of energy consumption data. These considerations exist, unrelated to the smart grid, but smart grid aspects fundamentally change their impact.

5.3.1 General Privacy Issues Related to Smart Grid Data

The primary privacy issue related to the deployment of smart grid technologies is that the installation of advanced utility electric meters and associated devices and technology will result in the collection, transmittal and maintenance of personally identifiable data related to the nature and frequency of personal energy consumption and production in a more granular form. This concern arises when this type of data and extrapolations of this data are associated with individual consumers or locations.[16] Utilities have routinely collected energy consumption and personal billing data from customers for decades. The new privacy issues associated with advanced metering infrastructure are related to the behavioral inferences that can be drawn from the energy usage data collected by the meter at more granular frequencies and collected intervals. Additionally, smart meter data also raises potential surveillance issues relating to the methods by which the data is collected and transmitted (electronic collection transmittal rather than manual meter reading and compilation).

The ability to determine specific appliances or customer patterns depends on how often the meter is collecting information and what data the meter is collecting. Collecting energy usage data at more frequent intervals (rather than monthly meter reads using traditional meters) may enable one to infer more information about the activities within a dwelling or other premises than was available in the past.[17] At the time of this report, most residential smart meters in the United States are collecting either 15 minute interval or 1 hour interval consumption data.[18] The data that is measured is total consumption (kWh) during a particular period of time; the availability of

---

Google's disclosure of their own disclosures to law enforcement—http://www.google.com/transparencyreport/userdatarequests/ [accessed 8/11/2014].

Further primary sources of surveillance statistics—http://www.spyingstats.com/ [accessed 8/11/2014].

ACLU summary, "Cell Phone Location Tracking Public Records Request"—http://www.aclu.org/protecting-civil-liberties-digital-age/cell-phone-location-tracking-public-records-request [accessed 8/11/2014].

[16] For example, associating pieces of anonymized data with other publicly available non-anonymous data sets may actually reveal information about specific individuals. http://epic.org/privacy/reidentification/ [accessed 8/11/2014]

[17] Smart meter data are not read by the utility in real time, but are accumulated in the meter's memory. (The only exception is pre-pay meters so the customer can be warned when the power will be cut off.) Meters could be programmed to record energy every few seconds, but the internal memory would fill quickly unless the data are sent via the radio to the back office. Frequent data transmissions across a neighborhood area network would require sufficient bandwidth, which inherently has limitations. However, some smart meters can be programmed remotely, so it is possible the frequency of meter reading can be changed after the meter is installed.

[18] Per interviews with subject matter experts conducted at the time of drafting.

that total consumption data over a period of time, combined with the educated knowledge necessary to identify and analyze specific and/or unique appliance/equipment signatures contained within that more granular total consumption data, is what may enable a Third Party to identify particular appliances or usage patterns. The meter itself is only measuring consumption, and any ability to identify specific appliances or usage patterns would require the data to be compared or applied against a pre-determined set of usage patterns or portfolios; the data itself does not identify a specific appliance. The meter may be capable of collecting additional usage information, such as voltage or frequency, but the utility must enable the meter to measure it and make that data available to the utility, customer, or authorized Third Party.

In addition, although many smart meters come pre-equipped with a second radio in order to enable a Home Area Network (HAN), such meters are not necessarily paired with devices installed and located inside a premise by a customer or customer-authorized Third Party by default.[19] When authorized by the utility, the HAN would be allowed to continuously poll the smart meter and obtain data that could continually feed an in-home display with real-time meter information. The connection of a meter to a HAN simply allows for the data to be collected at more frequent intervals, but it is still limited to polling intervals dictated by the meter's technical capability and/or what the meter is set up to provide. If a HAN device is given the polling capabilities of a meter, there could be programs developed to poll a meter for its usage or other readings in a way that may have not been technically enabled by the utility in accordance with the customer's preferences. If so requested or required, one way to minimize the exposure to such programs is to enable all meters to push specific information to a paired HAN device or gateway based on an interval set by the utility or customer. The HAN operators would coordinate with the utility for the initial setup to pair the meter with the HAN using certificates or some form of mutual authentication. Once established, the customer or authorized Third Party would be required to alter the permissions granted to the HAN in order to actively request any additional data from the meter.

With the application of a HAN, it may be possible to access additional information, such as voltage or frequency readings in one-second increments and to identify a particular appliance through data disaggregation of those readings and profiles, provided the utility has activated that ability. Nevertheless, the ability to access this HAN-enabled data is dependent on both the utility enabling this ability and the customer installing the necessary technology. Access to meter data is dependent on the utility. Access to the HAN data is not usually dependent on the utility but rather on the customer's HAN device/system.

Using nonintrusive appliance load monitoring (NALM) techniques, interval energy usage at different time periods can be used to infer individual appliances' portions of energy usage by comparison to libraries of known patterns matched to individual appliances (for an example, see

---

[19] According to interviews with subject matter experts, in all the known U.S. deployments to date, the smart meter is the network coordinator. Because the smart meter is the network coordinator, for a HAN device to pair to the ZigBee Smart Energy network, the customer would need to provision the HAN device to the smart meter using unique device-specific keys, MAC ID and installation code. The provisioning process may vary depending on the particular smart meter implementation at each utility. For example, in the Texas market, customers, and authorized customer agents (retail electric providers and other Third Parties) are able to provision devices through the use of the Smart Meter Texas web portal. In other areas the provisioning process may be managed through utility-specific portals. Because the customer must first provision the HAN device to the smart meter, it is not currently possible for a HAN device to automatically join the associated smart meter network. And a smart meter that used the Zigbee Smart Energy Profile (SEP) cannot automatically join the customer HAN without the cooperation of the customer. It is important to note that a smart meter isn't necessary for a customer to have a HAN; it is only necessary if the customer wants to access the real-time feed from their associated smart meter.

Figure 5-1 and Figure 5-2). NALM techniques have many beneficial uses for managing energy usage and demand, including pinpointing loads for purposes of load balancing or increasing energy efficiency. However, such detailed information about appliance use has the potential to indicate whether a building is occupied or vacant, show residency patterns over time, and potentially reflect private details of people's lives and activities inside their homes.

The proliferation of smart appliances and devices from entities other than utilities throughout the smart grid means an increase in the number of devices that may generate data beyond the utility's metering and billing systems. This data may also be outside the utility's responsibility. The privacy issues presented by the increase in these smart appliances and devices on the consumer side of the meter are expanded if such appliances and devices transmit data outside of the HAN or energy management system (EMS) and do not have documented security requirements (e.g., a smart appliance being able to send data back to the manufacturer via telematics), thereby effectively extending the reach of the system beyond the walls of the premises. An additional consideration is that new Third Party entities may also seek to collect, access, and use energy usage data directly from customers, rather than from the utility (e.g., vendors creating energy efficiency or demand response applications and services specifically for smart appliances, smart meters, and other building-based solutions). The ability of the customer to understand these risks may require customers to be better educated and informed on the privacy consequences of decisions regarding these Third Party services. However, customer education is not the only method to address Third Party access challenges. There is also a need to develop guidance that both service providers and Third Parties can leverage to conduct privacy risk analyses and explore mitigation options, which may include establishing effective default privacy settings, clear user interfaces, improved educational outreach to ensure that customers are fully aware and consent to Third Parties' use of their information, and establishing or pointing to existing privacy standards for Third Parties to use.

An additional issue is that as smart grid technologies collect more detailed data about households, law enforcement requests to access that data for criminal investigations may include requests for this more detailed energy usage data, which heretofore has generally been neither of interest nor use to law enforcement. Law enforcement agencies have already used monthly electricity consumption data in criminal investigations. For example, in *Kyllo* v. *United States*, 533 U.S. 27 (2001), the government relied on monthly electrical utility records to develop its case against a suspected marijuana grower.[20]

Unlike the traditional energy grid, the smart grid may be viewed by some as carrying private and/or confidential electronic communications between utilities and end-users, possibly between utilities and Third Parties, and between end-users and Third Parties. Current law both protects private electronic communications and permits government access to real-time and stored communications, as well as communications transactional records, using a variety of legal processes.[21] Law enforcement agencies may have an interest in establishing or confirming presence at an address or location at a certain critical time, or possibly establishing certain

---

[20] *Kyllo* v. *United States*, 809 F. Supp. 787, 790 (D. Or. 1992), aff'd, 190 F.3d 1041 (9th Cir. 1999), rev'd, 533 U.S. 27 (2001), page 30. The Supreme Court opinion in this case focuses on government agents' use of thermal imaging technology. However, the district court decision discusses other facts in the case, including that government agents issued a subpoena to the utility for the suspect's monthly power usage records. For more, *see* §5.3.2.2.

[21] See, e.g., Electronic Communications Privacy Act, 18 U.S.C. § 2510. http://www.law.cornell.edu/uscode/18/usc_sup_01_18_10_I_20_119.html [accessed 8/11/2014].

activities within the home —information that may be readily obtained from energy usage data collected, stored, and transmitted by new, more granular smart grid technologies, such as a HAN that accesses a smart meter capable of a real-time feed. Accordingly, these types of situations regarding smart grid data warrant review and consideration in comparison to similar restrictions on law enforcement access to other personal and private information under existing constitutional and statutory privacy requirements.[22]

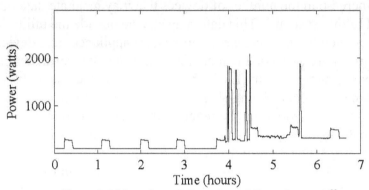

Figure 5-1 Meter Data Collected at 1 Minute Intervals[23]

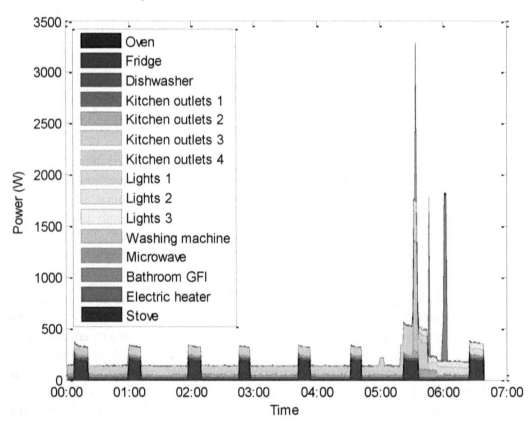

[22] For example *Kyllo* demonstrates that some subpoenas are illegal, whereas others are not. See also *Golden Valley*, p. 8. *See* footnote 26 for full reference for *Golden Valley*.

[23] O. Parson, S. Ghosh, M. Weal, and A. Rogers, "Non-intrusive Load Monitoring using Prior Models of General Appliance Types [extended abstract]," *1st International Workshop on Non-Intrusive Load Monitoring*, Pittsburgh, Pennsylvania, May 7, 2012, http://www.ices.cmu.edu/psii/nilm/abstracts/parson_Southampton_NILM2012_abstract.pdf [accessed 8/11/2014].

5.3.2 Existing Legal and Regulatory Frameworks

When considering the possible legal issues relating to smart grid privacy, it is important to note that general privacy laws currently in effect may or may not already apply to personal information generated by the smart grid even if the laws do not explicitly reference the smart grid (including unique smart grid data and/or technology). On the other hand, existing state-level smart grid and electricity delivery regulations may or may not explicitly reference privacy protections.

While it is uncertain how general privacy laws may or may not apply to energy usage data collected, stored, and transmitted by smart grid technologies, it is clear that the smart grid brings new challenges and privacy issues, which can lead to detailed information and additional insights about device usage, including medical devices and vehicle charging data that may be generated by new services and applications provided directly by third-parties to customers.[25] These new data items, and new uses of existing data may require additional study and public input to adapt to current laws or to shape new laws and regulations.

To understand the types of data items that may be protected within the smart grid by existing non-smart grid-specific privacy laws and regulations it is important to first consider some of the most prominent examples of existing laws and regulations that provide for privacy protection, which will be discussed in the following sections.

5.3.2.1 Overview of U.S. legal privacy protection approaches

There are generally four approaches in the U.S. to protecting privacy by law—

- **Constitutional Protections and Issues: General protections**. The First (freedom of speech), Fourth (search & seizure), Fifth (self-incrimination), and Fourteenth Amendments (equal protection), cover personal communications and activities.

- **Statutory, Regulatory and Case Law, both Federal and State**

- **Data-specific or technology-specific protections, including direct regulation of public utilities by state public utility commissions**. These protect specific information items such as credit card numbers and Social Security Numbers (SSN); or specific technologies such as phones or computers used for data storage or communication; or customer-specific billing and energy usage information used by public utilities to provide utility services. Other federal or state laws or regulations may apply privacy protections to information within the context of specific industries (e.g., Gramm-Leach-Bliley, Health Insurance Portability and Accountability Act (HIPAA), etc.).

- **Contractual and Agreement-related Protections and Issues: Specific protections**. These are protections specifically outlined within a wide range of business contracts, such as those between consumers and businesses.

---

[24] *Ibid.*

[25] For additional possible privacy concerns in different scenarios and settings, refer to the Privacy Subgroup's Privacy Matrix— http://collaborate.nist.gov/twikisggrid/pub/SmartGrid/CSCTGPrivacy/Smart_Grid_Privacy_Groupings_Nov_10_2010_v6.7.xls [accessed 8/11/2014].

Even though some states and public utilities commissions (PUCs) have laws and/or regulations in place to protect energy consumption data in some manner, some states, such as California and Colorado, have passed or implemented rules and regulations specifically focused on the energy consumption data produced by smart meters. Energy consumption patterns have historically not risen to the level of public concern given to financial or health data because (1) electric meters had to be physically accessed to obtain usage data directly from buildings, (2) the data showed energy usage over a longer time span such as a month and could not be analyzed to reveal usage by specific appliance, and (3) it was not possible or as easy for utilities to share this specific granular data in the ways that will now be possible with the smart grid. Public concerns for the related privacy impacts will likely change with implementation of the smart grid, because energy consumption data may reveal personal activities and the use of specific energy using or generating appliances[26], and because the data can be used or shared in ways that will impact privacy.

While some states have examined the privacy implications of the smart grid, most states had little or no documentation available for review by the Privacy Subgroup. Furthermore, enforcement of state privacy-related laws is often delegated to agencies other than PUCs, who have regulatory responsibility for electric utilities. However, state PUCs may be able to assert jurisdiction over utility privacy policies and practices because of their traditional jurisdiction and authority over the utility-retail customer relationship.[27]

5.3.2.2   Constitutional Protections and Considerations

Fourth Amendment Search and seizure considerations, Warrants and Subpoenas

Fourth Amendment provisions, pertaining to unreasonable search & seizure, have been applied to the ways government officials have attempted to obtain energy consumption data, although the ways in which utilities collect the data, such as through meters, is not at issue in such cases. In *Kyllo*, U.S. law enforcement's warrantless use of thermal imaging technology to monitor energy consumption was found to be an unlawful "search" under the Fourth Amendment.

How the Fourth Amendment might further apply to data collected about appliances and patterns of energy consumption, to the extent that energy usage data collected, stored, and transmitted by smart grid technologies reveals information about personal activities is yet to be determined.

Not all subpoenas, although issued by the US government and approved by a court, may be lawful. Higher courts have repeatedly found subpoenas issued by lower courts to be unlawful. Partially due to legal challenges to subpoenas, it may sometimes be unclear to smart grid service providers whether to comply with subpoenas or to appeal them to higher courts. This is a subject of the *Golden Valley*[28] decision.

---

[26] For more discussion on this, see §5.3.1

[27] For more information about how California and Colorado instituted their relevant rules, *see* Appendix C: Changing Regulatory Frameworks.

[28] *UNITED STATES OF AMERICA*, v. *GOLDEN VALLEY ELECTRIC ASSOCIATION*, Case No. 11-35195 (C.A. 9 2012), http://www.ca9.uscourts.gov/datastore/opinions/2012/08/07/11-35195.pdf [accessed 8/11/2014].

CALEA and Subpoenas (Data already collected and stored by Third Parties)

The Communications Assistance for Law Enforcement Act (CALEA) details how the U.S. government may obtain telecommunications and location data from telecommunications service providers through subpoenas without a Fourth Amendment violation. Under CALEA, the government may not compel Third Party communications service providers to collect data they would not otherwise collect. However, if they are already collecting and storing it, CALEA allows the government to compel them to hand it over. Thus, service providers must now consider carefully whether to collect "unnecessary" data which may seem interesting, but which may later expose consumers to privacy risks. It has not yet been determined by the courts if smart meters do or do not qualify as "telecommunications devices" for the purposes of CALEA.

Smart Grid Data Ownership

The legal ownership of smart grid energy data is the subject of much discussion. Various regulators and jurisdictions have treated the issue of who owns energy data differently. Data ownership is a very complex issue that may be viewed as a question of who should have what rights to the data. (e.g., right to control, right to exclude, etc.) These rights may be divided or shared among multiple entities. Alternatively, entities that have the ability to control or manage the data may have some responsibilities regarding the data, regardless of "ownership." Data ownership is an issue touched upon in the *Golden Valley* case discussed below under Case Law (§5.3.2.4).

National Security Letters

In 1994, an amendment to the Foreign Intelligence Surveillance Act of 1978 (FISA)[29] introduced National Security Letters ("NSLs"), broadening the government's scope in obtaining information relating to terrorist investigations without judicial oversight, in narrow circumstances. However, the power granted under FISA for these NSLs was significantly expanded in 2005. Since that time, constitutional challenges to NSLs have increased, again leaving "gray areas" when it comes to service providers' compliance.

Evidence and reporting of NSL abuse started in 2005, when the U.S. Department of Justice (DOJ) Inspector General's Office found widespread abuse. The *Washington Post* reported in 2010 that the "FBI illegally collected more than 2000 U.S. telephone call records," using methods that FBI general counsel Valerie Caproni admitted "technically violated the Electronic Communications in Privacy Act when agents invoked nonexistent emergencies to collect records."[30] The FBI admitted that "about half of the 4400 toll records collected in emergency situations... were done in technical violation of the law," and that "agents broadened their searches to gather numbers two and three degrees of separation from the original request." By October, 2013, 39 companies, including Google, Microsoft, Apple, Facebook, and Twitter, and 51 non-governmental organizations (NGOs), including the American Civil Liberties Union and Electronic Frontier Foundation (EFF), had signed a letter to President Obama protesting the gag NSLs ordered on their own and others' reporting, and urging

---

[29] *Foreign Intelligence Surveillance Act of 1978* ("FISA"; Pub.L. 95-511, 92 Stat. 1783, enacted October 25, 1978, 50 U.S.C. ch.36, S. 1566)

[30] J. Solomon and C. Johnson,"FBI broke law for years in phone record searches," *Washington Post*, January 19, 2010; A01 http://www.washingtonpost.com/wp-dyn/content/article/2010/01/18/AR2010011803982_pf.html [accessed 8/11/2014].

immediate and specific reforms.[31] "Basic information about how the government uses its various law enforcement–related investigative authorities has been published for years without any apparent disruption to criminal investigations," the letter noted. Recently, in March 2013, EFF won a landmark decision entitled *In Re National Security Letter* in the Northern District of California in which Judge Susan Illston declared one of the NSL statutes unconstitutional in its entirety.[32] It was noted that a judge may eliminate the gag order that an NSL carries only if they have "no reason to believe that disclosure may endanger the national security of the United States, interfere with a criminal counter-terrorism, or counterintelligence investigation, interfere with diplomatic relations, or endanger the life or physical safety of any person."[33] Most recently, several companies have been able to publish more accurate data on the number of NSLs and FISA court requests they have received in recent years, showing "a spike of affected accounts" between July and December 2012.[34]

5.3.2.3 U.S. Federal Privacy Laws and Regulations

U.S. federal privacy laws cover a wide range of industries and topics. It is currently not clear to what extent the following laws that provide privacy protections may apply, if at all, to the more revealing uses of consumer energy usage data that may be made possible by advanced smart grid technologies and identification techniques.[35]

- Healthcare: Examples include the Health Insurance Portability and Accountability Act (HIPAA) and the associated Health Information Technology for Economic and Clinical Health (HITECH) Act.

- Financial: Examples include the Gramm-Leach-Bliley Act (GLBA), the Fair Credit Reporting Act (FCRA), the Fair and Accurate Credit Transactions Act (FACTA), and the Equal Credit Opportunity Act (ECOA).

- Education: Examples include the Family Educational Rights and Privacy Act (FERPA) and the Children's Internet Protection Act (CIPA).

- Communications: Examples include the First Amendment to the U.S. Constitution, the Electronic Communications Privacy Act (ECPA), and the Telephone Consumer Protection Act (TCPA).

---

[31] "We, the undersigned, are writing to urge greater transparency around national security-related requests by the US government to Internet, telephone, and web-based service providers", July 18- September 30, 2013, https://www.cdt.org/files/pdfs/weneedtoknow-transparency-letter.pdf [accessed 8/11/2014].

[32] M. Zimmerman, "In Depth: The District Court's Remarkable Order Striking Down the NSL Statute," *Electronic Frontier Foundation* [Web site], March 18, 2013, https://www.eff.org/deeplinks/2013/03/depth-judge-illstons-remarkable-order-striking-down-nsl-statute [accessed 8/11/2014].

And see Hon. S. Illston, *"In Re National Security Letter,"* March 14, 2013, https://www.eff.org/sites/default/files/filenode/nsl_order_scan.pdf [accessed 8/11/2014].

[33] P. Elias, "National Security Letters Unconstitutional, Rules Judge," *The Huffington Post*, March 16, 2013, http://www.huffingtonpost.com/2013/03/16/national-security-letters_n_2892568.html [accessed 8/11/2014].

[34] S. Rosenblatt, "Tech firms reveal even more about FISA requests," *CNET*, February 3, 2014, http://news.cnet.com/8301-1009_3-57618266-83/tech-firms-reveal-even-more-about-fisa-requests/ [accessed 8/11/2014].

[35] As of May 28, 2013, there was only one adjudicated U.S. case related to privacy and energy usage data, *Friedman* v. *Maine PUC*.

- Government: Examples include the Privacy Act of 1974, the Computer Security Act of 1987, and the E-Government Act of 2002.

- Online Activities: Examples include the Controlling the Assault of Non-Solicited Pornography and Marketing (CAN-SPAM) Act and the Uniting and Strengthening America by Providing Appropriate Tools Required to Intercept and Obstruct Terrorism Act (USA PATRIOT Act, commonly known as the "Patriot Act").

- Privacy in the Home: Examples are the protections provided by the Fourth, Fifth, and Fourteenth Amendments to the U.S. Constitution.

- Employee and Labor Laws: Examples include the Americans with Disabilities Act (ADA) and the Equal Employment Opportunity (EEO) Act.

- General Business and Commerce: One example is Section 5 of the Federal Trade Commission Act, which prohibits unfair and deceptive practices, and has been used by the FTC to cover a wide variety of businesses.

5.3.2.4 State Privacy Laws and Regulations: Smart Grid-Specific

In 2012, according to the National Conference of State Legislatures,[36] "at least 13 states" (California, Illinois, Massachusetts, Maine, Michigan, New Hampshire, New Jersey, New York, Ohio, Oklahoma, Pennsylvania, Rhode Island and Vermont) took up consideration of 31 smart grid-specific bills. Several of these laws supplement pre-existing utility laws or regulations that already are intended to protected customer-specific information collected by utilities, such as billing and credit information, from unauthorized disclosure except where specifically required for purposes such as utility services, equal access by non-utility retail energy providers, or law enforcement pursuant to valid subpoenas.[37] The following seven States have enacted smart grid-specific privacy protection laws:

- California Senate Bill 1476 – customer data generated by smart meters is private and can only be shared with Third Parties upon consent of the customer, with the following exceptions: for basic utility purposes, at the direction of the California PUC, or to utility contractors implementing demand response, energy efficiency or energy management programs;

- Illinois S.B. 1652 - develop and implement an advanced smart grid metering deployment plan, which included the creation of a Smart Grid Advisory Council and H.B. 3036 Amended the smart grid infrastructure investment program and the Smart Grid Advisory Council;

- Maine H.B. 563 – directed the Public Utility Commission to investigate current cybersecurity and privacy issues related to smart meters;

---

[36] J. Pless, "2012 Smart Grid State Action," National Conference of State Legislatures [Web site], July 9, 2012, http://www.ncsl.org/research/energy/smart-grid-state-action-update.aspx [accessed 8/11/2014].

[37] See, e.g. California Public Utilities Commission Decision No. 11-07-056, Attachment B, "List of Current Statutes, Regulations, Decisions and Protocols Related to Customer Privacy Applicable to California Energy Utilities," July 28, 2011, http://docs.cpuc.ca.gov/PublishedDocs/PUBLISHED/GRAPHICS/140370.PDF [accessed 8/11/2014].

- New Hampshire - S.B. 266 prohibition on utility installation of smart meters without the property owners' consent. Utilities must disclose in writing the installation of a smart meter;

- Ohio S.B. 315 – encourages innovation and market access for cost effective smart grid programs and H.B. 331 – creates a Cybersecurity, Education and Economic Development Council to help improve state infrastructure for cybersecurity;

- Oklahoma Law H.B. 1079 – established the Electronic Usage Data Protection Act that directs utilities to provide customers with access to and protection of smart grid consumer data;

- Vermont S.B. 78 – promote statewide smart grid deployment and S.B. 214/Act 170 – directs the Public Utility Board to set terms and conditions for access to wireless smart meters. The law also requires consumers' written consent prior to smart meter installation and requires removal of smart meters upon request/cost-free opt-out of Smart Meters.

U.S. Case Law Relevant to the Smart Grid

Two U.S. cases have recently been decided applying to energy consumption data and evolving technology, joining *Kyllo*:

- *US* v. *Golden Valley*- US 9th Circuit[38] - 8/7/12

- *Friedman* v. *Maine PUC* - Supreme Court of Maine[39]- 7/12/12

In *Golden Valley*, a non-profit rural electric cooperative lost an appeal in the 9th Circuit federal court, and was required to comply with an administrative subpoena to provide consumer records pursuant to a DEA investigation. Golden Valley opposed the petition, primarily relying on a company policy of protecting the confidentiality of its members' records. The district court granted the petition to enforce the subpoena. Golden Valley complied but appealed the subpoena, which it felt was unlawful, on the grounds that it was:

- Irrelevant to the investigation;

- Inadequately following DEA and judicial oversight procedures; was an administrative subpoena with a lower burden of cause;

- Overbroad; and

- Violating 4th amendment search and seizure principles.

Golden Valley Electric Association argued that fluctuating energy consumption is "not unusual" in its area and so "not obviously relevant" to a drug crime. The Ninth Circuit rejected Golden Valley's arguments, upholding the district court order enforcing the subpoena. The Court referenced a view that consumers do not own their own energy consumption data. This view is based on the contract which consumer signs, allowing the utility use of the data. Other opinions, however, have disagreed with this approach, arguing it significantly erodes privacy. For

---

[38] See Footnote 26 for full citation.

[39] *ED FRIEDMAN et al.* v. *PUBLIC UTILITIES COMMISSION et al.*, PUC-11-532 (S. CT MAINE 2012), http://www.courts.state.me.us/opinions_orders/supreme/lawcourt/2012/12me90fr.pdf [accessed 8/11/2014].

example, earlier this year, Supreme Court Justice Sotomayor noted in her concurring opinion[40] in *United States* v. *Jones,* a case dealing with GPS data, that the elimination of privacy rights in information voluntarily turned over to Third Parties is "ill-suited for the digital age we live in today."

Although it ruled against Golden Valley, the 9th Circuit indicated a possible new legal approach. Specifically, the court said that in some circumstances "a company's guarantee to its customers that it will safeguard the privacy of their records might suffice to justify resisting an administrative subpoena."[41] The Court did note that the outcome might have been different if Golden Valley had entered into a contract with its customers specifically agreeing to keep such business records confidential.[42]

In 2012, the first court case discussing privacy in the context of the smart grid was tried in the Maine Supreme Court. In *Friedman*, the Maine Supreme Court partially invalidated the Maine Public Utilities Commission's ("Maine PUC") dismissal of plaintiff Friedman's objections to a Smart Meter opt-out penalty. First, the court rejected the Maine PUC's arguments that Friedman's health and safety concerns had been "resolved" by its opt-out investigations in another proceeding, because the Commission had explicitly declined in those proceedings to make any determination on health and safety -- instead deferring to the jurisdiction of the Federal Communications Commission (FCC). The court held the Maine PUC could not explicitly decline to make determinations on health and safety in the opt-out investigations proceedings, and then attempt to treat the issues as "resolved" in this proceeding. Having never determined whether the smart-meter technology is safe, it could not conclude whether the opt-out fee was "unreasonable or unjustly discriminatory."

Second, the Maine Supreme Court concluded that the Maine PUC had resolved the privacy, trespass, and Fourth Amendment claims against the utility, but did not state exactly how the Maine PUC concluded that was the case.

Finally, the Maine Supreme Court also affirmed that the plaintiffs' constitutional Fourth and Fifth Amendment claims brought against the Maine PUC were properly dismissed as without merit. Therefore, the Maine Supreme Court invalidated the portion of the Maine PUC's decision regarding health and safety, remanding it back to the Maine PUC for further proceedings to resolve that issue, and otherwise affirmed the rest of its decision.

5.3.2.5   Contractual Approaches and Issues Related to Consumer Agreements

Opt-Out Provisions

In response to both potential privacy and health concerns, some state legislatures and regulatory commissions have required that the customer be given the option to opt-out of smart meter implementation as part of a contract for service with a utility, or to have an installed smart meter

---

[40] *United States v. Jones*, 565 US ___, 132 S.Ct. 945 (2012), p. 3 (Justice Sotomayor's concurring opinion
  https://www.eff.org/node/69475, p.5).

[41] Golden Valley, 8922.

[42] Golden Valley, 8922.

removed.[43] Additionally, some utilities have voluntarily offered this option for their customers.[44] The *Friedman* case discussed above reviewed the procedural grounds for a Maine PUC decision regarding proposed opt-out provisions.

5.3.3 Applicability of Existing Data Protection Laws and Regulations to the Smart Grid

Personally identifiable information (PII) has no single, authoritative, legal definition. Fair Information Practice Principles (FIPPs) provide the most generally accepted, rather than legal, definition. However, as noted in above, there are a number of laws and regulations, each of which protects different specific types of information. A number of these were previously noted, such as HIPAA, which defines individually identifiable health information, arguably the widest definition by many organizations throughout the U.S. of what constitutes PII within the existing U.S. federal regulations. State attorneys general have pointed to HIPAA as providing a standard for defining personal information. In one case, the State of Texas has adopted the HIPAA requirements for protected health information to be applicable to all types of organizations, including all those based outside of Texas.[45] This is an example of how a federal law regarding one industry (i.e., healthcare) has been generally adopted at the state level as a law to protect the information of citizens (in this case, health information) regardless of the industry of organizations handling that information.

Private industry's definition of personally identifiable information predates legislation and is generally legally defined[46] in a two-step manner, as *x* data (e.g., SSN) in conjunction with *y* data (e.g., name.) This is the legal concept of "personally identifiable information" or PII.

For example, the Massachusetts breach notice law,[47] in line with some other state breach notice laws, defines the following data items as being personal information:

First name and last name or first initial and last name in combination with any one or more of the following:

---

[43] N.H. Rev. Ann. Stat. § 374:62 (prohibiting electric utilities from installing and maintaining smart meter gateway devices without a property owner's consent); Vt. Stat. Ann. tit. 30, § 8001 (requiring public service board to establish terms and conditions governing the installation of wireless smart meters). See also, Nev. P.S.C. Case 11-10007 (February 29, 2012) (adopting recommendation that Nevada Energy provide opt-out opportunity for residential customers); and Texas P.U.C. Case 40199 (May 17, 2012) (refusing to initiate rulemaking requiring opt-out options for smart meter deployment).

[44] See Cal. P.U.C. Case No. A. 11-03-014 (February 1, 2012) (approving Pacific Gas & Electric's SmartMeter program, allowing residential customers to opt-out of smart meter deployment); Pursuing the Smart Meter Initiative, Me. P.U.C. Docket No. 2010-345 (May 19, 2011) (approving Central Maine Power's customer opt-out program); P.S.B. Vt. Tariff 8317 (March 8, 2012) (approving Central Vermont Public Service Smart Power Wireless Meter Opt-Out tariff); and P.S.B. Vt. Tariff 9298 (March 8, 2012) (approving Green Mountain Power smart meter opt-out policy).

[45] For example, the Texas Appellate Court stated that the HIPAA Privacy rule applies to the entire State of Texas. See Abbott v. Texas Department of Mental Health and Mental Retardation for details, or refer to the discussion in P. MacKoul, "Impact of the Attorney General Opinion GA-0519 on Medical Information & HIPAA," 2007, http://www.hipaasolutions.org/white_papers/HIPAA%20Solutions,%20LC%20White%20Paper%20-Texas%20AG%20Opinion%20On%20Privacy%20And%20HIPAA.pdf [accessed 8/11/2014].

[46] For example, most of the U.S. state breach notice laws define personal information to be first name or first initial and last name in combination with any one or more of other specified data elements. See a listing of the laws, with links to the regulatory text, at "Security Breach Notification Laws" (National Conference of State Legislatures), http://www.ncsl.org/research/telecommunications-and-information-technology/security-breach-notification-laws.aspx, [accessed 8/11/2014].

[47] See text of the Massachusetts breach notice law, "An Act Relative to Security Freezes and Notification of Data Breaches," *Chapter 82*, 2007, http://www.mass.gov/legis/laws/seslaw07/sl070082.htm [accessed 8/11/2014].

- Social Security number;

- Driver's license number or state-issued identification card number; or

- Financial account number.

As noted at the outset of Section 5.3 above, businesses often store SSNs and financial account numbers in their payroll or billing systems. For instance, utilities have been obligated to follow the associated legal requirements for safeguarding this data for many years. For all organizations that handle energy usage data, the sharing and storage capabilities that the smart grid network brings to bear creates the need to protect not only the items specifically named within existing laws, but in addition to protect new types of personal information that are created using smart grid data.

There is also the possibility of utilities possessing new types of data as a result of the smart grid for which they have not to date been custodians. These new types of data may be protected by regulations from other industries that utilities did not previously have to follow. As revealed by the privacy impact assessment (PIA) found in Section 5.4, there may be a lack of privacy laws or policies directly applicable to the smart grid. Privacy subgroup research indicates that, in general, many state utility commissions currently lack formal privacy policies or standards related to the smart grid.[48] Comprehensive and consistent definitions of privacy-affecting information with respect to the smart grid typically do not exist at state or federal regulatory levels, or within the utility industry. However, existing privacy laws and regulations regarding consumer usage information may or may not be applicable to energy usage information related to smart grid technologies. These laws and regulations may not be applicable if a customer shares its information with organizations other than utilities.

5.4. CONSUMER-TO-UTILITY PRIVACY IMPACT ASSESSMENT

A PIA is a comprehensive process for determining the privacy, confidentiality, and security risks associated with the collection, use, and disclosure of personal information. PIAs also define the measures that may be used to mitigate and, wherever possible, eliminate the identified risks. The smart grid PIA activity provides a structured, repeatable analysis aimed at determining how collected data can reveal personal information about individuals or groups of individuals. The scope of the PIA can vary from the entire grid to a segment within the grid. Privacy risks may be addressed and mitigated by policies and practices that are instituted throughout the implementation, evolution, and ongoing management of the smart grid.

The Privacy Subgroup conducted a PIA for the consumer-to-utility portion of the smart grid during August and September 2009. In the months following the PIA, the group considered additional privacy impacts and risks throughout the entire smart grid structure.

The focus of the Privacy Subgroup has been on: (1) determining the types of information that may be collected or created that can then reveal information about individuals or activities within specific premises (primarily residential); (2) determining how these different types of information may be exploited; and (3) recommending business/organization information security and privacy policies and practices to mitigate the identified privacy risks. Entities of all types

---

[48] Most public utility commissions have significant customer privacy policies that predate the smart grid. It is not clear whether and to what extent these privacy policies would apply to smart grid data, or the extent to which they would need to be updated to reflect the new uses of smart grid data as they affect these traditional privacy issues.

that provide, use, or obtain data from the smart grid can also benefit from performing PIAs to determine privacy risks and then take action to mitigate those risks.

The following questions were identified and addressed in the process of performing the consumer-to-utility PIA and in the follow-on discussion of the findings:

1. What personal information may be generated, stored, transmitted, or maintained by components and entities that are part of the smart grid?

2. How is this personal information new or unique compared with personal information in other types of systems and networks?

3. How is the use of personal information within the smart grid new or different from the uses of the information in other types of systems and networks?

4. What are the new and unique types of privacy risks that may be created by smart grid components and entities?

5. What is the potential that existing laws, regulations, and standards apply to the personal information collected by, created within, and flowing through the smart grid components?

6. What could privacy practice standards look like for all entities using the smart grid so that following them could help to protect privacy and reduce associated risks?

5.4.1 Consumer-to-Utility PIA Basis and Methodology

In developing a basis for the consumer-to-utility PIA, the Privacy Subgroup reviewed the available documentation for use cases for the Advanced Metering Infrastructure (AMI)[49] and other published smart grid plans covering the interactions between the consumers of services and the providers of those services. The group also reviewed numerous data protection requirements and considered global information security and privacy protection laws, regulations, and standards to assemble the criteria against which to evaluate the consumer-to-utility aspects of smart grid operations. Taken into account were numerous U.S. federal data protection requirements and FIPPs, also often called "Privacy Principles," that are the framework for many modern privacy laws around the world. Several versions of the Fair Information Practice Principles have been developed through government studies, federal agencies, and international organizations.

For the purposes of this PIA, the group used the American Institute of Certified Public Accounts (AICPA) Generally Accepted Privacy Principles (GAPPs),[50] the Organisation for Economic Cooperation and Development (OECD) Privacy Principles, and information security management principles from the International Organization for Standardization (ISO) and

---

[49] *See* "AMI Systems Use Cases" at http://collaborate.nist.gov/twiki-sggrid/pub/SmartGrid/AugustWorkshop/All_of_the_Diagrams_in_one_document.pdf [accessed 8/11/2014].

[50] *See* D. Cornelius, "AICPA's Generally Accepted Privacy Principles," *Compliance Building* [Web site], January 9, 2009, http://www.compliancebuilding.com/2009/01/09/aicpas-generally-accepted-privacy-principles/ [accessed 8/11/2014].

International Electrotechnical Commission (IEC) Joint Technical Committee (JTC) *International Standard ISO/IEC 27001*[51] as its primary evaluation criteria:[52]

- The ten AICPA principles are entitled Management, Notice, Choice and Consent, Collection, Use and Retention, Access, Disclosure to Third Parties, Security for Privacy, Quality, and Monitoring and Enforcement.

- With respect to the *OECD Guidelines on the Protection of Privacy and Transborder Flows of Personal Data,*[53] the group's particular focus was on the *Annex to the Recommendation of the Council of 23rd September 1980: Guidelines Governing the Protection of Privacy and Transborder Flows of Personal Data,*[54] wherein paragraphs 7–14 of Part Two[55] outline the basic principles of national application, and on the "Explanatory Memorandum,"[56] wherein those principles are amplified (by paragraph number) in subsection II.B.[57] The enumerated OECD principles relate to Collection Limitation, Data Quality, Purpose Specification, Use Limitation, Openness, and Individual Participation.

- *International Standard ISO/IEC 27001* provides a model for establishing, implementing, operating, monitoring, reviewing, maintaining, and improving an Information Security Management System (ISMS).

The general privacy principles and ISMS described here and adopted for use in the PIA are designed to be applicable across a broad range of industries and are considered internationally to be best practices but are generally not mandatory. However, most privacy experts agree that data protection laws throughout the world have been built around the OECD privacy principles.[58][59]

---

[51] *See* International Standards Organization/International Electrotechnical Commission, *Information technology—Security techniques—Information security management system—Requirements,* ISO/IEC 27001:2013, http://www.iso.org/iso/home/store/catalogue_tc/catalogue_detail.htm?csnumber=54534 [accessed 8/11/2014].

[52] Since the PIA was conducted in 2009, more documents have been published that may be useful in conducting a PIA. Two of these are the Consumer Privacy Bill of Rights (Feb 2012) and NIST Special Publication 800-53 Revision 4 Appendix J (Apr 2013, including updates as of 1/15/2014).

[53] The *Guidelines* document has since been added to the OECD's 2013 Privacy Guidelines. *See* http://www.oecd.org/sti/ieconomy/privacy.htm#newguidelines [accessed 8/11/2014].

[54] *Id.* at http://www.oecd.org/document/18/0,3343,en_2649_34255_1815186_1_1_1_1,00.html#guidelines [accessed 8/11/2014].

[55] *Id.* at http://www.oecd.org/document/18/0,3343,en_2649_34255_1815186_1_1_1_1,00.html#part2 [accessed 8/11/2014].

[56] *Id.* at http://www.oecd.org/document/18/0,3343,en_2649_34255_1815186_1_1_1_1,00.html#memorandum [accessed 8/11/2014].

[57] *Id.* at http://www.oecd.org/document/18/0,3343,en_2649_34255_1815186_1_1_1_1,00.html#comments [accessed 8/11/2014].

[58] Per the *OECD Privacy Principles*, http://oecdprivacy.org/, "Internationally, the OECD Privacy Principles provide the most commonly used privacy framework, they are reflected in existing and emerging privacy and data protection laws, and serve as the basis for the creation of leading practice privacy programs and additional principles."

[59] Alternatively, one could use the Fair Information Practice Principles (FIPPs) found in Appendix A of the *National Strategy for Trusted Identities in Cyberspace*, developed since the original issuance of this document. Appendix A is available at: http://www.nist.gov/nstic/NSTIC-FIPPs.pdf [accessed 8/11/2014]. Rooted in the United States Department of Health, Education and Welfare's seminal 1973 report, "Records, Computers and the Rights of Citizens" (1973), these principles are at the core of the Privacy Act of 1974 and are mirrored in the laws of many U.S. states, as well as in those of many foreign nations and international organizations. A number of private and not-for-profit organizations have also incorporated these principles into their privacy policies.

5.4.2 Summary PIA Findings and Recommendations

The consumer-to-utility PIA conducted by the Privacy Subgroup revealed valuable insights about the general consumer-to-utility data flow and privacy concerns, and indicated that significant areas of concern remain to be addressed within each localized domain of the smart grid. For example, as smart grid implementations collect more granular, detailed, and potentially personal information, this information may reveal business activities, manufacturing procedures, and personal activities in a given location. It will therefore be important for utilities to consider establishing privacy practices to protect this information.

As noted in Section 5.3,[60] which focuses on privacy laws and legal considerations, the PIA also revealed the lack of privacy laws or policies directly applicable to the smart grid. Accordingly, opportunities remain for developing processes and practices to identify and address smart grid privacy risks.

Organizations that collect or use smart grid data can use the Privacy group's PIA findings to guide their own use of PIAs and develop appropriate systems and processes for protecting smart grid data. Organizations can also use the six questions listed in Section 5.4 when conducting their own PIAs and then examine their findings with the ten privacy principles listed in Appendix F. The answers to these questions are essential both for efficient data management in general and for developing an approach that will address privacy impacts in alignment with all other organizational policies regarding consumer data. Where an organization has defined privacy responsibilities, policies, and procedures, that organization should consider reviewing its responsibilities and updating or potentially augmenting its policies and procedures associated with the use of smart grid data in new ways that can cause privacy concerns. Each entity within the smart grid can follow a similar methodology to perform its own PIAs to ensure privacy is appropriately addressed for its smart grid activities.

The PIA Findings and Recommendations Summary of the Smart Grid High-Level Consumer-to-Utility Privacy Impact Assessment[61] used the privacy principles as the basis for the PIA. Within the summary, each privacy principle statement is followed by the related findings from the PIA and the suggested privacy practices that may serve to mitigate the privacy risks associated with each principle.

Privacy Practices Recommendations:

- **Policy challenge procedures**. Organizations collecting energy data, and all other entities with access to that data, should establish procedures that allow smart grid consumers to have the opportunity and process to challenge the organization's compliance with their published privacy policies as well as their actual privacy practices.

- **Perform regular privacy impact assessments**. Any organization collecting energy data from or about consumer locations should perform periodic PIAs with the proper

---

[60] *See* 5.3.2, Existing Legal and Regulatory Frameworks, and 5.3.3, Applicability of Existing Data Protection Laws and Regulations to the Smart Grid.

[61] See the summary of the Smart Grid High-Level Consumer-to-Utility Privacy Impact Assessment in Appendix F. See the full "NIST Smart Grid High-Level Consumer-to-Utility Privacy Impact Assessment," September 10, 2009, at https://collaborate.nist.gov/twiki-sggrid/pub/SmartGrid/CSCTGPrivacy/NIST_High_Level_PIA_Report_FINAL_-_Herold_Sept_10_2009.pdf. [accessed 8/11/2014].

time frames, to be determined by the utility and the appropriate regulator, based upon the associated risks and any recent process changes and/or security incidents. The organizations should consider sending the PIA results for review by an impartial Third Party and making a summary of the results available to the public. This will help to promote compliance with the organization's privacy obligations and provide an accessible public record to demonstrate the organization's privacy compliance activities. Organizations should also perform a PIA on each new system, network, or smart grid application and consider providing a copy of the results in similar fashion to that mentioned above.

- **Establish breach notice practices**. Any organization with smart grid data should establish or amend policies and procedures to identify breaches and misuse of the data, along with expanding or establishing procedures and plans for notifying the affected individuals in a timely manner with appropriate details about the breach. This becomes particularly important with new possible transmissions of consumer data between utilities and other entities providing services in a smart grid environment (e.g., Third Party service providers).

5.5. PERSONAL INFORMATION IN THE SMART GRID

As shown in the PIA, energy data and personal information can reveal something either explicitly or implicitly about specific individuals, groups of individuals, or activities of those individuals. Smart grid data such as energy usage measurements, combined with the increased frequency of usage reporting, energy generation data, and the use of appliances and devices capable of energy consumption reporting, provide new sources of personal information.

The personal information traditionally collected by utility companies can be used to identify individuals through such data as house number and/or street address; homeowner or resident's first, middle, or last name; date of birth; and last four digits of the SSN. Smart grid data elements that reflect the timing and amount of energy used, when correlated with traditional personal information data elements, can provide insights into the lifestyle of residential consumers and the business operations of commercial and industrial consumers.[62]

With a few exceptions (e.g., SSN and credit card numbers), rarely does a single piece of information or a single source permit the identification of an individual or group of individuals. However, it has been shown through multiple research studies[63] and incidents[64] that a piece of

---

[62] The ability to determine personal activities according to energy consumption data alone was demonstrated recently in quotes from a Siemens representative in a Reuters news article: "We, Siemens, have the technology to record it (energy consumption) every minute, second, microsecond, more or less live," said Martin Pollock of Siemens Energy, an arm of the German engineering giant, which provides metering services. "From that we can infer how many people are in the house, what they do, whether they're upstairs, downstairs, do you have a dog, when do you habitually get up, when did you get up this morning, when do you have a shower: masses of private data." *See* "Privacy concerns challenge smart grid rollout," *Reuters*, June 25, 2010, http://www.reuters.com/article/idUSLDE65N2CI20100625 [accessed 8/11/2014].

[63] *See* A. Narayanan and V. Shmatikov, "Myths and Fallacies of 'Personally Identifiable Information'," *Communications of the ACM* 53(6), June 2010, pp. 24-26, http://dx.doi.org/10.1145/1743546.1743558. This article points out multiple incidents and studies that have shown how combinations of data items that are anonymous individually can be linked to specific individuals when combined with other anonymous data items and "quasi-identifiers" or a piece of auxiliary information. "Consumption preferences" is specifically named as a type of human characteristic data that, when combined with other items, can point to individuals.

[64] In addition to the incidents discussed in the Narayanan and Shmatikov article previously referenced, another specific example to consider is that in 2006, AOL released anonymous information about search data that was re-identified linking to individuals by

seemingly anonymous data (date of birth, gender, zip code) that on its own cannot uniquely identify an individual may reveal an individual when combined with other types of anonymous data. If different datasets that contain anonymized data have at least one type of information that is the same, the separate sets of anonymized information may have records that are easily matched and then linked to an individual. It is also possible the potential matches to an individual may be narrowed because of situational circumstances to the point that linking becomes an easy task.[65] (This may particularly be seen in sparsely populated geographical areas or for premises with unique characteristics.)

Another study published in 2009 illustrates the increasing ease of disaggregating data into personally identifiable information. Carnegie Mellon researchers Alessandro Acquisti and Ralph Gross assessed the predictability of SSNs by knowing the date and geographic location of an individual subject's birth and found that they could predict the first five digits for 44 % of those born after 1988 on the first attempt and 61 % within two attempts.[66]

There are potential unintended consequences of seemingly anonymous smart grid data being compiled, stored, and cross-linked. While current privacy and security anonymization practices tend to focus on the removal of specific personal information data items, the studies referenced in this section show that re-identification[67] and linking to an individual may still occur. This issue of data re-identification becomes potentially more significant as the amount and granularity of the data being gathered during smart grid operations increases with the deployment of more smart grid components. It then becomes important, from a privacy standpoint, for utilities and Third Parties participating in the smart grid to determine which data items will remove the ability to link to specific addresses or individuals whenever they perform their data anonymization[68] activities.

Table 5-1 identifies and describes potential data elements within the smart grid that could impact privacy if not properly safeguarded. This is not an exhaustive list of all data elements about customers that could pose a privacy risk. There is additional risk outside of the smart grid around the access of certain data elements.

---

a NY Times reporter. This incident led to a complaint filed by the Electronic Frontier Foundation (EFF) with the Federal Trade Commission against AOL for violating the Federal Trade Commission Act. *See* M. Barbaro and T. Zeller, Jr., "A Face is Exposed for AOL Searcher No. 4417749," *The New York Times*, August 9, 2006, http://www.nytimes.com/2006/08/09/technology/09aol.html?ex=1312776000 [accessed 8/11/2014].

[65] L. Sweeney, "k-anonymity: A Model for Protecting Privacy," *International Journal of Uncertainty, Fuzziness and Knowledge-based Systems* 10(5), October 2002, pp. 557-570, http://dx.doi.org/10.1142/S0218488502001648. Sweeney gathered data from the Massachusetts Group Insurance Commission (GIC), which purchases health insurance for state employees. GIC released insurer records to the researcher, but before doing so, with the support of the Governor's office, they removed names, addresses, SSNs, and other "identifying information" in order to protect the privacy of the employees. Sweeney then purchased voter rolls, which included the name, zip code, address, sex, and birth date of voters in Cambridge. Matched with the voter rolls, the GIC database showed only six people in Cambridge were born on the same day as the Governor, half of them were men, and the Governor was the only one who lived in the zip code provided by the voter rolls. Correlating information in the voter rolls with the GIC database made it possible to re-identify the Governor's records in the GIC data, including his prescriptions and diagnoses.

[66] A. Acquisti and R. Gross, "Predicting Social Security numbers from public data," *PNAS: Proceedings of the National Academy of Sciences* 106(27), July 7, 2009, pp. 10975-10980, http://dx.doi.org/10.1073/pnas.0904891106.

[67] Re-identification is the process of relating unique and specific entities to seemingly anonymous data, resulting in the identification of individuals and/or groups of individuals.

[68] Data Anonymization is a process, manual or automated, that removes, or replaces with dummy data, information that could identify an individual or a group of individuals from a communication, data record, or database.

Table 5-1 Information Potentially Available Through the Smart Grid

Data Element(s)	Description
Name	Party responsible for the account
Address	Location where service is being provided
Account Number	Unique identifier for the account
Meter reading	kWh energy consumption recorded between 15 to 60 minute intervals and once daily intervals during the current billing cycle
Financial information	Current or past meter reads, bills, and balances available, including history of late payments/failure to pay, if any
Lifestyle	When the home is occupied and unoccupied, when occupants are awake and asleep, how much various appliances are used[69]
Distributed resources	The presence of on-site generation and/or storage devices, operational status, net supply to or consumption from the grid, usage patterns
Meter Unique Identifiers	The Internet Protocol (IP) address, media access control (MAC) address, or other network identifiers for the meter, if applicable

5.6. IN-DEPTH LOOK AT SMART GRID PRIVACY CONCERNS

As outlined in the results of the PIA described earlier, there is a wide range of privacy concerns to address within the smart grid. These may impact the implementation of smart grid systems or their effectiveness. For example, a lack of consumer confidence in the security and privacy of their energy consumption data may result in a lack of consumer acceptance and participation, if not outright litigation.

In general, privacy concerns about the smart grid fall into one of two broad categories:

Category 1: Personal information not previously readily obtainable; and

Category 2: Mechanisms that did not previously exist for obtaining (or manipulating) personal information.

Examples of the first category include detailed information on the appliances and equipment in use at a given location, including the use of specific medical devices and other electronic devices that indicate personal patterns and timings of legal and potentially illegal operations within the location, and finely grained time series data on power consumption at metered locations and from individual appliances.

The second category includes instances where personal information is available from other sources, and the smart grid may present a new source for that same information. For example, an individual's physical location can be tracked through their credit card and cell phone records today. Charging PEVs raises the possibility of tracking physical location through new energy consumption data.

---

[69] For discussion on this topic, see §5.3.1.

Detailed profiles of activities within a house or building can be derived from "equipment electricity signatures"[70] and their time patterns. Such signatures and patterns can provide a basis for making assumptions about occupant activities (e.g., when the premise was unoccupied).[71]

While technology to communicate directly with appliances and other energy consumption elements already exists, smart grid implementation may create broader incentives for their use. Appliances so equipped may deliver detailed energy consumption information to both their owners and operators and to outside parties.

Table 5-2 outlines some of the possible areas of privacy concern and provides some analysis of the nature of the concern according to the categories given above. While this is not an exhaustive list, it serves to help categorize the concerns noted.

Table 5-2 Potential Privacy Concerns and Descriptions

Privacy Concern	Discussion	Categorization Category 1: Personal information not previously readily obtainable. Category 2: Mechanisms that did not previously exist for obtaining (or manipulating) personal information.
Personal data exposure	Unauthorized exposure of energy consumption or other personal information.	Category 2: The traditional method of reading consumer meters (either manual recording or electronically via "drive-by" remote meter reading systems) may allow less opportunity for data manipulation or exposure without collusion with the personnel handling the data.
Determine Personal Behavior Patterns / Appliances Used	Smart meters, combined with home automation networks or other enabling technologies, may track the use of specific appliances. Access to data-use profiles that can reveal specific times and locations of electricity use in specific areas of the home can also indicate the types of activities and/or appliances used[72]. Possible uses for this information include: • Appliance manufacturers product reliability and warranty purposes; • Targeted marketing.	Category 1: The type of data made available by smart grid implementation may be both more granular and available on a broader scale.

---

[70] This is a term coined by the Privacy Subgroup and not one that is officially used by any regulatory or standards group.

[71] While using NALM techniques to compare appliance signatures against total consumption data can provide a basis for assumptions regarding the number of individuals in a given location, such techniques cannot conclusively reveal the number of individuals in a location. For example, even if NALM techniques can reveal that a toaster (or hot water heater) was used at 8am, 10am, and 12noon, it cannot distinguish between 3 toast-eaters (or shower-takers) and 1 toast- (or shower-) loving person.

[72] For discussion on this topic, see §5.1.

Privacy Concern	Discussion	Categorization Category 1: Personal information not previously readily obtainable. Category 2: Mechanisms that did not previously exist for obtaining (or manipulating) personal information.
Perform Real-Time Remote Surveillance	Access to live energy use data can potentially reveal such things as if people are in a facility or residence, what they are doing, waking and sleeping patterns, where they are in the structure, and how many are in the structure.	Category 2: Many methods of real-time surveillance currently exist. The availability of computerized real-time or near-real-time energy usage data would create another way in which such surveillance could be conducted.
Non-Grid Commercial Uses of Data	Customer energy usage data storage may reveal lifestyle information that could be of value to many entities, including vendors of a wide range of products and services. Vendors may obtain attribute lists for targeted sales and marketing campaigns that may not be welcomed by those targets. Data may be used for insurance purposes.	Category 2: Under the existing metering and billing systems, meter data is not sufficiently granular in most cases to reveal any detail about activities. However, with smart meters, time of use and demand rates, and direct load control of equipment may create detailed data that could be sold and used for energy management analyses and peer comparisons. While this information has beneficial value to Third Parties, consumer education about protecting that data has considerable positive outcomes.

5.6.1 Data Collection and Availability

A detailed sense of activities within a house or building can be derived from equipment electricity signatures, individual appliance usage data, time patterns of usage, and other data, as illustrated earlier in this chapter (see §5.3.1). Especially when collected and analyzed over a period of time, this information can provide a basis for determining occupant activities and lifestyle. For example, a forecast may be made about occupancy, sleep schedules, work schedules, and other personal routines.[73]

While technology that communicates directly with appliances and other energy consumption elements already exists, smart grid implementation may create broader incentives for its use and provide easier access by interested parties. Appliances so equipped may deliver granular energy consumption data to both their owners and operators, as well as to outside parties. The increased collection of and access to granular energy usage data will create new uses for that data: for

---

[73] *See* M.A. Lisovich, D.K. Mulligan, and S.B. Wicker, "Inferring Personal Information from Demand-Response Systems," *IEEE Security & Privacy* 8(1), January-February 2010, pp. 11-20, http://dx.doi.org/10.1109/MSP.2010.40 (presenting the results of an initial study in the types of information than can be inferred from granular energy consumption data); *see also* Footnote 65.

example, residential demand-response systems,[74] marketing,[75] and law enforcement.[76] Many of these new uses will be innovative and provide individual and consumer benefits, some will impact privacy, and many will do both.

The listing of "Potential Privacy Concerns and Descriptions" shown earlier (Table 5-2), outlines some of the privacy concerns that may arise from potential uses of smart grid data. The table also lists a variety of parties that may use smart grid data. Many of these uses are legitimate and beneficial. However, all parties that collect and use smart grid data should be aware of uses that impact privacy, and should develop appropriate plans for data stewardship, security, and data use.

Any party with access to customers' personal data could intentionally or unintentionally be the source of data that is misused or that is used in a way that has negative effects on consumer privacy. "Intentional" privacy compromises might occur through voluntary disclosure of data to Third Parties who then share the data with others or use the data in unexpected ways, while "unintentional" impacts might arise through data breaches or criminal attacks. It is important that all smart grid entities handling personal information are aware of various potential uses of the data, and that they consider these factors when developing processes for data collection, handling, and disclosure.

Many potential uses arise from the generation of granular energy data when it is combined with personal information. Table 5-3 broadly illustrates the various industries that may be interested in smart grid data. While this is not an exhaustive listing, it serves to help categorize the various concerns.

---

[74] Federal Energy Regulatory Commission, *2008 Assessment of Demand Response and Advanced Metering: Staff Report*, December 2008, http://www.ferc.gov/legal/staff-reports/12-08-demand-response.pdf [accessed 8/11/2014] (discussing various types of demand-response systems and pricing schemes, including those for residential *customers)*.

[75] E. Protalinkski, "Facebook, Opower, NRDC launch energy use app," *ZDNet*, April 3, 2012, http://www.zdnet.com/blog/facebook/facebook-opower-nrdc-launch-energy-use-app/11332 [accessed 8/11/2014].

[76] Law enforcement already uses energy consumption data to try to identify potentially criminal activity, like drug cultivation. *See e.g., United States v. Golden Valley Electric Association*, No. 11-35195, http://www.ca9.uscourts.gov/datastore/opinions/2012/08/07/11-35195.pdf [accessed 8/11/2014]. More granular data will provide law enforcement with more valuable information that may be able to identify a wider range of illegal activities.

Table 5-3 Potential Privacy Impacts that Arise from the Collection and Use of Smart Grid Data

Type of Data	Privacy-Related Information Potentially Revealed by this Type of Data	Parties Potentially Collecting or Using this Type of Data	Type of Potential Use[77]	Specific Potential Uses of this Type of Data
Detailed energy usage at a location, whether in real-time or on a delayed basis.	*Personal Behavior Patterns and Activities Inside the Home*[78] Behavioral patterns, habits, and activities taking place inside the home by monitoring electricity usage patterns and appliance use, including activities like sleeping, eating, showering, and watching TV.	Utilities	Primary	Load monitoring and forecasting; demand response; efficiency analysis and monitoring, billing.
		Edge Services[79]		Efficiency analysis and monitoring; demand-response, public or limited disclosure to promote conservation, energy awareness, etc. (e.g., posting energy usage to social media).
	Patterns over time to determine number of people in the household, work schedule, sleeping habits, vacation, health, affluence, or other lifestyle details and habits.	Insurance Companies	Secondary	Determine premiums (e.g., specific behavior patterns, like erratic sleep).
		Marketers		Profile for targeted advertisements.
	When specific appliances are being used in a home, or when industrial equipment is in use, via granular energy data and appliance energy consumption profiles.	Law Enforcement		Identify suspicious or illegal activity; investigations; real-time surveillance to determine if residents are present and current activities inside the home.
		Civil Litigation		Determine when someone was home or the number of people present.
		Landlord/Lessor		Use tenants' energy profiles to verify lease compliance.
	Real-Time Surveillance Information Via real-time energy use data, determine if anyone is home, potentially what they are doing.	Private Investigators		Investigations; monitoring for specific events.
		The Press		Public interest in the activities of famous individuals.[80]

---

[77] "Primary" uses of smart grid data are those used to provide direct services to customers that are directly based on that data, including energy generation services or load monitoring services. "Secondary" uses of data are uses that apply smart grid data to other business purposes, such as insurance adjustment or marketing, or to nonbusiness purposes, such as government investigations or civil litigation. "Illicit" uses of data are uses that are never authorized and are often criminal.

[78] For more discussion on this, see §5.3.1.

[79] Edge services include businesses providing services based directly upon electrical usage but not providing services related to the actual generation, transportation, or distribution of electricity. Some examples of edge services would include apps built to utilize Green Button data, or consulting services based upon electricity usage.

[80] For example, there were numerous news stories about the amount of electricity used by Al Gore's Tennessee home. *See e.g.*, "Gore's High Energy-Use Home Target of Critical Report," FoxNews.com, February 28, 2007, http://www.foxnews.com/story/2007/02/28/gore-high-energy-use-home-target-critical-report/ [accessed 8/11/2014].

Type of Data	Privacy-Related Information Potentially Revealed by this Type of Data	Parties Potentially Collecting or Using this Type of Data	Type of Potential Use[77]	Specific Potential Uses of this Type of Data
	and where they are located in the home.	Creditors		Determine behavior that seems to indicate creditworthiness or changes in credit risk.[81]
		Criminals and Other Unauthorized Users	Illicit	Identify the best times for a burglary; determine if residents are present; identify assets that might be present; commit fraud; corporate espionage—determine confidential processes or proprietary data.
Location / recharge information for PEVs or other location-aware appliances.	*Determine Location Information* Historical PEV data, which can be used to determine range of use since last recharge.	Utilities/Energy Service Provider	Primary	Bill energy consumption to owner of the PEV; distributed energy resource management; emergency response.
		Insurance Companies	Secondary	Determine premiums based on driving habits and recharge location.
	Location of active PEV charging activities, which can be used to determine the location of driver.	Marketers		Profile and market based on driving habits and PEV condition.
		Private Investigators Law Enforcement/ Agencies		Investigations; locating or creating tracking histories for persons of interest.
		Civil Litigation		Determine when someone was home or at a different location.
		PEV Lessor		Verify a lessee's compliance regarding the mileage of a lease agreement.
Consumer-owned equipment and capabilities.	*Identify Household Appliances* Identifying information (such as a MAC address); directly reported usage information	Utilities	Primary	Load monitoring and forecasting; efficiency analysis and monitoring; reliability; demand response; distributed energy resource management; emergency response.

---

[81] Sudden changes in when residents are home could indicate the loss of a job. Erratic sleep patterns could indicate possible stress and increased likelihood of job loss. *See e.g.*, C. Duhigg, "What Does Your Credit-Card Company Know About You?" *New York Times Magazine*, May 12, 2009, http://www.nytimes.com/2009/05/17/magazine/17credit-t.html [accessed 8/11/2014].

Type of Data	Privacy-Related Information Potentially Revealed by this Type of Data	Parties Potentially Collecting or Using this Type of Data	Type of Potential Use[77]	Specific Potential Uses of this Type of Data
	provided by "smart" appliances. Data revealed from HAN or appliance.	Edge Services		Efficiency analysis and monitoring; broadcasting appliance use to social media.
		Insurance Companies	Secondary	Make claim adjustments (e.g., determine if claimant actually owned appliances that were claimed to have been destroyed by house fire); determine or modify premiums based upon the presence of appliances that might indicate increased risk; identify activities that might change risk profiles.
		Appliance Manufacturers		Determine usage and/or condition of appliances, potentially in order to offer repair, replacement, and/or warranty services.
		Marketers		Profile for targeted advertisements based upon owned and un-owned appliances or activities indicated by appliance use.
		Law Enforcement		Substantiate energy usage that may indicate illegal activity; identify activities on premises.
		Civil Litigation		Identify property; identify activities on premises.
		Criminals & Other Unauthorized Users	Illicit	Identify what assets may be present to target for theft; introduce a virus or other attack to collect personal information.

As seen in the table, such data might be used in ways that raise privacy concerns. For example, granular smart grid data may allow numerous assumptions about the health of a dwelling's resident in which some insurance companies, employers, the press, civil litigants, and others could be interested. Most directly, specific medical devices may be uniquely identified through serial numbers or MAC addresses, or may have unique electrical signatures; if associated with data that identifies an individual resident, either could indicate that the resident suffers from a particular disease or condition that requires the device.[82] More generally, inferences might be used to determine health patterns and risk. For example, the amount of time the computer or television is on could be compared to the amount of time the treadmill is used.[83] Electricity usage data could also reveal how much the resident sleeps and whether he gets up in the middle of the night.[84] Similarly, appliance usage data could indicate how often meals are cooked with the microwave, the stove, or not cooked at all, as well as implying the frequency of meals.[85] Many of the parties listed in the "Potential Privacy Impacts" table (Table 5-3) will not be interested in the health of the resident and will wish to use the data for purposes such as efficiency monitoring, but some parties may be interested in the behavioral assumptions that could be made with such data.

5.6.2 Wireless Access to Smart Meters and Secondary Devices

Future designs for some smart meters and many secondary devices (e.g., smart appliances and smaller devices) may incorporate wireless-enabled technology to collect and transmit energy usage information for homes or businesses.[86] Should designers and manufacturers of smart meters or secondary devices decide to incorporate wireless technology for the purpose of communicating energy usage information, then that data must be securely transmitted and have privacy protection.[87] There are well-known vulnerabilities related to wireless sensors and networks,[88] and breaches of wireless technology that may result in breaches of privacy.[89] For example, "war driving" is a popular technique used to locate, exploit, or attack insufficiently

---

[82] S. Lyon and J. Roche, "Smart Grid Privacy Tips Part 2: Anticipate the Unanticipated," *SmartGridNews.com*, February 9, 2010, http://www.SmartGridnews.com/artman/publish/Business_Policy_Regulation_News/Smart-Grid-Privacy-Tips-Part-2-Anticipate-the-Unanticipated-1873.html [accessed 8/11/2014]. To be clear, the data being discussed would be customer energy usage data that may be used to infer the presence of certain health-related equipment or appliances, and not specific health data. For a discussion about granularity of this data and what is possible to infer from it, see §5.3.1.

[83] Elias Quinn mentions an Alabama tax provision that requires obese state employees to pay for health insurance unless they work to reduce their body mass index (E.L. Quinn, "Privacy and the New Energy Infrastructure," CEES Working Paper No. 09-001, Fall 2008, p. 31, http://papers.ssrn.com/sol3/papers.cfm?abstract_id=1370731 [accessed 8/11/2014]). He suggests that smart grid data could be used to see how often a treadmill was being used in the home.

[84] From Privacy by Design: Information and Privacy Commissioner of Ontario, and The Future of Privacy Forum, *SmartPrivacy For the Smart Grid: Embedding Privacy into the Design of Electricity Conservation*, November 2009, 27 pp., http://www.ipc.on.ca/images/Resources/pbd-smartpriv-Smart Grid.pdf [accessed 8/11/2014] (describing the types of information that could be gleaned from combining personal information with granular energy consumption data).

[85] Id. at page 11.

[86] Office of the National Coordinator for Smart Grid Interoperability, *NIST Framework and Roadmap for Smart Grid Interoperability Standards, Release 2.0*, NIST Special Publication 1108R2, National Institute of Standards and Technology, February 2012, p. 24, http://nist.gov/smartgrid/upload/NIST_Framework_Release_2-0_corr.pdf [accessed 8/11/2014].

[87] *See* Table 5-2 Potential Privacy Concerns and Descriptions.

[88] *See, e.g.*, M.F. Foley, "Data Privacy and Security Issues for Advanced Metering Systems (Part 2)," *SmartGridNews.com*, July 1, 2008, http://www.smartgridnews.com/artman/publish/industry/Data_Privacy_and_Security_Issues_for_Advanced_Metering_Systems_Part_2.html [accessed 8/11/2014].

[89] Id.

protected or improperly configured wireless systems.[90] Readily available portable computing devices are used to detect signals emanating from wireless technology. If wireless technology is used to transmit energy consumption information for a unique location or dwelling, then that usage data should be protected from unauthorized use, modification, or theft, even if it is being transmitted for purposes of later aggregating to protect privacy.[91]

Since the utilities most frequently would not be receiving usage data from secondary devices, such as smart appliances, that data would not necessarily be protected in the same manner as usage data collected from a smart meter. For a discussion on recommended privacy protection practices for Third Parties not receiving the data from a utility, see §5.7.

5.6.3 Commissioning, Registration, and Enrollment for Smart Devices[92]

This subsection describes a method for implementing demand response using load control through an energy management system linked to a utility or a Third Party service provider offering remote energy management. As explained in §3.7, it is possible to protect consumer privacy by implementing demand response without a direct data connection between the energy service provider and home devices.

Privacy issues that should be addressed related to the registration of these devices with Third Parties include:

- Determining the types of information that is involved with these registration situations;

- Controlling the connections which transmit the data to the Third Party, such as wireless transmissions from home area networks;[93] and

- Determining how the registration information is used, where it is stored, and with whom it is shared.

To create a home area network, devices must, at a minimum, scan for networks to join, request admission, and exchange device parameters. This initial process is called "commissioning" and allows devices to exchange a limited amount of information (including, but not limited to, network keys, device type, device ID, and initial path) and to receive public broadcast information. This process is initiated by the "installer" powering-on the device and following the

---

[90] *See* M. Bierlein, "Policing the Wireless World: Access Liability in the Open Wi-Fi Era," *Ohio State Law Journal* 67(5), 2012, pp. 1123-1185, http://moritzlaw.osu.edu/students/groups/oslj/files/2012/04/67.5.bierlein.pdf [accessed 8/11/2014].

[91] For a discussion on how data aggregation was addressed in the healthcare industry, *see* "Standards for Privacy of Individually Identifiable Health Information; Final Rule," *67 FR 53181*, August 14, 2002, http://www.hhs.gov/ocr/privacy/hipaa/administrative/privacyrule/privrruletxt.txt [accessed 8/11/2014]. There may also be efficiencies that can be gained by the smart grid when aggregating data from transmission and processing that save money for utilities (*see* H. Li, H. Yu, B. Yang, and A. Liu, "Timing control for delay-constrained data aggregation in wireless sensor networks: Research Articles," *International Journal of Communication Systems – Energy-Efficient Network Protocols and Algorithms for Wireless Sensor Networks* 20(7), July 2007, pp. 875-887, http://dx.doi.org/10.1002/dac.849). This may create a greater incentive to aggregate data. If this is the case, then proper aggregation to protect PII or sensitive data should be incorporated into the plan for data aggregation.

[92] The first four paragraphs of this subsection are taken from OpenHAN v1.95: UCA International Users Group, *UCAIug Home Area Network System Requirements Specification,* Draft v1.95, May 21, 2010, http://www.smartgridug.net/sgsystems/openhan/Shared%20Documents/OpenHAN%202.0/UCAIug%20OpenHAN%20SRS%20-%20v1.95%20clean.doc [accessed 8/11/2014].

[93] The other chapters within NISTIR 7628 include recommendations for securing wireless transmissions, such as those from OpenHAN networks, to smart grid entities, as well as to Third Parties.

manufacturer's instruction. Once a HAN device has completed the commissioning process, it may go through an additional process called "registration."

The registration process is a further step involving "mutual authentication" and authorizing a commissioned HAN device to exchange secure information with other registered devices and with a smart energy industrial provider. Registration creates a trust relationship between the HAN device and the smart energy industrial provider and governs the rights granted to the HAN device. This process is more complex than commissioning and requires coordination between the installer and the service provider. In some instances, commissioning and registration are combined into one process called "provisioning."

The final process is "enrollment." This process is applicable only when the consumer wants to sign up their HAN device for a specific service provider program, such as a demand-response, PEV special rate, or a prepay program. In this process, the consumer selects a service provider program and grants the service provider certain rights to communicate with or control their HAN device. A HAN device must be commissioned and registered prior to initiating the enrollment process. This process requires coordination between the consumer and the service provider. Each of these processes is discrete but may be combined by a service provider in order to provide a seamless consumer experience.

At each step in this process, the consumer, utility, and Third Party provider must ensure that data flows have been identified and classified, and that privacy issues are addressed throughout, from initial commissioning up through service-provider-delivered service. Since each step in the process, including commissioning, registration, and enrollment, may contain personal information, sufficient privacy protections should be in place to minimize the potential for a privacy breach.

5.7. SMART GRID DATA ACCESS BY THIRD PARTIES

In September 2010, the CSWG Privacy subgroup began looking at the issue of Third Parties gaining access to customer energy usage data (CEUD) and any resulting privacy concerns. The primary purpose was to ascertain what gaps there might be in existing guidelines or standards for the obligations of Third Parties to protect privacy, and how they get and handle CEUD. Although the membership of the Third Party Recommended Practices Team was somewhat fluid throughout the process, it was generally composed of individuals representing utilities, state public utilities commissions, vendors, privacy advocacy organizations, and NIST.

5.7.1 Change in Group Charter

The charter of the group was to address a perceived gap in standards, regulations and best practices that might apply to how Third Parties receive and handle CEUD, and how they protect the privacy of the related customers. The focus was on consumer data, rather than commercial. Initially, the group reviewed the California Public Utilities Commission (CPUC) Rules on CEUD privacy[94], the NAESB REQ.22 Standard, *Third Party Access to Smart Meter-based*

---

[94] "Decision Adopting Rules to Protect the Privacy and Security of the Electricity Usage Data of the Customers of Pacific Gas and Electric Company, Southern California Edison Company, and San Diego Gas & Electric Company," Decision 11-07-056, issued July 29, 2011 ("CPUC Decision"), http://docs.cpuc.ca.gov/PublishedDocs/WORD_PDF/FINAL_DECISION/140369.PDF [accessed 8/11/2014].

Information Model Business Practices (MBPs) [95] (2011), and the Advanced Security Acceleration Project for the Smart Grid (ASAP-SG) Third Party Access Security Profile v1.0. From these three primary documents, a fourth document was put together as an all-encompassing set of recommended practices for Third Party CEUD usage. Due largely to the work accomplished by NAESB on REQ.22, which addresses data given to Third Parties by utilities, a more narrow focus for this group was later adopted. The initial work of the group clearly had overlap with the NAESB requirements, and so as to not give utilities potentially conflicting advice, this team sought to address only data Third Parties received from non-utility sources, such as in-home devices.

5.7.2 Additional Scope Determinations for Recommended Privacy Practices

While there may exist uncertainty over the extent to which any one government agency has regulatory oversight of Third Parties using CEUD, many agree that energy usage data (that will soon become more prevalent as the electric grid gains increased intelligence) can potentially be sensitive, privacy-impacting data in need of protection. This is particularly true when CEUD is combined with other data, such as an account number or smart meter IP address that then makes it identifiable to one premise or customer. The recommended privacy practices seek to provide suggestions as to how CEUD, and the data combined with it as just described, is best protected in order to protect personal privacy. The recommendations also may help educate consumers on what they should expect out of Third Parties with which they choose to share their data.

For purposes of these recommended practices, data provided to Third Parties by electric utilities or electricity providers was excluded. The distinction is also made between companies that are under contract to a utility or Third Party (Contracted Agents) and companies that do not have a contractual relationship with a utility (Third Party). Definitions from other sources were utilized where available.

In the present document, recommendations for how to protect privacy are made utilizing Fair Information Practice Principles (FIPPs). The basis for FIPPs is material found in the Privacy Act of 1974.[96] There are several versions of FIPPs commonly in use. The set used in this document includes Management and Accountability; Notice and Purpose; Choice and Consent; Collection and Scope; Use and Retention; Individual Access; Disclosure and Limiting Use; Security and Safeguards. When considering what recommendations might be made for Third Parties, the FIPPs provided the basic structure and baseline ideas for what should be done.

5.7.3 Recommended Privacy Practices

The full set of recommendations is found in Appendix D: Recommended Privacy Practices for Customer/Consumer Smart Grid Energy Usage Data Obtained Directly by Third Parties. The following provides a basic summary of the recommendations.

Privacy Notices

Third Parties should provide a privacy notice to customers prior to sharing CEUD with another party, or in the case of a significant change in organizational structure, such as merger, bankruptcy, or outsourcing, if it could impact the security or privacy of the data. Privacy policy

---

[95] Available for purchase at https://www.naesb.org/retail_standards.asp.

[96] 5 U.S.C §552a As Amended, http://www.justice.gov/opcl/privacy-act-1974 [accessed 8/11/2014].

notices should include information about how the Third Party will access, collect, use, store, disclose, retain, dispose of, and safeguard CEUD. The privacy notice should also detail how the customer may address complaints and/or revoke their authorization for the Third Party to have and use their CEUD.

Customer Authorization for Disclosures

Third parties should seek customer authorization prior to disclosing CEUD to other parties unless the service for which the data disclosure is necessary has been previously authorized by the customer. Customers should have access to their CEUD, and should be able to request corrections to the CEUD be made.

Data Disclosure and Minimization

In following with the FIPPs, a Third Party should not be collecting more than what is required to fulfill the agreed upon service, and a separate customer authorization should be obtained before CEUD is used in a materially different manner. There are, however, some exceptions that may be made. Aggregated data may be shared to provide an authorized service without disclosure to the customer. There may also be instances in which law enforcement seeks data via subpoena or court order, or perhaps situations in which there is a risk of imminent threat to life or property. In these instances, data may be disclosed without prior notice.

Customer Education & Awareness

Third Parties should educate customers about the Third Party's CEUD privacy protection policies and practices, including the steps the Third Party is taking to protect privacy. Customers should also be provided with a notice that the data they collect via in-home devices (or data from the meter that has not yet been validated) may differ from what the customer may receive on their bill from the Utility.

Data Quality

Data should be as accurate and complete as possible, recognizing that the data will be only as accurate and complete as the information received.

Data Security

Third parties should have clear data security policies that should be periodically reviewed and updated. They should have specific personnel to handle these policies and to ensure that their privacy practices are transparent to customers.

Privacy Practices Risk Assessment

Periodic assessments of the privacy practices should be performed. Assessments should also be considered in the case of a significant change in organizational structure that may impact privacy, when new privacy-related laws or regulations become effective, or when an event occurs that may impact privacy, such as unauthorized disclosure of data. The development of privacy use cases may prove a helpful tool, not just for the Third Party, but also for those within the smart grid community that may be able learn from the experiences of others.

Data Retention and Disposal

Third parties should have clear policies and practices on how long data will be retained, as well as when and how CEUD will be disposed of. This should be detailed in the privacy notice given to the customer.

Data Breaches

Third parties should be aware of and adhere to any laws or requirements with regard to data breaches. These rules may apply to Third Parties or to Contracted Agents.

Employee Training

Employees of Third Parties and their Contracted Agents should be trained on the security and privacy practices necessary to protect customer CEUD.

Audits

Finally, the recommended practices discuss the use of independent Third Party audits of security and privacy practices. These audits may be useful in helping to identify issues before they become legitimate problems.

5.8. INTRODUCTION TO PLUG-IN ELECTRIC VEHICLES COMMUNICATION ISSUES

5.8.1 Background – Vehicle Data Systems

In recent years, embedded computers have become an integral part of automotive systems. The modern vehicle includes an interconnected network of dozens of embedded microcomputers wired together by a Control Area Network (CAN) bus defined by an array of International Organization for Standardization (ISO) and Society of Automotive Engineers (SAE) standards. These microcomputers are dedicated to specific functions such as automatic braking, ignition systems, engine functions, lighting controls, fuel delivery, on-board diagnostics (OBD), and "black box" data recorders. More recently, vehicle on-board entertainment and Global Positioning Systems (GPS) navigation systems have also become part of the vehicle's on-board computer network. Until recently, this on-board network has not been connected to the world outside the vehicle, except for a single OBD connector for plugging into repair shop diagnostic equipment.[97] Vehicle "black box"-stored data has been subject to subpoena by courts in litigation related to a variety of situations involving insurance claims, accident investigations, or other matters.[98] Otherwise the data has historically remained under the control of the individual using the vehicle.

5.8.2 New Electric Vehicle Privacy and Security Risks

With the introduction of plug-in electric vehicles (PEVs), this situation is poised to change dramatically. PEVs need to plug into premises-based charging equipment, commonly referred to as Electric Vehicle Service Equipment (EVSE), and need to communicate such parameters as the vehicle's battery state-of-charge to the premises charger in order to properly manage charging

---

[97] An exception is the case of the GMC *OnStar*™ system installed in certain models, a cellular phone-based communication system for automatic crash response, navigation, roadside assistance and vehicle diagnostics.

[98] For more on this topic, see §5.3.2.2.

(and potentially, discharging back into the premises or into the electric grid). However, once such a data connection is established, there is currently no technical limitation on the amount or type of data that may be acquired from the vehicle's computers or "black boxes." In theory, depending on how the vehicle is equipped, it is possible to learn where the vehicle had traveled, how fast, where it stopped, for how long, how many were in the vehicle, what they listened to, etc.

PEVs change how society fuels their vehicles. With this change comes the promise of increased use of cleaner and renewable energy resources. This promise, coupled with limited traditional energy resources and societal changes, is pushing nations toward greater use of PEVs. PEVs provide for freedom of travel without the total reliance on motor fuel to keep them going, as is the case with traditional vehicles. Rather, PEVs harness electrical power and store it in the vehicle for future use. Instead of merely "filling up," these vehicles "plug-in" to the power of the electric grid allowing individuals to re-energize their vehicles at home, work, the mall—wherever people are able to find a charging station.

PEVs are also raising privacy concerns. The internal memory of a PEV may contain information about the vehicle user's name, address, VIN#, location, maintenance history, driving patterns, and more. Hundreds of these data items are available to be viewed by anyone with access to the PEV's internal memory. A number of potential privacy impacts put the vehicle users at risk if these data items are not appropriately safeguarded. For example, the vehicle's location history could pinpoint a location pattern for the vehicle, and thus may put the driver in greater danger of being tracked or harassed if, for one possible example, his or her estranged spouse has access to the vehicle's data. Maintenance history could share relevant information about the vehicle user's adherence to the maintenance schedule, which could be pertinent to the manufacturer's warranty responsibilities. Because of these types of issues and the impacts they potentially have on individual privacy, it is important to understand how PEVs affect privacy, and what steps are necessary to mitigate the privacy risks associated with owning and operating a PEV.

All PEVs will have the ability to have two-way communication with other systems. PEVs need to communicate with EVSE in order to communicate with a charging station. This communication is necessary for charging to occur safely. For instance, the charging station needs the current state of charge of the PEV in order to compute its charging schedule.

PEVs may also have a need to communicate with a system in order to resolve billing for a charging service. When charging at a "home" station, differential rates may be used for PEVs. When at a remote charging station, it will frequently be needed for billing. There are a number of ways this communication may occur depending on several factors. At the time of publication, there is no large PEV charging infrastructure in place, partially due to the difficulties associated with determining how billing for a charging service will be handled.

For instance, one scenario is that the local charging facility is responsible for collecting payment, and in turn, is also responsible for paying an energy distributor for the energy used. In this case, it is very likely that the PEV will only communicate with the local charging facility's system, and the bill will be resolved much like paying for gasoline at a local station.

However, another scenario being proposed within the industry is to have the bill for charging services at a remote facility be added to the PEV user's "home" utility bill. In this case, data about the PEV, including some sort of identifying information, will need to travel through the local charging station's system to the "home" utility's systems. The data will cross many systems during this process. There likely will be multiple telecommunications companies involved in transmitting this data to the correct recipient. There may be some sort of intermediate clearinghouse used to help properly route the data. If not, the local facility would need to be able to handle routing the data to 1 of over 3300 utilities in the U.S. The data may cross geographical and legal boundaries that likely will have implications for how the data should be handled, and possibly stored. This model quickly becomes more complicated than merely paying for gasoline at the pump.

Yet another scenario being proposed is that PEV users would have an account with an electric vehicle service provider (EVSP). As there were fewer than ten EVSPs in the U.S. at the time of publication, the routing of data from a local charging station to a billing system would be much simpler than trying to route such data to a particular utility. However, the data would still need to cross multiple systems with possible legal boundary and other issues in order to reach the EVSP's billing system.

The latter two scenarios have more potential challenges for protecting PEV consumer privacy. An identifier could be used to bill the correct person, which is a primary source of privacy concerns. Every time data travels from one system to another, the risk of that data being compromised or inappropriately accessed increases.

An alternative to charging is electric grid support through PEV "parking lots" in which vehicles are not only charged, but discharged to provide temporary grid support in times of peak demand. When used in discharge mode, credit on the home electric bill is a possibility, requiring many of the same billing considerations as remote station charging.

PEVs are also capable of sending information via telematics directly to manufacturers or other entities, bypassing utilities and the electric grid completely. However, since this communication capability does not involve smart grid entities, this is not within the scope of this document.

5.8.3 Potential Privacy Issues and Risks -- Possible Information Elements

When considering potential privacy risks, there are certain specific types of information that are likely to be of particular concern. These include—

1. VIN# or other identifier – a type of personal information

2. Charging history/state of charge – identifies whereabouts and home charging station

3. Location history – identifies patterns in daily activities

4. Driving behavior history – identifies patterns in driving behavior

5. Maintenance history – identifies how often the PEV is serviced and how the vehicle user maintains the vehicle

6. Utility account(s) information – contains personal information, such as address

7. Point-of-service payment information – identifies financial information which may include credit card or bank account information; types of personal information

8. Other account information (i.e., parking garages, etc.) – identifies possible information regarding the PEV user

9. IP or MAC address (if applicable) – can be used to spoof IP address for hacking or identity theft

10. PEV purchase information/history – private or proprietary information, resale history

Any one of these pieces of information could pose a privacy risk by themselves. But when two or more of these elements are combined a greater potential privacy risk may exist. For example—

1. VIN# and charging locations/duration – May be used to track the travel times, locations, and patterns for the PEV user.

2. Name/identifier and PEV purchase information – Can notify potential thieves of location and type of vehicle, can enable inferences about income, can enable targeted advertising (e.g. charging facilities, etc.). Can also provide unfair competitive advantage to commercial entities when purchasing fleet vehicles.

3. Identifier, driving behavior history, and maintenance history – Can enable inferences for insurance and warranties, can enable targeted advertising for car-related services (e.g., mechanic services, high-risk insurance companies, etc.).

4. Utility account information and point-of-service payment information – can provide insight to personal information as well as account information, allowing the possibility of identity theft and/or credit card fraud.

5.8.4 Approaches to Mitigation of Risks

The new data privacy and security risks introduced with PEVs extends the discussion about smart meter data privacy into a larger dimension. Although the issue is potentially complex, two basic approaches can be used to help address the privacy risks, as in the case of other home appliances and networks:

1. Structurally contain the vehicle data within a home or premises network, and constrain access to it under the control of a premises gateway/firewall that enforces data privacy and security policies.
2. Establish legal, regulatory, and/or industry voluntary enforcement of privacy policies.

The first approach was identified in NISTIR 7628 (2010) Volume 2, pp. 37-38 with regard to consumer energy management systems (EMS). It is also the approach taken by recent regulatory initiatives in Germany and The Netherlands mandating an independent standardized gateway that controls and manages all access to all metering devices and other home energy applications and appliances (including PEVs) to ensure consumer data privacy and security.[99] For example, the

---

[99] Bundesamt für Sicherheit in der Informatioinstechnik [Federal Office for Information Security] (BSI), *Protection Profile for the Gateway of a Smart Metering System*, v1.3 (final release), March 31, 2014, http://www.commoncriteriaportal.org/files/ppfiles/pp0073b_pdf.pdf [accessed 8/11/2014].

Privacy and Security Working Group, Netbeheer Nederland (NN), *Privacy and Security of the Advanced Metering Infrastructure*. Anahem, The Netherlands: NN, 2011. It may be worth noting that different countries have different market requirements and structures, such as state commission authorities, small municipal, or co-op structures, which may significantly limit the options when considering global implementations.

vehicle user could have the right and ability to erase, limit, or block data from being stored or transferred beyond the vehicle or premises such as is being done in the case of some computer browsers (e.g., *CCleaner* removes browsing history recorded by Firefox and Explorer browsers).

5.8.5 Looking Forward

Technical standards for premises systems and vehicle systems are currently under development that could support both privacy risk mitigation approaches. Currently regarding PEVs, there are essentially no technical safeguards to protect data stored in internal memory. Policy makers have the opportunity now to identify policies and to guide standards development in a way that could avoid future problems.

Specific solutions or mitigations for these potential privacy issues will need to be explored as technology solutions are deployed going forward. System and infrastructure architects and engineers should, in the meantime, stay aware of these potential issues. The Privacy Subgroup will endeavor to conduct more research in this area before the next revision of this document occurs.

5.9. AWARENESS AND TRAINING

Providing effective information security and privacy training and awareness not only supports privacy principles but also helps to ensure that workers, throughout all entities within the smart grid, have the knowledge necessary to keep personal information and energy usage data assets appropriately secured during their daily work activities. There is also a growing number of laws and regulations that include requirements for organizations to provide some type of information security and privacy training and awareness communications to not only their personnel, but also in some instances to their customers and consumers. Just a few examples of these include the Health Insurance Portability and Accountability Act (HIPAA), the Fair Credit Reporting Act (FCRA) and the Gramm Leach Bliley Act (GLBA).

In addition to employee education, consumer education on privacy supports informed decisions related to participating in the deployment of smart grid technologies and granting access to the information such technologies enables. Concerns related to privacy can result in consumers opting out of smart meter deployment or in limiting access to customer energy usage data collected using smart grid technologies. All stakeholders have an important role in educating consumers on their rights as someone that will have their data collected to promote confidence in the way that such information is used and safeguarded from unauthorized use. To promote these objectives, information on privacy protections should be incorporated conspicuously into communications with consumers.

Likewise, raising awareness of privacy concerns for customer and energy usage data, and showing how those concerns are being addressed, may be an important aspect of managing relationships between various stakeholders. The audience for this training could include consumer advocates, legislators, state regulatory commissions, and utility companies.

It is important to note that while training and awareness are critical to overall understanding and acceptance of smart meter technologies, state PUCs/PSCs may not be the best avenue for seeking training. There are multiple areas where a PUC/PSC may lack in training abilities including resource and budget constraints, lack of jurisdiction, or political constraints stemming from public perceptions of their state utility commission. In general, state PUCs/PSCs where smart grid functionalities exist may make an effort to educate customers using non-direct methods such as FAQ pages on their website, but should not be expected to roll out a public outreach campaign similar to the outreach programs created by utilities and/or Third Parties. PSCs/PUCs often mandate that utilities should create and execute well-defined public outreach campaigns that focus on educating customers about smart grid technologies as a part of their cost recovery stipulation. While not directly a product of state commissions, these campaigns are generally reviewed and approved by state commissions as being acceptable for public dissemination.

Through the efforts of several stakeholder categories, training slide sets have been developed by the CSWG Privacy Subgroup to assist various organizations with training employees, contracted workers, government entities, the private sector, and the general public on privacy implications and protections specific to the smart grid. These slide sets[100] include training materials for the following groups:

- Utilities

- State PUCs/PSCs

- Third Party Service Providers

- Consumer Advocacy Groups

These training and awareness slides may be used by organizations as a starting point for those within organizations planning information security and privacy education programs as they relate to smart grid privacy. These slides provide information as a way to help "train the trainer" -- providing advice and assistance for the organizations to create their own awareness and training content. There is significant additional information within the speaker notes, along with many pointers to other information resources, that organizations may wish to use when delivering their own tailored training.

The slide sets were created to assist organizations in developing their own training regimen and should not be considered as legal advice under any circumstances. Note that these slides are not endorsed by NIST, nor are they required to be used under any existing law or regulation.

5.10. MITIGATING PRIVACY CONCERNS WITHIN THE SMART GRID

Many of the concerns relating to the smart grid and privacy may be addressed by limiting the information required to that which operationally necessary.

Where there is an operational need for information, controls should be implemented to ensure that data is collected only where such a need exists. Organizations will benefit by developing policies to determine the consumer and premises information that should be safeguarded and how that information should be retained, distributed internally, shared with Third Parties, and secured against breach. As noted in other parts of this report, training employees is critical to implementing this policy. Similarly, recipients of smart grid services should be informed as to what information the organization is collecting and how that information will be used, shared, and secured. Service recipients may also need the ability to inspect collected information for accuracy and quality, as recommended in the privacy principles described in the PIA material

---

[100] See https://collaborate.nist.gov/twiki-sggrid/bin/view/SmartGrid/CSCTGPrivacy#Privacy_Training_Slides [accessed 8/11/2014].

(see Appendix F: Summary of the Smart Grid High-Level Consumer-to-Utility Privacy Impact Assessment).

Existing business rules, standards, laws, and regulations previously considered relevant to other sectors of the economy might, if not directly applicable, be usable as models to provide protection against certain areas of concern described in §5.6, Table 5-2.[101] However, because of the current technology used for the collection of the data, some concerns may need to be addressed by other means.

Many of the concerns relating to the smart grid and privacy may be addressed by limiting the information required from an operational standpoint. For example, many existing implementations of demand response use direct load control, where the utility has a communications channel to thermostats, water heaters, and other appliances at consumer premises. Although most direct load control today is one-way, if two-way communications are implemented, the pathway from the consumer may allow granular monitoring of energy consumption by appliance. Such direct monitoring may provide more accurate load management, but could also pose certain privacy risks.

There are other methods that use demand response for distributed load control where the utility or Third Party energy service provider delivers pricing and energy data to a consumer Energy Management System (EMS) through a gateway. Intelligent appliances and/or the consumer EMS use this pricing and energy information to optimize energy consumption according to consumer preferences. With the insertion of a gateway and local intelligence, any feedback to the utility could include aggregated load control results for the entire household, rather than individual appliance data. To mitigate privacy concerns, these results need to be averaged over a long enough time interval to prevent pattern recognition against known load profiles, as explained in §5.3.1. Thus, it is possible to protect consumer privacy at a macro level by choosing a system design that minimizes frequent access to granular data from outside the consumer premises.

5.10.1 Existing Privacy Standards and Frameworks

The following represents a list of some existing standards and frameworks that can supplement the use cases documented here that applied the OECD Privacy Guidelines (see Appendix E).

1. *ISO/IEC 27002: Information technology — Security techniques — Code of practice for information security management: Section 15.* The International Organization for Standardization (ISO), and the International Electrotechnical Commission (IEC) jointly issued this international standard, last updated and published in December 2005. It is part of a growing family of ISO/IEC Information Security Management Systems (ISMS) standards. It is the Security Compliance Standard. ISO/IEC 27002 provides a security framework. Section 15 covers Compliance, including legal requirements; security policies and standards and technical compliance; and Information systems audit considerations. It is part of a growing family of ISO/IEC Information Security Management Systems (ISMS) standards.

2. *ISO/IEC 29100: Information technology — Security techniques — Privacy framework.* This international standard published in December 2011 provides a privacy framework which specifies a common privacy terminology; defines the actors and their roles in

---

[101] For a discussion regarding current legal and regulatory developments regarding energy usage data, see §5.3.

45

processing personally identifiable information (PII); describes privacy safeguarding considerations; and provides references to known privacy principles for information technology.

3. *ISO/IEC 15944-8: Information technology — Business Operational View —Part 8: Identification of privacy protection requirements as external constraints on business transactions.* Modeling business transactions using scenarios and scenario components is done by specifying the applicable constraints on the data content using explicitly stated rules. External constraints apply to most business transactions. This part of ISO/IEC 15944 describes the business semantic descriptive techniques needed to support privacy protection requirements when modeling business transactions using the external constraints of jurisdictional domains. It was published in April 2012.

4. *Fair Information Practice Principles (FIPPs).* The FIPPs are a set of principles that are rooted in the tenets of the Privacy Act of 1974. Several slightly different versions are used by various U.S. Federal Agencies, including the Department of Homeland Security (DHS), the Federal Trade Commission (FTC), and the Department of Commerce (DOC). For DHS, the FIPPs are Transparency, Individual Participation, Purpose Specification, Data Minimization, Use Limitation, Data Quality and Integrity, Security, and Accountability and Auditing. For the FTC, they are Notice/Awareness, Choice/Consent, Access/Participation, Integrity/Security, and Enforcement/Redress.

5. *American Institute of Certified Public Accountants (AICPA)/Canadian Institute of Chartered Accountants (CICA) Generally Accepted Privacy Principles (GAPP) (a.k.a. AICPA/CICA GAPP).* These privacy tools include a universal framework for CPAs to conduct risk assessments and provide criteria to protect the privacy of personal information. The AICPA/CICA GAPP's Security for Privacy Principles has been mapped to ISO/IEC 27002. [102]

6. *European Union (EU) privacy framework.* The European Commission has proposed reforms to existing 1995 data protection rules that include a single set of rules on data protection that include a policy communication, a regulation setting out a general EU framework for data protection, and a directive to protect personal data processed for judicial activities.[103]

7. *APEC Privacy Framework.* Published in 2005, this framework establishes and promotes an approach to protecting privacy when sharing information throughout Asia-Pacific Economic Cooperation (APEC) member countries, with a goal of removing barriers to the free flow of information.[104]

8. *Privacy by Design (PbD).* This is a privacy framework by Ann Cavoukian, PhD, Information & Privacy Commissioner of Ontario. PbD promotes the proactive incorporation of privacy as the default and data protections embedded throughout the

---

[102] See http://www.aicpa.org/INTERESTAREAS/INFORMATIONTECHNOLOGY/RESOURCES/PRIVACY/Pages/default.aspx [accessed 8/11/2014].

[103] See http://ec.europa.eu/justice/data-protection/index_en.htm [accessed 8/11/2014].

[104] See more at http://www.apec.org/Groups/Committee-on-Trade-and-Investment/~/media/Files/Groups/ECSG/05_ecsg_privacyframewk.ashx [accessed 8/11/2014].

entire lifecycle of systems and technologies. The 7 Foundational Principles of PbD were published in August 2009 and revised in January 2011.[105]

9. *FTC Privacy Framework*. The Federal Trade Commission, America's chief privacy policy and enforcement agency, issued this final report setting forth best practices for businesses to protect the privacy of American consumers and give them greater control over the collection and use of their personal data. The final privacy report expands on a preliminary staff report the FTC issued in December 2010.[106]

10. *The Consumer Privacy Bill of Rights*. The Obama Administration released this document in February 2012, as part of a comprehensive blueprint to improve consumers' privacy protections and ensure that the Internet remains an engine for innovation and economic growth. The blueprint will guide efforts to give users more control over how their personal information is used on the Internet and to help businesses maintain consumer trust and grow in the rapidly changing digital environment.[107]

11. NIST Special Publication (SP) 800-53 Revision 4, *Security and Privacy Controls for Federal Information Systems and Organizations, Appendix J, Privacy Control Catalog*. The purpose of this publication is to provide guidelines for selecting and specifying security controls for organizations and information systems supporting the executive agencies of the federal government to meet the requirements of FIPS Publication 200, *Minimum Security Requirements for Federal Information and Information Systems*.[108]

5.10.2 Privacy Mitigation Tools and Activities

The mitigation of privacy risks is a process that seeks to minimize negative impacts to privacy. It encompasses a wide range of privacy management activities that identify threats and vulnerabilities to privacy for each business activity. Once a risk is identified, privacy mitigation processes attempt to match proportionate privacy controls for each relevant business activity that creates a risk to privacy. Described below are three widely used privacy mitigation processes: Privacy Impact Assessments, Privacy Audits, and Privacy Use Cases.

Privacy Impact Assessments.

A privacy impact assessment (PIA) is a structured process used to identify risks involved with—

- Fulfilling legal and regulatory obligations for managing, using, and sharing personal information.

- Collecting and using personal information only for the intended purposes.

- Ensuring the information is timely and accurate.

---

[105] See more at http://privacybydesign.ca/ [accessed 8/11/2014].

[106] "FTC Issues Final Commission Report on Protecting Consumer Privacy: Agency Calls on Companies to Adopt Best Privacy Practices," Federal Trade Commission [Press release], March 26, 2012, http://www.ftc.gov/news-events/press-releases/2012/03/ftc-issues-final-commission-report-protecting-consumer-privacy [accessed 8/11/2014].

[107] "We Can't Wait: Obama Administration Unveils Blueprint for a "Privacy Bill of Rights" to Protect Consumers Online," The White House [Press release], February 23, 2012, http://www.whitehouse.gov/the-press-office/2012/02/23/we-can-t-wait-obama-administration-unveils-blueprint-privacy-bill-rights [accessed 8/11/2014].

[108] See http://dx.doi.org/10.6028/NIST.SP.800-53r4.

- Ensuring the information is protected according to applicable laws and regulations while in the organization's possession.

- Determining the impact of the information systems on individual privacy.

- Ensuring individuals (e.g., employees, customers, etc.) are aware of the information the organization collects and how the information is used.

Any organization that collects personal information, or information that can reveal information about personal activities, can identify areas where privacy protections are necessary by performing a PIA. A PIA can be performed internal to the organization, or by an objective independent entity.

Audits.

An audit is a structured evaluation of a person, organization, system, process, enterprise, project or product. Audits can be used to determine compliance levels with legal requirements, identify areas where policies are not being followed, and so on. An audit should ideally be performed by an objective entity that is independent of the entity being audited.

Privacy Use Cases.

A Privacy Use Case is a method of looking at data flows that will help entities within the smart grid to rigorously track data flows and the privacy implications of collecting and using data. It is intended to help organizations address and mitigate the associated privacy risks within common technical design and business practices. Use cases can help smart grid architects and engineers build privacy protections into the smart grid. Privacy protection designed into a system is preferable to a privacy patch or "work around" in an attempt to remedy a limitation or omission.

The Privacy Use Cases presented in Appendix E of this document are focused on data privacy in selected smart grid scenarios[109], making them unique amongst the many tools, frameworks, and standards that are noted above. These Privacy Use Cases reflect the electricity value chain and the impacts that smart grid technologies, new policies, new markets, and new consumer interactions will have on the privacy of personal data. The Privacy Use Cases can serve as a valuable tool for all types of smart grid entities to better understand the implications of smart grid changes to existing processes and procedures. These smart grid entities include utilities; energy service companies (ESCOs); vendors of products and services that may include collection, storage, or communication of personal data; and policy-makers.

When the general privacy concerns have been identified, the entities within each part of the smart grid can then look at their associated smart grid business processes and technical components to determine which privacy concerns exist within their scope of smart grid use and participation. Privacy use cases may be utilized to represent generalizations of specific scenarios within the smart grid that require interoperability between systems and smart grid participants in support of business processes and workflow. Through structured and repeatable analysis, business use cases can be elaborated upon as interoperability/technical privacy use cases to be implemented by the associated entities within the smart grid. The resulting details will allow

---

[109] The key Use Cases deemed architecturally significant with respect to security requirements for the smart grid in NISTIR 7628 (August 2010). The CSWG Privacy Subgroup took those use cases verbatim and added the privacy considerations for each associated use case.

those responsible for creating, implementing, and managing the controls that impact privacy to do so more effectively and consistently.

5.10.3 Privacy Use Case Scenarios

The Privacy Subgroup spent many months creating a few different methods for expanding the existing NIST collection of use cases[110] to include consideration of privacy concerns. When considering which set of FIPPS to use for creating privacy use cases, it was decided to use the Organisation for Economic Co-operation and Development (OECD) Privacy Guidelines. They are—

- Long-established and widely recognized;

- Freely available; and

- Straightforward concepts that will be more easily and consistently utilized when building privacy controls into processes.

The larger set of principles used to conduct the smart grid PIA was chosen because they better served the purposes of identifying where, within an identified system or process, the most comprehensive set of privacy concerns exist. Typically, PIAs are performed by a specific individual or specialized group within an organization, and the PIAs look at a broader scope within a system or process and go less in-depth than a privacy use case.

Privacy use cases are typically utilized by a broader community and are repeatedly used to examine a specific, narrow scope. By keeping the privacy use case process limited to one set of accepted privacy principles such as the OECD Privacy Guidelines, it will be simpler and more feasible for the privacy use cases to be consistently used and applied by the broader community.

Appendix E contains the full set of privacy use cases.

5.11. EMERGING SMART GRID PRIVACY RISKS

Seamless and rapid access to energy usage data can benefit consumers by helping them to manage costs and to conserve energy but may also introduce additional privacy risks. In addition to addressing the other current risks identified within this report as a whole, organizations and consumers utilizing smart grid systems, applications, and related technologies should also be aware that new threats to privacy, and vulnerabilities within new technologies and practices, will continue to emerge over time and as capabilities and technologies evolve. Interconnected networks (e.g., smart phones that utilize cloud services) expand the opportunities for privacy data breaches. While such risks are not unique to the smart grid, they may introduce new types of issues that will need to be addressed as the smart grid evolves. Some of the new and emerging technologies and activities that were not yet widely deployed or in existence within the smart grid at the time of this report, but that are being discussed and could introduce different privacy challenges, include:

---

[110] See the collection of use cases that the Privacy Subgroup considered and chose as representative use cases: http://collaborate.nist.gov/twiki-sggrid/bin/view/SmartGrid/UseCases [accessed 8/11/2014].

1. **Customer energy usage data (CEUD) and personal consumer data being sent to smart phones and other mobile computing devices.** Sending data from centrally controlled and secured systems to such devices as smart phones and mobile computers puts that data under the control of the associated users. While such information can be very useful to those users, if the data is not appropriately secured, the data can be breached. This type of decentralization of sensitive and personal data has led to significant privacy breaches through mobile computing devices[111]. Additionally, CEUD and personal consumer data stored on mobile computing devices are difficult to track and maintain.

2. **CEUD and personal consumer data being sent to social media sites, or social media sites being used to control end devices.**[112] In recent years, data that used to be stored only on secured business servers have been put onto social media sites, resulting in unauthorized disclosure and the loss of trust in the organizations responsible for the data. Often workers with authorized access to the sensitive data have been careless, or lacked appropriate privacy and security training.[113]

3. **CEUD and personal consumer data being stored, managed, or otherwise accessed from cloud services.** Sensitive data stored and managed by cloud services have been breached on numerous occasions. In a recent study, over half of the organizations surveyed are not currently using cloud services because of the related security concerns.[114] Organizations within the smart grid should be aware of the risks related to the use of cloud services if or when they consider moving some smart grid activities to such cloud services.

4. **The creation of new applications (apps) that collect CEUD and personal consumer data.** According to a recent study, most workers now are spending a significant amount of time each day using apps on mobile devices and are expected to spend more time doing so than browsing the Internet on those devices.[115] There is a growing number of apps, and the

---

[111] As reported in the Pew Research Center report, *Privacy and Data Management on Mobile Devices* (September 5, 2012), "smartphone owners are also twice as likely as other cell owners to have experienced someone accessing their phone in a way that made them feel like their privacy had been invaded. Owners of smartphones and more basic phones are equally likely to say their phone has been lost or stolen." See http://pewinternet.org/~/media//Files/Reports/2012/PIP_MobilePrivacyManagement.pdf, p. 3 [accessed 8/11/2014].

[112] S. Soundation, *4 Channel Arduino-based Twitter control for home appliances!*, January 11, 2012. http://www.youtube.com/watch?v=n3S5CDm7IPk [accessed 8/11/2014].

[113] According to a Ponemon Institute survey report, *The Human Factor in Data Protection* (January 2012), employees are the root cause of many data breaches due to their negligence or malicious behavior, and 78 % of the survey respondents indicate that employee behaviors, both intentional and accidental, were cited as leading to at least one data breach within their organizations over the past two years. One of the primary reasons listed was the "use of social media in the workplace." See http://www.trendmicro.com/cloud-content/us/pdfs/security-intelligence/reports/rpt_trend-micro_ponemon-executive-summary.pdf [accessed 8/11/2014].

[114] According to a global cloud survey conducted by Trend Micro in August, 2012, more than half (53 %) of decision makers surveyed said that data security was a key factor in their decision to "put the brakes on" cloud adoption. See S. Hoffman, "Study: Data Security Biggest Cloud Inhibitor," *ChannelNomics.com*, August 30, 2012, http://channelnomics.com/2012/08/30/study-security-biggest-cloud-inhibitor/ [accessed 8/11/2014].

[115] According to a September 12, 2012 Flurry Analytics report, mobile phone users spend over 1.5 hours a day on average on applications, and the number continues to grow. The time spent by users on apps is now beginning to surpass the time spent on the Internet on mobile devices. See P. Depuy, "Surfing your smartphone: who's watching you?" *Prime Social Marketing*, September 12, 2012, http://www.primesocialmarketing.com/surfing-your-smartphone-whos-watching-you.html#.U_YMoWOFlHo [accessed 8/11/2014].

quality of the security built into these apps varies widely. A growing number post information to online sites without the app users' knowledge.[116]

5. **Smart meter reading capabilities for individual premises so that a home area network (HAN) or other device may monitor in smaller intervals, as well as in real-time**. As discussed in other areas of this report, the more frequently energy usage readings occur, the more detailed information can be inferred about the related personal activities. As customers consider installing advanced technology, all parties involved should consider the potential privacy impacts of using that technology or service.

6. **Including CEUD and energy consumer data in "Big Data"[117] files and their associated analysis activities**. Seemingly benign data can have consequences when amassed, analyzed, cross-referenced, and correlated with other databases. Analyzing energy usage data and/or consumer personal data may reveal information about the associated individuals' activities, habits, and lifestyles. When this data is combined with other data in Big Data repositories, it may enable useful and needed energy management breakthroughs that benefit both the individual and society by using powerful Big Data analytics. However, the activities may also reveal personal information about individuals that, until the advent of Big Data and associated analytics, had not yet been able to be accomplished.[118] If smart grid entities consider the use of Big Data, they should also consider the associated new ways in which Big Data analytics can reveal consumer information and energy consumption activities. In addition, regulators and other legal authorities may wish to consider Big Data analytics and possible consequences.

7. **Connecting smart appliances and HANs directly to the smart grid**. Utilities are already seeing the benefits of consumers using their HANs to help self-manage their energy use, as well as improving the ability for utilities to manage service to customers.[119] If smart grid entities continue along this path, they should also consider the associated privacy risks that will accompany connections of consumer HANs to smart meters or other smart grid components.

8. **Green Button developments that bring privacy risks**. Utilities are working with software companies to enable energy customers to transfer their own energy data to authorized Third Parties using new Green Button energy application program interfaces (APIs) and data sets. The Green Button initiative is resulting in innovations, and possibly new types of

---

[116] Secure.me analyzed approximately 500,000 Facebook apps and found 63 % of those apps ask for the ability to post on the app user's behalf. See C. Taylor, "Most Facebook Apps Can Post Behind Your Back [updated]," *Mashable*, September 4, 2012, http://mashable.com/2012/09/04/most-facebook-apps-post-behind-your-back-exclusive/ [accessed 8/11/2014].

[117] The term "Big Data" refers to digital data volume, velocity and/or variety that can enable novel approaches to frontier questions previously inaccessible or impractical using current or conventional methods; and/or exceed the capacity or capability of legacy or conventional methods and systems.

[118] In Microsoft's *Trustworthy Computing Next* report, an entire section is devoted to discussing privacy issues related to Big Data that are similar to this. See S. Charney, *Trustworthy Computing Next*, version 1.01, Microsoft Corporation, February 28, 2012, http://blogs.technet.com/b/security/archive/2012/08/27/computing-trends-cloud-big-data-and-the-evolving-threat-landscape.aspx [accessed 8/11/2014].

[119] L. Margonelli, "Could the Smart Grid Finally Do Some Good for Consumers?" *Pacific Standard*, September 26, 2012, http://www.psmag.com/environment/could-the-smart-grid-finally-do-some-good-for-consumers-46882/ [accessed 8/11/2014].

technologies, to provide energy data transfer paths to authorized Third Parties.[120] The vendors creating these new Green Button technology solutions should build in controls to address any new types of privacy risks that emerge with the new technology solutions.

9. **Linking or tracking (e.g., GPS) consumer activities and movements with energy usage data**. Law enforcement and investigators have been tracking vehicle activities through the use of GPS for several years to help with cases and solving crimes. There are now GPS devices that track fuel use as it relates to driving behavior.[121] If these types of monitoring tools are expanded to tracking PEVs, and then connected to other networks that are part of the smart grid, the related privacy issues need to be addressed. Likewise, if any other types of mobile energy-using appliances or other devices are connected to a HAN or other smart grid components, the impact of combining the GPS and related locational data with the energy usage data should be assessed for new privacy risks.

10. **Sharing smart grid data across national borders**. Energy usage data, focused at the transmission and distribution level, but not individual consumer, is currently shared from the U.S. to Canada. Energy data is also currently shared across borders throughout the European Union (EU),[122] as well as other locations throughout the world. If the U.S. plans to share more types of data that would involve individual consumer data, created through any of the smart grid components with another country, then the privacy impacts of such new types of cross border data flows should be evaluated.

11. **Wireless smart grid data transmissions, including near field communications (NFC) as well as wide area wireless communications**. Smart meters and associated devices may collect energy usage data from inside the home, store it, and send it to the utilities through wireless Internet or other connections. If plans emerge to start transmitting energy usage and/or customer data from HANs into smart meters, or other types of existing or future smart grid components, then those wireless transmissions will bring privacy risks, and controls should be established to protect the transmissions from inappropriate use.

12. **Linking biometrics with the smart grid**. Biometrics are currently used to accomplish strong authentication for secured networks and systems. Biometric encryption is currently being used within Canada to secure smart meter and other smart grid transmissions.[123] Biometrics provide a strong way to perform authentication and encryption. However, the biometric identifier itself provides information about an individual that needs to be strongly controlled and secured. If utilities and smart grid vendors start exploring biometric

---

[120] See "3 promising developments on the road to energy empowerment," *SmartGridNews.com,* October 2, 2012, http://www.smartgridnews.com/artman/publish/Business_Consumer_Engagement/3-promising-developments-on-the-road-to-energy-empowerment-5162.html/#.UHsRZMXA9V4 [accessed 8/11/2014].

[121] See A. Chang, "Tracking Behavior Behind the Wheel," *Forbes.com*, September 27, 2012, http://www.forbes.com/sites/altheachang/2012/09/27/tracking-behavior-behind-the-wheel/ [accessed 8/11/2014].

[122] See "Smart grids: Making connections," EurActiv.com, December 22, 2011, http://www.euractiv.com/energy/smart-grids-making-connections-linksdossier-509908 [accessed 8/11/2014].

[123] See K. Anderson, "Practical Privacy by Design: Examples of Success," [Presentation], June 13, 2012, http://www.pcpd.org.hk/pbdconference/files/Anderson_Part2.pdf [accessed 8/11/2014].

authentication and/or encryption methods for use within the smart grid, then they should determine how to acceptably secure those biometric data files.

13. **New types of malware within the smart grid**. There are ever increasing types of malware throughout all systems and networks. Many types of mobile malware exist whose sole purpose is to steal data from mobile devices, with the goal of obtaining as much personal data as possible.[124] Many of these privacy-stealing malware are delivered through apps, while others are delivered through online sites. It is a growing occurrence for personal data stealing malware to be represented as anti-malware tools.[125] As new apps, tools, and technologies emerge for smart grid components, organizations should be vigilant for new types of malware created to steal data collected through various smart grid technologies such as smart meters and smart appliances.

14. **New risks created by adding other utilities (e.g., water, gas, etc.) into the smart grid.** Many utilities also currently provide water and/or gas services. Usage data from those services may provide additional insights into personal activities, possibly creating additional privacy risks. If water and gas data are combined with electricity usage data within the smart grid, more information about lifestyles and individual activities may be revealed. Additional research should be used to identify any additional privacy risks accompanying the incorporation of water and gas usage within the smart grid.

15. **Ensuring "intelligent" systems that react to smart grid activities do not invade privacy as an after-effect**. Intelligent software that has the ability to control and make changes to different components within the smart grid, based upon systems settings, patterns, and other factors, can provide great benefit to managing energy usage. However, as has already been demonstrated,[126] if the intelligent systems are compromised, such as through the supporting code or through access to the systems themselves, potentially immeasurable amounts of damage could occur. Some of this damage could include access to customer and/or energy usage data, and making data and energy usage alterations that impact dwelling environments and the individuals within them. As intelligent systems are created for use within the smart grid, attention should be given to how the planned systems can impact privacy.

All utilities and smart grid vendors that are planning to pursue any of these activities and technologies should keep privacy in mind, and address the associated privacy risks as they develop such services and solutions. Consumers considering making use of these advanced technologies and services should also be aware of the potential privacy trade-offs of using those technologies or services.

---

[124] See more information in L. Seltzer, "Mobile Malware Exists to Steal Your Data," *InformationWeek Government,* March 6, 2012, http://www.informationweek.com/byte/personal-tech/mobile-applications/mobile-malware-exists-to-steal-your-data/232602097 [accessed 8/11/2014].

[125] See more information in the thread "Removal Instructions for Privacy Protection," *Malwarebytes.org,* started November 6, 2011, http://forums.malwarebytes.org/index.php?showtopic=99247 [accessed 8/11/2014].

[126] See more information in "Cyber Security Risk to Smart Grids and Intelligent Buildings," *ScienceDaily.com,* August 13, 2012, http://www.sciencedaily.com/releases/2012/08/120813115448.htm [accessed 8/11/2014].

5.12. SMART GRID PRIVACY SUMMARY AND RECOMMENDATIONS

Based upon the work and research conducted since June 2009, and since the publication of the first version of NISTIR 7628 Volume 2 (August 2010), the Privacy Subgroup identified significant new privacy issues to address, created a number of tools for smart grid entities to use, and made a number of recommendations to mitigate privacy risks.

Creating a smart grid privacy principles program that individuals are willing to use continues to be a challenge. The goal is to have individuals participate in the smart grid, allowing the electric sector to thrive and innovation to occur. An indicator of success is the degree to which effective and transparent privacy practices are consistently implemented, followed, and enforced within the smart grid. To create this transparency and obtain the trust of smart grid participants—and based on the conclusions and the details of the associated findings—recommendations were made throughout this volume for all entities that participate within the smart grid. The following provides a summary listing of all the recommendations from within this volume that can be used for quick reference by organizations to assist with their privacy mitigation efforts. This list provides only a brief description of each recommendation. For more details refer to the associated section as indicated below—

Sections 5.1 - 5.3

- No recommendations within these sections.

Section 5.4 and Appendix F Consumer-to-Utility Privacy Impact Assessment

1. **Management and Accountability**.

   - **Assign privacy responsibility.** Each organization collecting or using smart grid data from or about consumer locations should create (or augment) a position or person with responsibility to ensure that privacy policies and practices exist and are followed.

   - **Establish privacy audits.** Audit functions should be modified to monitor all privacy-related energy data access.

   - **Establish or amend incident response and law enforcement request policies and procedures.** Organizations accessing, storing, or processing energy data should include specific documented incident response procedures for incidents involving energy data.

2. **Notice and Purpose**.

   - **Provide notification for the personal information collected.** Any organization collecting energy data from or about consumers should establish a process to notify consumer account inhabitants and person(s) paying the bills (which may be different entities), when appropriate, in a clearly worded description of the data being collected, why it is necessary to collect the data, and the intended use, retention, and sharing of the data.

   - **Provide notification for new information use purposes and collection.** Organizations should update consumer notifications whenever they want to start using existing collected data for materially different purposes other than those the consumer has previously authorized.

3. **Choice and Consent**.

- **Provide notification about choices.** The consumer notification should include a clearly worded description to the recipients of services notifying them of (1) any choices available to them about information being collected and obtaining explicit consent when possible; and (2) explaining when and why data items are or may be collected and used without obtaining consent, such as when certain pieces of information are needed to restore service in a timely fashion.

4. **Collection and Scope**.

- **Limit the collection of data to only that necessary for smart grid operations,** including planning and management, improving energy use and efficiency, account management, and billing.

- **Obtain the data by lawful and fair means and, where appropriate and possible, with the knowledge or consent of the customer.**

5. **Use and Retention**.

- **Review privacy policies and procedures.** Every organization with access to smart grid data should review existing information security and privacy policies to determine how they may need to be modified.

- **Limit information retention.** Data collection that exceeds the purposes for which the data were originally collected can have financial consequences. For example, the existence and contents of databases about customers may be subject to civil and criminal discovery. Service providers may be obligated to hire staff to cull these databases in order to fulfill court orders. Data, and subsequently created information that reveals personal information or activities from and about a specific consumer location, should be retained only for as long as necessary to fulfill the purposes that have been communicated to the energy consumers. After the appropriate retention period, data should be aggregated or destroyed.

6. **Individual Access**.

- **Access to energy usage data.** Any organization possessing energy data about consumers should provide a process to allow consumers access to the corresponding energy data for their utilities account.

- **Dispute resolution.** Smart grid entities should establish documented dispute resolution procedures for energy consumers to follow.

7. **Disclosure and Limiting Use**.

- **Limit information use.** Data on energy or other smart grid service activities should be used or disclosed only for the authorized purposes for which it was collected.

- **Disclosure.** Data should be divulged to or shared only with those parties authorized to receive it and with whom the organizations have told the recipients of services it would be shared.

8. Security and Safeguards.

- **Associate energy data with individuals only when and where required.** For example, only link equipment data with a location or consumer account when needed for billing, service restoration, or other operational needs.

- **De-identify information.** Energy data and any resulting information, such as monthly charges for service, collected as a result of smart grid operations should be aggregated and anonymized by removing personal information elements wherever possible to ensure that energy data from specific consumer locations is limited appropriately. This may not be possible for some business activities, such as for billing.

- **Safeguard personal information.** All organizations collecting, processing, or handling energy data and other personal information from or about consumer locations should ensure that all information collected and subsequently created about the recipients of smart grid services is appropriately protected in all forms from loss, theft, unauthorized access, disclosure, copying, use, or modification.

- **Do not use personal information for research purposes.** Any organization collecting energy data and other personal information from or about consumer locations should refrain from using actual consumer data for research until it has been anonymized and/or sufficiently aggregated to assure to a reasonable degree the inability to link detailed data to individuals.

9. Accuracy and Quality.

- **Keep information accurate and complete.** Any organization collecting energy data from or about consumer locations should establish policies and procedures to ensure that the smart grid data collected from and subsequently created about recipients of services is accurate, complete, and relevant for the identified purposes for which they were obtained, and that it remains accurate throughout the life of the smart grid data within the control of the organization.

10. Openness, Monitoring, and Challenging Compliance.

- **Policy challenge procedures.** Organizations collecting energy data, and all other entities throughout the smart grid, should establish procedures that allow consumers to have the opportunity and process to challenge the organization's compliance with their published privacy policies as well as their actual privacy practices.

- **Perform regular privacy impact assessments.** Any organization collecting energy data from or about consumer locations should perform periodic PIAs with the appropriate time frames, to be determined by the utility and the appropriate regulator, based upon the associated risks and any recent process changes and/or security incidents.

- **Establish breach notice practices.** Any organization with smart grid data should establish policies and procedures to identify breaches and misuse of smart srid data, along with expanding or establishing procedures and plans for notifying the affected individuals in a timely manner with appropriate details about the breach.

Section 5.5 Personal Information in the Smart Grid

All organizations participating in the smart grid should determine which data items will significantly lessen or remove the ability to link to specific addresses or individuals whenever they perform their data anonymization activities.

Section 5.6 In-depth Look at Smart Grid Privacy Concerns

5.6.7 Wireless Access to Smart Meters and Secondary Devices

If future wireless technology is used to transmit aggregate home or business energy consumption information for a unique location or dwelling, then that usage data should also be protected from unauthorized use, modification, or theft prior to sufficient aggregation to protect privacy.

5.6.8 Commissioning, Registration, and Enrollment for Smart Devices

- Privacy issues that should be addressed related to the registration of these devices with Third Parties include: determining the types of information that are involved with these registration situations; controlling the connections which transmit the data to the Third Party, such as wireless transmissions from home area networks; and determining how the registration information is used, where it is stored, and with whom it is shared.

- At each step in this process, the consumer, utility, and Third Party provider should ensure that data flows have been identified and classified, and that privacy issues are addressed throughout, from initial commissioning up through service-provider-delivered service.

Section 5.7 and Appendix D Smart Grid Data Access by Third Parties

For the full set of recommendations, see Appendix D. A concise overview of the recommendations is contained below.

- **Privacy Notices.** Third Parties should provide a privacy notice to customers prior to sharing customer energy usage data (CEUD) with another party, or in the case of a significant change in organizational structure, such as a merger, bankruptcy, or outsourcing.

- **Customer Authorization for Disclosures.** Third Parties should seek customer authorization prior to disclosing CEUD to other parties unless the service for which the data disclosure is necessary has been previously authorized by the customer.

- **Data Disclosure.** A Third Party should not be collecting more than what is required to fulfill the agreed upon service, and a separate authorization should be obtained before CEUD is used in a different manner.

- **Customer Education & Awareness.** Third Parties should educate customers about the Third Party's CEUD privacy protection policies and practices, including the steps the Third Party is taking to protect privacy.

- **Data Minimization.** In following with the FIPPs, Third Parties should collect only the CEUD they need to provide the service they offer and have an authorization for.

- **Data Quality.** Data should as accurate and complete as possible.

- **Data Security.** Third Parties should have clear data security policies that should be periodically reviewed and updated.

- **Privacy Practices Risk Assessment.** Periodic assessments of the privacy practices should be performed.

- **Data Retention and Disposal.** Third Parties should have clear policies on how long data will be retained, as well as when and how CEUD will be disposed of.

- **Data Breaches.** Third Parties should be aware of any laws or requirements with regard to data breaches. These rules may apply, not just to the Third Party, but also to their Contracted Agents.

- **Employee Training.** Employees of Third Parties and their Contracted Agents should be trained on the security and privacy practices necessary to protect customer CEUD.

- **Audits.** The recommended practices discuss the use of independent Third Party audits of security and privacy practices. These audits may be useful in helping to identify issues before they become legitimate problems.

Section 5.8 Plug-in Electric Vehicles Privacy Concerns

Specific solutions or mitigations for PEV potential privacy issues should be explored as technology solutions are deployed going forward. System and infrastructure architects and engineers should stay aware of potential issues.

Section 5.9 Awareness and Training

Organizations involved within the smart grid should provide privacy and information security training, supported by ongoing awareness communications, to their workers that have job responsibilities involving customer and energy usage data. Organizations should also consider providing information to their customers and the public to help them to better understand the privacy issues related to the smart grid, along with how the organization is working to mitigate the associated risks, and also steps the public can take to better protect their own privacy. Utilities, State PUCs/PSCs, Third Party providers, and consumer advocacy groups should consider using these as a starting point to help them effectively and efficiently plan for privacy education programs as they may relate to smart grid privacy.

Section 5.10 Mitigating Privacy Concerns within the Smart Grid

- **Perform privacy impact assessments (PIAs).** Any organization that collects personal information, or information that can reveal information about personal activities, can identify areas where privacy protections are necessary by performing a PIA. A PIA can be performed internal to the organization, or by an objective outside entity.

- **Perform Audits.** An audit is a structured evaluation of a person, organization, system, process, enterprise, project or product. Audits can be used to determine compliance levels with legal requirements, to identify areas where policies are not being followed, and so on. An audit should ideally be performed by an objective entity that is not a member of the area being audited.

- **Utilize the Privacy Use Cases.** Use cases can help smart grid architects and engineers build privacy protections into the smart grid. The Privacy Use Cases in this document are focused on data privacy in selected smart grid scenarios, making them unique amongst the many tools, frameworks, and standards that are noted above.

Section 5.11 Emerging Smart Grid Privacy Risks

- Entities should remain aware of emerging smart grid privacy risks.

Given these realities, findings, and recommendations, the Privacy Subgroup hopes that the information contained in this volume will serve as a useful guide and reference for the wide variety of smart grid stakeholders, policymakers, and lawmakers who have, or may have in the future, responsibility for consumers' personal information, including energy consumption data.

5.13. NIST PRIVACY-RELATED WORK

5.13.1 National Strategy for Trustworthy Identities in Cyberspace Concerns

In April 2011, President Barack Obama issued the National Strategy for Trusted Identities in Cyberspace[127] (NSTIC). NSTIC calls for the development of interoperable technology standards and policies — an "Identity Ecosystem" — where individuals, organizations, and underlying infrastructure can be authoritatively authenticated in cyberspace. The goals of the NSTIC include protecting against cyber crimes (i.e. identity theft, fraud), while simultaneously helping to ensure that the Internet continues to support the innovation of products and ideas.[128]

The Identity Ecosystem promotes the secure validation of identities when performing sensitive transactions (such as obtaining financial, health or energy usage data) while simultaneously allowing for anonymity in other situations (such as casually surfing the Web). The Identity Ecosystem could protect individual privacy by reducing the need to share personally identifiable information (PII) at multiple web sites and by establishing policies about how organizations use and manage PII in the Identity Ecosystem.[129]

Additional benefits of the Identity Ecosystem may include:

- **Speed**: One user and one key credential would authorize any password-protected website the user delegates. This feature is very similar to the existing banking structure that allows a client to use their PIN for ATM transactions here and abroad.

- **Convenience**: Individuals, business, and government agencies could perform secured and sensitive transactions online that now are conducted in person.

---

[127] "National Strategy for Trusted Identities in Cyberspace: Enhancing Online Choice, Efficiency, Security, and Privacy," *The White House*, April 2011, http://www.whitehouse.gov/sites/default/files/rss_viewer/NSTICstrategy_041511.pdf [accessed 8/11/2014].

[128] "About NSTIC," [Web page], http://www.nist.gov/nstic/about-nstic.html [accessed 8/11/2014].

[129] *Ibid.*

- **Privacy**: Credentials would be intended to share only the amount of personal information necessary for the transaction, but allows for a choice of when to use or not to use a trusted ID.[130]

While the key framework of NSTIC calls for development by the private sector, the Department of Commerce established a National Program Office (NPO) to coordinate related federal activities that will advance the project's objectives.

As of May 2014, the NPO has taken two major steps forward. First, it contracted with a private organization to jump-start the public-private collaboration in August 2012. The Identity Ecosystem Steering Group has since established itself as a non-profit corporation and has held eight publicly open plenary sessions. It is in the process of developing the Identity Ecosystem Framework necessary to meet the NSTIC's goals. Second, the NPO has awarded twelve pilot projects that are intended to test or demonstrate new solutions, models or frameworks, motivated by the recognition that market forces alone have not been able to overcome various barriers to innovation. Such barriers include, but are not limited to:

- A lack of commonly accepted technical standards to ensure interoperability among different authentication solutions.

- Complex economic issues, including a lack of clarity related to liability (i.e., "who is liable if something goes wrong in a transaction?" "How – if at all – should transactions be monetized?").

- No common standards for privacy protections and data re-use.

- Challenges with usability of some strong authentication technologies.[131]

To help overcome some of these barriers, the Identity Ecosystem Framework promotes developing "policies for verifying identity and identity credentials; procedures for how identity credentials are used and verified through online authentication transactions; standards and technical specifications for conveying and securing identity information online, and; accountability measures to ensure all participants operate in accordance with defined rules."[132] The NSTIC NPO is currently reviewing applications for a third round of pilot projects to be awarded in the fall of 2014.

There are those that question the need for government action. A common criticism is that NSTIC will lead to an online national (or even worldwide) identity system that could discourage constitutionally protected speech and association, (such as anonymous speech). In addition, the Identity Ecosystem could create additional security and privacy concerns. For example, the Identity Ecosystem strategy could be compared to "creating a single skeleton key that, if cracked, could allow for a much greater security issue than a single site password breach."[133] Related

---

[130] "National Strategy for Trusted Identities in Cyberspace," [Web page], http://www.nist.gov/nstic/ [accessed 8/11/2014].

[131] "Announcement of Federal Funding Opportunity (FFO), National Strategy for Trusted Identities in Cyberspace (NSTIC) Pilot Grant Program," February 1, 2012, p. 5, http://www.nist.gov/nstic/2012-nstic-ffo-01.pdf [accessed 8/11/2014].

[132] Identity Ecosystem Steering Group (IESG), "The Proposed Identity Ecosystem Steering Group Workplan Outline," [August 3, 2012], p. 1, http://www.nist.gov/nstic/reports/IESG_Workplan_Outline.pdf [accessed 8/11/2014].

[133] K. Hickey, "Trusted Identities: Single sign-on or single point of failure?" *GCN*, February 1, 2011, http://gcn.com/articles/2011/02/01/trusted-identities-single-point-of-failure.aspx?m=2. [accessed 8/11/2014].

thereto, even though the process is entirely voluntary for the user, the increased acceptance of and preference for credentials by commercial websites could pressure even reluctant consumers to obtain NSTIC credentials, thereby greatly expanding the risks associated with such credentials.

Another chief privacy concern regarding the use of a single NSTIC credential to access multiple sites is that such credentials could be used to identify and track each unique user's online activity. Finally, credential issuing authorities could obtain leverage over website owners and consumers through not only their power to issue, but also potentially their ability to revoke credentials as well. There also is concern that since the system is being introduced by the government "individuals may be lulled into a false sense of security, believing it has appropriate safeguards in place to prevent security and privacy issues."[134]

The NSTIC NPO has addressed these concerns by developing a governance structure under a "multi-stakeholder" process that engages companies, government and consumer advocacy organizations on equal levels, and that currently has active participation and leadership from a number of privacy and consumer advocates. Under the Identity Ecosystem, relying parties would be dependent on identity providers, those that issue credentials, to validate the identity of users visiting the relying party's site. Accordingly, logic and history indicate that it may be difficult to initially recruit significant numbers of relying parties.[135]

To the extent NSTIC is implemented, the possibilities for incorporating the Identity Ecosystem into smart grid systems could be significant. For example, the NSTIC framework has the potential to affect utilities in multiple areas. In operations, NSTIC could allow field staff trusted access to company equipment using pre-authorized credentials without the need for additional verification from the management office. From the consumer's perspective, a user may have the ability to pay their utility bill without revealing credit card information simply by using the same credentials authorized by their financial institution, as well as have more secure access to Green Button[136] information. However, there are also likely to exist both additional positive and negative utility impacts that will not be known unless the NSTIC Identity Ecosystem comes to fruition.

In sum, the NSTIC Identity Ecosystem could change the paradigm for how energy usage information is accessed and shared, as well as if and when PII would be used or retained for identification purposes.

5.13.2 Privacy Engineering

NIST has begun a Privacy Engineering initiative that seeks to establish an outcome-oriented design framework for enhancing privacy within information systems. Process-oriented principles such as the Fair Information Practice Principles are an important component of an overall privacy framework, but on their own they do not achieve consistent and measurable results in privacy protection. In the security field, risk management models, along with technical standards

---

[134] *Ibid.*

[135] J. Fontana, "On 1-year anniversary, organized NSTIC looking for fast track," *ZDNet*, April 18, 2012, http://www.zdnet.com/blog/identity/on-1-year-anniversary-organized-nstic-looking-for-fast-track/424 [accessed 8/11/2014].

[136] Green Button is an industry-led effort that responds to a White House call-to-action: provide electricity customers with easy access to their energy usage data in a consumer-friendly and computer-friendly format. For more information, refer to: http://greenbuttondata.org [accessed 8/11/2014].

and best practices, are key components of improving security. Similarly, the safety risk management field also has well-developed models, technical standards and best practices. To date, the privacy field has lagged behind in the development of analogous components.

NIST's objective is to provide system owners, developers, and engineers with reusable, standards-based tools and privacy engineering practices that can be used to mitigate the risk of privacy harm in a measurable way within an organization's overall risk management process. The Smart Grid, like many other complex efforts, requires coordination across a wide range of disciplines – from engineers and system designers to legal and policy professionals. The Privacy Engineering initiative is intended to improve the ability of interdisciplinary teams to implement effective privacy practices, in part, by providing a common language that can be used across organizations.

NIST will engage a broad community of stakeholders to facilitate this work. To capture the findings from this outreach, NIST will produce a report that identifies challenges in privacy engineering, and proposes a framework for understanding privacy risk and a methodology for designing privacy-enabled systems that would support outcome-driven privacy design and engineering practices. NIST will hold workshops and formal public comment periods to maximize input from interested stakeholders. As the development of reusable tools and privacy engineering practices evolves, NIST may produce additional supporting materials.

APPENDIX C: CHANGING REGULATORY FRAMEWORKS

Beginning in 2010, the public utility commissions of California and Colorado conducted rulemaking proceedings to address privacy issues for customer energy usage data. Both proceedings involved collaborative processes and broad stakeholder involvement.

On September 29, 2010, California passed SB 1476 (California Public Utilities Code Secs. 8380 and 8381), which outlined privacy protections for electricity and natural gas usage data. Cal. P.U. Code Secs. 8380 and 8381 provide privacy protections for data generated by electrical and natural gas advanced meters used by both investor-owned and publicly owned utilities. Utilities cannot share, disclose or make available to a Third Party a customer's electricity or gas usage data generated by an advanced metering infrastructure without the consent of the customer, with limited exceptions. Those exceptions are when the data is used "for system, grid or operational needs, or [in] the implementation of demand response, energy management, or energy efficiency programs," or "as required or permitted under state or federal law or by an order of the" California Public Utilities Commission (CPUC). (California Public Utilities Code Section 8380(e)(2) and (3).) All other purposes, deemed "secondary purposes," require the consent of the customer. In addition, SB 1476 requires utilities to use "reasonable security procedures and practices" to protect a customer's unencrypted electric and gas usage data from unauthorized access, use or disclosure. SB 1476 also prohibits utilities from selling a customer's electric or gas usage data or any other personally identifiable information for any purpose.

SB 1476 was an update of and supplement to existing privacy statutes, regulations and tariffs dating from the early 1990s and already applicable to customer data held by utilities, such as Public Utilities Code Sections 394.4 (privacy protection for customer usage data obtained by non-utility electric service providers from utilities) and 2894 (privacy protections for customer information collected by telecommunications providers), and CPUC Decision No. 90-12-121, 39 CPUC 2d 173 (1990) (restrictions on Third Party access to confidential customer information possessed by utilities unless customer consent is obtained or a valid warrant or subpoena is obtained for law enforcement access). In response to the new statute, the CPUC initiated a new phase of their smart grid Rulemaking to develop updated privacy rules to implement SB 1476. The CPUC held several workshops and invited many interested parties, including utilities, consumer advocates, Third Party vendors and privacy advocates to make recommendations on what new rules the CPUC should adopt to implement SB 1476 and protect customer privacy. In addition to these workshops, the parties also met on their own to develop a consensus set of privacy requirements based on the Fair Information Practice Principles (FIPPS), which formed the basis of the rules ultimately adopted by the CPUC.

On July 28, 2011, the CPUC approved Decision 11-07-056 which adopted a set of "Rules Regarding Privacy and Security Protections for Energy Usage Data."[137] These rules, based on the FIPPS, and input from parties, maintained the "primary/secondary purpose" structure adopted by SB 1476. The Privacy Rules apply to utilities, Third Party contractors of the utility, and customer authorized Third Parties who obtain data from the utility; the Privacy Rules do not

---

[137] D.11-07-056 at Attachment D (Privacy Rules). This decision only applied to electrical utilities, a subsequent decision, D.12-08-045 (August 23, 2012), adopted the privacy rules to cover natural gas data generated by advanced meters.

apply to Third Parties who obtain customer data from the customer. [138] The Privacy Rules direct utilities to provide customers with a notice of what data is collected, and for what purpose the data is used.[139] The Rules direct the utilities to provide this notice yearly to all customers, be available on the utilities' home page, and provide a link to the privacy notice on all email to customers. [140] The Privacy Rules also provide the customer the ability to access their usage information, and allows customers to control access to their usage information. Consistent with the FIPPS, the Privacy Rules adopt a "Data Minimization" strategy for utilities and their contractors; specifically, Third Parties should only get the data necessary to accomplish the primary purpose and should hold on to the data for only as long as reasonably necessary. The Privacy Rules also contain requirements regarding the security of customer data, a requirement to notify customers and the CPUC upon a security or data breach affecting 1000 or more customers, and direct the utilities to implement periodic audits of their privacy and security practices and annually disclose the number of contractors and other Third Parties who obtain customer data.

The CPUC's Decision 11-07-056 also initiated a separate phase of the smart grid proceeding requiring investor-owned electric utilities to provide third-parties with electronic access to a customer's usage data via the utility's "backhaul" data storage and communications systems when authorized by the customer. The Third Party access must be consistent with the CPUC's privacy rules and must allow the CPUC to exercise oversight over Third Parties receiving customer data. The CPUC adopted the utility data access proposals on September 19, 2013.[141] This decision adopts a process for the oversight of Third Parties that obtain customer usage information from the utility via these utility processes. In order for a Third Party to obtain customer usage information, the Third Party must show 1) that the Third Party has obtained the customer's authorization, 2) the Third Party must meet the technical requirements of the standard, 3) acknowledge receipt of the utility tariffs and applicable rules, and 4) are not otherwise prohibited by the CPUC from receiving information. The process allows for a utility to notify the CPUC of a potential violation of the CPUC's privacy rules, whereby the CPUC will initiate an investigation of the utility's claims. Access to customer usage information will continue unless the CPUC finds the Third Party in violation of the CPUC's rules, whereupon access to customer usage information by that Third Party will cease. Additionally, a Third Party found in violation of the CPUC's rules will be identified as a company ineligible for obtaining customer usage information. Finally, this decision adopted a modified customer information service request form for those parties seeking only usage information.

Colorado's development of new customer privacy rules involved similar collaborative aspects. In November of 2010, the Colorado Public Utilities Commission (CoPUC) filed a notice of proposed rulemaking (NOPR) with the stated goal of establishing a substantial, thoughtful, and

---

[138] In 2013, California adopted AB 1274, codified at California Civil Code Section 1798.98-99, which provides privacy protection of customer usage data over Third Parties not covered by the CPUC's rules or SB 1476.

[139] Data covered by the rules is defined as "any usage information obtained through [an advanced meter] when associated with any information that can reasonably be used to identify an individual, family, household, residence, or non-residential customer." Privacy Rules at Section 1(b).

[140] For example, PG&E's Privacy Policy and "Notice of Accessing, Collecting, Storing, Using and Disclosing Energy Usage Information" can be found at http://www.pge.com/en/about/company/privacy/customer/index.page [accessed 8/11/2014].

[141] California Public Utilities Commission, In the Matter of Pacific Gas and Electric Company for Adoption of its Customer Data Access Project, et al., Decision 13-09-025 (September 19, 2013).

proactive privacy regime for the protection of customer data.[142] In response to initial comments from stakeholders to its NOPR, the CoPUC staff convened nine public workshops and one public hearing where stakeholders discussed the proposed rule language, proposed edits the language, raised related issues and debated their relative merits. At the end of this process, a proposed set of rules was filed in the proceeding that reflected either consensus of the entire group, or agreement from a majority of the involved stakeholders. Individual stakeholders then filed comments on the specific rule provisions and participated in further public hearings. These comments and testimony was considered by the administrative law judge (ALJ), which proposed a recommended decision on the rules for consideration by the CoPUC. The CoPUC adopted final rules on October 26, 2011, and those rules were effective February 14, 2012.

The CoPUC focused on the balancing of two competing but valid interests: (1) protecting the privacy interests of customers; and (2) developing a mechanism where customer-specific energy usage data could be provided to local governments, Third Parties and commercial interests. In the recommended decision adopting the new rules the ALJ found that, "(t)he bedrock for issues arising from innovations regarding energy usage is the direct regulatory authority over the essential utility-customer relationship. These considerations drive the appropriate adoption of policies to protect customer information from unauthorized disclosure while fostering customer access to information. Should a customer of record desire to authorize access by any Third Party, they may do so through informed consent provided for in these rules."[143] Specifically, the rules:

- Clarify that a utility is only authorized to use customer data to provide regulated utility service in the ordinary course of business (primary purpose).

- Affirm that utilities can share customer energy usage data with Contracted Agents without first obtaining customer consent, but only where such sharing is related to the primary purpose and the utility has secured an agreement with the Contracted Agents prohibiting use of customer energy usage data for a secondary purpose. Additionally, the Contracted Agent's data security procedures and practices must be equal to or greater those data security procedures and practices used by the utility. Affirm that a utility can release customer energy usage data if required by law or CoPUC rule.

- Create an annual privacy notice requirement for the utility addressing customer energy usage data use, access and release.

- Create a Commission-produced uniform customer consent form for use by customers to authorize the disclosure of customer energy usage data to Third Parties for a secondary purpose.

- Require the utility to validate the customer consent form prior to the release of customer energy usage data to a Third Party.

- Define aggregated customer energy usage data to be a minimum of fifteen customers, with no single customer representing fifteen percent or more of the total data set (15/15

---

[142] Colorado Public Utilities Commission, In the Matter of the Proposed Rules Relating to Smart Grid Data Privacy for Electric Utilities, 4 Code of Colorado Regulations 723-3, Docket No. 10R-799E, Notice of Proposed Rulemaking, Paragraph 5. All filings in Docket No. 10R-799E are available from www.dora.state.co.us.

[143] Ibid., Paragraph 17.

rule). Notwithstanding, the 15/15 Rule, a utility would not be required to disclose aggregated data if the disclosure would compromise the individual customer's privacy or the security of the utility's system.

- Require the utility to file a tariff identifying its customer energy usage data and aggregated customer energy usage data services, and related costs for non-standard data services.

- Provide civil enforcement and civil penalties in the event customer energy usage data is released without customer authorization.

The California and Colorado privacy regulations for customer energy usage data have many similarities. However, areas of distinction include:

- **Scope:** California's rules apply to "covered information" which is defined as information obtained through the use of Advanced Metering Infrastructure that is identifiable to an individual. Colorado's rules apply to any "customer information" which is defined more broadly to apply to energy usage data and program participation, regardless of the metering technology used to collect such information.

- **Jurisdiction Over Third Parties**: The CPUC's decision asserts jurisdiction over Third Parties that obtain customer usage information from the utility, but defers a decision on whether the CPUC has authority to directly regulate Third Parties which obtain customer usage information from the customer. Since utility tariffs cover the exchange of data between the utility and a Third Party, the CPUC has authority over the utility tariffs. Subsequent legislation provides for an additional level of privacy protection over those Third Parties not covered by the CPUC's rules. In general, CoPUC did not assert jurisdiction over the data practices of Third Parties, other than to require that the utility's Contracted Agents must have security equal to or exceeding that of the utility.   The customer consent form required by the CoPUC for Third Parties to obtain customer consent does, however, provide an explicit disclaimer putting customers on notice that the utility does not have any obligation to protect the data once it leaves their control.

- **Restrictions on Third Parties:** The CPUC's regulations provide that all Third Parties are limited to collecting only that data necessary to implement the purpose for which data is needed. Consistent with customer privacy rules adopted in the early 1990s, non-utility contractors and other Third Parties are also required to obtain customer consent prior to accessing customer usage information. Customer consent can be currently obtained through the use of a utility's tariffed Customer Information Service Request form, which has been in use by California utilities for twenty years for customer authorization of access to billing records. There are no direct CPUC restrictions on Third Parties that obtain data from the customer, but other California privacy laws applicable to privacy in general do apply. Colorado also places restrictions on the utility regarding the release of the customer's data. Since the utility is the ultimate gatekeeper on information, the utility is treated as the final arbiter of whether the consent forms were incomplete or non-compliant. Thus, while CoPUC does not place restrictions directly on Third Parties, there are requirements that the utility will oversee and the utility is ultimately overseen by the CoPUC.

- **Demand Side Management Programs:** California's rules provide an exception to the customer consent process for Third Parties assisting utilities or the CPUC with planning, implementing or evaluating demand side management programs, such as energy efficiency or demand response programs where authorized by the CPUC. Colorado's rules do not contain an explicit exemption for such data use, but do generally allow the utility to release customer energy usage data to comply with a CoPUC order.

- **Aggregated Data:** California defines aggregated customer energy usage data as a data set where all personally-identifiable information has been removed, and where the release will not disclose or reveal specific customer information because of the size of the group, rate classification, or nature of the information. Colorado incorporates into its rules the presumption that information is sufficiently anonymous if aggregated consistent with a 15/15 Rule.

- **Dispute Process**: California provides a dispute mechanism for customers to challenge the accuracy or completeness of customer energy usage data, and to request corrections or amendments. Colorado's rules do not specifically address this type of dispute but a complaint can always be filed with the Commission if a customer has a specific concern.

- **Data Breach**: As a supplement to existing federal and California "red flag" data breach disclosure laws, California requires utilities to make contemporaneous reports of data breaches affecting 1000 or more customers to the CPUC, and to file an annual report of all such incidents each year. The CoPUC's rules do not require a data breach report to the commission, but there is a state statute covering the utility's obligation to report data breaches to impacted individuals.

Appendix D: Recommended Privacy Practices for Customer/Consumer Smart Grid Energy Usage Data Obtained Directly by Third Parties

D-1 Preamble

The Customer/Consumer Energy Usage Data Privacy Protection team under the Privacy Subgroup has developed the following recommended privacy practices for application to energy customers and the Third Parties with whom they share Customer/Consumer Energy Usage Data (CEUD). While the work of this group began early in 2011, the bulk of the work on these recommended privacy practices occurred after the California Public Utilities Commission (CPUC) issued its smart grid data access rules, the North American Energy Standards Board (NAESB) released its guidelines (REQ 22) on this subject, and the Advanced Security Acceleration Project for the Smart Grid (ASAP-SG) group released their recommendations. Those efforts applied to utilities and Third Parties obtaining access to data from those utilities. The purpose of this group's effort was to apply the same type of recommended protections to Third Parties that gain access to CEUD directly from customers or customer-owned devices, bypassing the utility and the smart meter. The goal of the group was to expand upon the good work already done.

These are recommended privacy practices that should be implemented in a comprehensive manner and not considered individually. If individual recommendations are taken out of context, they may not stand on their own. While there may exist uncertainty over the extent to which any one government agency has regulatory oversight of Third Parties using CEUD, many agree that energy usage data (that will soon become more prevalent as the electric grid gains increased intelligence) can potentially be sensitive, privacy-impacting, data in need of protection. This is particularly true when CEUD is combined with other data, such as an account number or AMI IP address,that then makes it identifiable to one premise or customer. These recommended privacy practices seek to provide suggestions as to how CEUD, and the data combined with it as just described, is best protected in order to protect personal privacy.

D-2 Definitions

Customer: Any entity that takes electric service for its own consumption.

Third Party: An entity — other than the electric utility or other electricity provider for a given premise, the applicable regulatory authority, an independent system operator (ISO) or another regional entity— that performs services or provides products using CEUD. This definition does not include Contracted Agents of an electric utility or electricity provider.

Contracted Agent: An entity under contract with the Third Party to perform services or provide products using CEUD. In some industries, Contracted Agents are referred to as Business Partners or Business Associates.

Customer/Consumer[144] **Energy Usage Data (CEUD):** Energy usage information and data identifiable to a premise or an individual customer obtained without the involvement of the utility.

Privacy Use Case: A method of looking at data flows that will help Third Parties to rigorously track data flows and the privacy implications of collecting and using data, and will help the organization to address and mitigate the associated privacy risks within common technical design and business practices. Use cases can help smart grid architects and engineers build privacy protections into the smart grid.

D-3   Recommended Privacy Practices

D-3.1 Privacy Notices

When a Privacy Notice Is Issued

- Prior to sharing CEUD, Third Parties should provide clear and conspicuous[145] notice to customers regarding data treatment and that CEUD will not be disclosed to other Third Parties unless authorized by the customer (with all exceptions listed).

- Notice to the customer of all intended disclosures should be re-issued at least annually.

- Re-issue should occur when significant changes are made to operational or organizational structure of the company that may impact privacy or security of the data. A few examples may include:

    1) a merger or acquisition of the company

    2) when declaring bankruptcy[146]

    3) when services are outsourced, which were not previously.

- Re-issue should also occur when major changes occur within the organization that may reasonably impact the company's data privacy practices relating to disclosing CEUD to Third Parties or Third Party's Contracted Agents, such as when new applicable laws and/or regulations become effective.

---

[144] There may be a legal issue in terms of who has access to this data. There may be situations in which the Customer and the consumer are not the same and that one might want to restrict access to the CEUD. These recommended practices are not designed to determine legal issues.

[145] For one example of what is considered "clear and conspicuous," see the Federal Trade Commission's document entitled "Dot Com Disclosures: Information About Online Advertising," page 5, at http://www.ftc.gov/sites/default/files/attachments/press-releases/ftc-staff-revises-online-advertising-disclosure-guidelines/130312dotcomdisclosures.pdf.

[146] http://www.wilmerhale.com/publications/whPubsDetail.aspx?publication=2180, and http://epic.org/privacy/airtravel/clear/.

- Customer notice should come from the Third Party with which the customer has a business relationship. Any entity that is not directly involved with the transaction being considered need not send a separate notice.[147]

What Should Be Included In a Privacy Policy Notice

- Privacy policy notices should include information about how the Third Party will access, collect, use, store, disclose, retain, dispose of, and safeguard CEUD.

- Information about data access that will or may be given to a Third Party's Contracted Agent should be provided in the initial notice to the customer. The notice may be listed by service (e.g., data formatting, billing) instead of contractor's company name.

- Separate notice should not be necessary for the sharing of CEUD with a Third Party's Contracted Agent, unless the purpose is materially different than has been previously authorized.

- Third Parties should provide customers with a process for addressing their CEUD privacy complaints. This process, which may include existing procedures established or approved by the applicable regulatory authority or other legal requirements, should be discussed in the notices to the customer.

- A customer's right to revoke authorization should be reiterated in the periodic privacy notice sent to customers.

- Breach notification processes should be communicated to customers by the Third Party as part of the periodic privacy notice.[148]

- All information privacy policies regarding disclosure to other Third Parties or the Third Party's Contracted Agents should be clear, concise (notice should be no longer than is necessary to convey the requisite information), understandable, and easily accessible.

D-3.2 Customer Authorization for Disclosures

- Data should not be disclosed to other Third Parties unless there is an authorization to do so by the customer. This authorization should notify the customer of the identity of the other Third Parties.

- When the Third Party obtains the customer's authorization, it should identify any choices available to the customer regarding CEUD disclosure as part of the authorization process (e.g., the ability to opt-out of disclosure).

---

[147] This is to clarify who among the common actors (Third Parties and Contracted Agents) needs to send a privacy policy notice to Customers.

[148] It is assumed that companies will comply with relevant breach notification laws. This is to make certain that a description of what the Customer should expect if a breach occurs is conveyed to the Customer.

Disclosure to Contracted Agents

- Third Parties and Third Party's Contracted Agents do not need further customer authorization in order to provide services or products, or to fulfill other obligations to customers, that have already been authorized by the customer.[149]

- Before releasing CEUD to a Third Party's Contracted Agent, Third Parties should receive confirmation that the Third Party's Contracted Agent has security and privacy safeguards in place at least equal to those implemented by the Third Party.

Customer Access to Their Data

- A Third Party should develop and communicate processes for a customer to have access to their CEUD and to be able to request that the CEUD be corrected where inaccuracies exist. The process for gaining data access should be a relatively simple process for the typical customer. This process, which may include existing procedures established or approved by the applicable regulatory authority or other legal requirements, should be discussed in the notices to the customer. The data provided to the customer should be provided in a form that is reasonably understandable by the average customer.

Customer Authorization & Data Accuracy

- Third Parties should provide customers with reasonable mechanisms for:

  1) granting and revoking authorization for access to their CEUD;

  2) providing feedback regarding the disclosure of CEUD; and

  3) requesting corrections to the CEUD.

D-3.3 Data Disclosure

- CEUD collected by a Third Party should be limited to only that data necessary to fulfill the purpose specified in the customer's authorization[150].

- A separate customer authorization should be obtained before CEUD is used in a materially different manner than previously authorized.

Aggregated or De-identified CEUD[151]

- If the customer has already authorized a particular service or product, and a Third Party or Third Party's Contracted Agent needs to disclose aggregated or de-identified information in order to produce that service or product, the Third Party or Third Party's Contracted Agent should not need a new authorization to disclose the aggregated or de-

---

[150] There may be a legal issue in terms of who has access to this data. There may be situations in which the Customer and the consumer are not the same and that one might want to restrict access to the CEUD. These recommended practices are not designed to determine legal issues.

[151] There are currently no known standards for determining what constitutes de-identified CEUD. The typical intention is that all identifying information has been removed.

identified information so long as that information cannot be tracked back to an individual or used to identify a customer.

- Third Parties should specify that any other Third Party or Contracted Agent receiving CEUD that has been anonymized or de-identified should not attempt to re-identify the data or otherwise identify an individual premise or customer.

Legal Disclosure for Law Enforcement

- Third Parties should have procedures in place to provide data access to law enforcement when presented with legal obligations to do so. These procedures should include validation that the necessary legal requirements have been met (e.g., subpoena, court order, etc.).

Disclosure of Information in Situations of Imminent Threat to Life or Property

- These practices do not apply to emergency disclosures of information provided to emergency responders in situations involving an imminent threat to life or property. What constitutes an emergency disclosure should be determined by appropriate authorities.

D-3.4 Customer Education & Awareness

- Third Parties should develop and implement customer education and awareness plans to inform the relevant customers about the Third Party's CEUD privacy protection policies and practices.

- The Third Party should provide its customers with educational and awareness materials that summarize the steps that the organization is taking to reduce potential risks associated with unauthorized use of CEUD, and describe the steps that customers can take to help reduce their own risk.

- The customer should be made aware that CEUD may unavoidably differ somewhat from different sources based on such factors as differences in technology, timing, and validation. For example, potential exists that data from a HAN device may differ from an aggregated view provided by a utility.

D-3.5 Data Minimization

- Collection of CEUD by Third Parties should be limited to only that information necessary to fulfill the purpose (e.g., to provide a service or product, etc.) as set forth in the customer's authorization.

D-3.6 Data Quality

- Third Parties and Third Party's Contracted Agents using CEUD should endeavor to ensure that the data is accurate and complete. It should be recognized that the data is only as accurate and complete as the information received if the holder is not the original collector. This should not preclude a Third Party or Third Party's Contracted Agents from modifying or enhancing CEUD, provided that it is clear that modifications or enhancements have been made when such information is disclosed.

D-3.7 Data Security & Governance

- Third Parties should protect information under their control from unauthorized access, copying, modification, inappropriate disclosure, or loss by having information privacy protections in policies, procedures, and practices relating to data security and to disclosure and accuracy of data disclosed to the Third Party's Contracted Agents, or to other Third Parties.

- These policies or procedures should periodically be reviewed, assessed, and updated, as necessary, to ensure CEUD is properly addressed.

- Third Parties should appoint positions and/or personnel to ensure that security and privacy policies are properly maintained, updated, and followed.

- Privacy practices should be transparent.

D-3.8 Privacy Practices Risk Assessment

- Third Parties should conduct and document periodic privacy impact and risk assessments and analyses associated with their processes for disclosing CEUD to Third Party's Contracted Agents. They should use these risk analyses and privacy impact assessments to update, when appropriate, the applicable policies and practices. Such risk analyses and privacy impact assessments should be considered at least annually or when:

  - Major changes occur within their organization that may reasonably impact the company's data privacy practices relating to disclosing CEUD to Third Parties or Third Party's Contracted Agents;

  - New applicable laws and/or regulations become effective;

  - An event related to the unauthorized disclosure of CEUD occurs at the company; and

  - Any other circumstance occurs that the Third Party or Third Party's Contracted Agent determines warrants such risk analysis.

- Third Party's Contracted Agents should conduct similar analyses and provide the results of their analyses/assessments to the Third Party in a timely manner.

- In developing and updating policies and practices, Third Parties should develop a set of Privacy Use Cases as a method to track information flows and the privacy implications of collecting and using data to help the organization to address and mitigate the associated privacy risks within common technical design practices and business practices.[152]

- Third Parties should share solutions to common privacy-related problems with other smart grid market participants in some appropriate manner (e.g., trade forums, associations, public policy, public out-reach, external coordination, etc.).

---

[152] For an example of smart grid use cases, see NISTIR 7628 Rev. 1 Volume 3, Chapter 10.

D-3.9 Data Retention and Disposal

- Unless authorized differently, Third Parties should keep CEUD no longer than is necessary to fulfill the business purposes for which it was collected, and as reasonably interpreted to be required to comply with legal or regulatory requirements.

- If CEUD is to be used for research, then policies and procedures should be established for retention and de-identification related to these activities.

- Third Parties should inform the customers of their data retention policies as part of their notice to customers.

- Third Parties' data retention policies should include when and how data should be irreversibly disposed of, including after revocation of a customer's authorization to collect or keep CEUD.

D-3.10 Data Breaches

- Third Parties should identify any state or federal requirements for disclosure or data breach notification that may be applicable to a Third Party or Contracted Agent.

- Consider including CEUD as data that may require a notice for any unauthorized breach dependent upon the granularity of the data and applicable legal breach notification requirements.

D-3.11 Employee Training

- Third Parties and Third Party's Contracted Agents should develop, disseminate, and periodically review and update a formally documented security and privacy awareness and training policy (which specifically includes the protection of CEUD) with documented supporting implementation procedures.

- The organization should document, maintain, and monitor each employee's security and privacy training activities on an individual basis, including basic security and privacy awareness training in accordance with the organization's security and privacy policies.

D-3.12 Audits

- Each Third Party should conduct a periodic independent audit of Third Party's data privacy and security practices.

- Each Third Party should periodically verify the privacy and security practices of Third Party's Contracted Agents. This may occur in one or more ways. Some examples are:

    1. Conducting an audit of the Third Party's Contracted Agents' privacy and security practices.
    2. Requiring the Contracted Agent to provide Third Party with an independent audit of its privacy and security practices.

3. Examining the results of an independent audit[153] of the Third Party's Contracted Agents' privacy and security practices.
4. Examine the results of a recent SSAE-16[154] audit.
5. Review any existing Information Security Management System (ISMS)[155] certifications.
6. Review any recent privacy impact assessments that have been performed.

---

[153] "Independent Audit" is described in F. Gallegos, "IT Audit Independence: What Does it Mean?" *ISACA Journal* vol. 6, 2003, http://www.isaca.org/Journal/Past-Issues/2003/Volume-6/Pages/IT-Audit-Independence-What-Does-It-Mean-.aspx [accessed 8/11/2014]. Previously known as the Information Systems Audit and Control Association, ISACA now goes by its acronym only, to reflect the broad range of IT governance professionals it serves.

[154] Statement on Standards for Attestation Engagements (SSAE) No. 16 replaced the SAS70 Type II audit. "SSAE 16 is an attestation standard geared towards addressing engagements conducted by practitioners (known as "service auditors") on service organizations for purposes of reporting on the design of controls and their operating effectiveness." See more in C. Denyer, "SSAE 16 | Introduction to Statement on Standards for Attestation Engagements (SSAE) No. 16," in *The SSAE 16 Resource Guide,* NDB LLP, http://www.ssae16.org/what-is-ssae-16/introduction-to-ssae-16.html [accessed 8/11/2014].

[155] A certified Information Security Management System (ISMS) is described at "ISO/IEC 27001 Information Security Management," *BSI Group* [Web page], http://www.bsigroup.com/en/Assessment-and-certification-services/management-systems/Standards-and-Schemes/ISO-IEC-27001/ [accessed 8/11/2014].

APPENDIX E: PRIVACY USE CASES

Category: AMI	Privacy Use Case #1

Scenario: Meter sends information

Category Description

AMI systems consist of the hardware, software, and associated system and data management applications that create a communications network between end systems at customer premises (including meters, gateways, and other equipment) and diverse business and operational systems of utilities and Third Parties. AMI systems provide the technology to allow the exchange of information between customer end systems and those other utility and Third Party systems. In order to protect this critical infrastructure, end-to-end security must be provided across the AMI systems, encompassing the customer end systems as well as the utility and Third Party systems that are interfaced to the AMI systems.

Scenario Description

A meter sends automated energy usage information to the Utility (e.g. meter read (usage data). The automated send of energy usage information is initiated by the meter and is sent to the Advanced Metering Infrastructure (AMI) Head End System (HES). The HES message flows to the Meter Reading and Control (MRC). The MRC evaluates the message. The MRC archives the automated energy usage information and forwards the information onto the meter Data Management Systems (MDMS).
- Meter configuration information
- Periodic meter Reading
- On-Demand meter Reading

Net metering for distributed energy resources (DER) and plug in electric vehicle (PEV)

Smart Grid Characteristics	Cybersecurity Objectives/Requirements	Potential Stakeholder Issues
<ul><li>Enables active participation by consumers</li><li>Enables new products, services and markets</li><li>Optimizes asset utilization and operates efficiently</li></ul>	<ul><li>Confidentiality (privacy) of customer metering data over the AMI system, metering database, and billing database to avoid serious breaches of privacy and potential legal repercussions</li><li>Integrity of meter data is important, but the impact of incorrect data is not large</li><li>Availability of meter data is not critical in real-time</li></ul>	<ul><li>Customer data privacy and security</li><li>Third Party or party acting as an agent of the utility access to energy usage information for market and/or consumer services</li><li>Third Party or party acting on behalf of the utility reliable data</li><li>Customer data access</li><li>Reliable data for billing</li></ul>

1.1	**Data Privacy Recommendations** Any individually negotiated purchase agreement that contains or is associated with personally identifiable customer data should be subject to the same privacy and security applications as personally identifiable data.
1.2	Meter read data should be evaluated to determine if it should be protected data regardless of type of service or tariff or scheduled meter read frequency and the same policy notice can apply. Similarly, the same choice and consent information can be used across all scenarios noted above, with the caveat that if any Contracted Agents are involved, the individual has been notified and consented to the Contracted Agent's access to the data identified as necessary for that activity. This notice may happen within the initial privacy notice given at account set up.

			Applies: X	
1.3	Customer access to data in real-time or near-real-time, particularly for net metering/feed in tariff (FiT) data is important for many customers to optimize performance of assets that generate or store electricity. This access should be limited to the consumer associated with the meter, the utility for operational and billing purposes or their authorized agents, and consumer-authorized Third Parties. (The OECD principle for access indicates that individuals should have access to data associated with them.)			
1.4	Meter reading is an ongoing activity, so it is important that utilities create a monitoring and enforcement process that ensures compliance on a continuous basis.			
1.5	Utility-authorized agents and/or Third Parties may be given access to meter reading data for various customer peer performance/comparison purposes. These agents or Third Parties should also conform and comply with utility privacy policies, and customers should consent to the disclosure of their information to these agents or Third Parties.			

	AICPA Principle	Applies: X	Notes
1.6	**Management Principle**	X	An individual, team or department should be assigned responsibility for ensuring policies and procedures exist that cover the situations involved within this use case scenario.
1.7	**Notice Principle**	X	Should be provided for all meter reading, regular consumption and net metering scenarios.
1.8	**Choice and Consent Principle**	X	Ensure that when customers sign up for service that this choice and consent requirement is met.
1.9	**Collection Principle**	X	Over time, data collection may change as new applications, technologies, or correlations of data are made available. Utility policy should indicate that collection purposes may change over time and that utilities will notify customers of any proposed changes that may impact collection in order to secure an updated choice and consent.
1.10	**Use and Retention Principle**	X	Retention may be impacted by time frames to record and compensate for net metering scenarios. Data retention may also be impacted by local, state, or federal laws/regulations/requirements outside of utility operational needs.
1.11	**Access Principle**	X	Access to the meter usage data, and any associated data that could reveal personal data, should be limited to only those who need such access to perform their job activities.
1.12	**Disclosure to Third Parties Principle**	X	Utility net metering payments to customers may be considered revenue or income and thus subject to tax laws, or garnishments for child support, legal claims, etc. Requests may come from law enforcement agencies or other entities that make requests for information from utilities. Some of the legal implications may not require implicit or explicit consent.

1.13	**Security for Privacy Principle**	X	Safeguards should be applied as appropriate to mitigate associated risks to an acceptable level.[156]
1.14	**Quality Principle**	X	Controls should be established to ensure meter usage data is as accurate as necessary for the purposes for which it is being collected.
1.15	**Monitoring and Enforcement Principle**	X	This should not be just a once and done audit on a yearly basis since meter reading is an ongoing activity. Utilities should create a practice of regular compliance monitoring on a rolling basis to completely cover the customer records on a several times a year frequency.

---

[156] For more discussion on identifying and selecting applicable security requirements for a smart grid information system, see Chapter 3, High-Level Security Requirements.

Category: AMI	**Privacy Use Case #2**

Scenario: Utility sends operational command to meter

Category Description
AMI systems consist of the hardware, software, and associated system and data management applications that create a communications network between end systems at customer premises (including meters, gateways, and other equipment) and diverse business and operational systems of utilities, utility-authorized agents, and Third Parties. AMI systems provide the technology to allow the exchange of information between customer end systems and those other utility and Third Party systems. In order to protect this critical infrastructure, end-to-end security must be provided across the AMI systems, encompassing the customer end systems, as well as the utility and Third Party systems that are interfaced to the AMI systems.

Scenario Description
A utility requires an operational command be sent to the meter, such as a disconnect or reconnect of an electric smart meter. The command flows to the Meter Reading and Control (MRC) that looks up the meter associated with the customer and then instructs the Advanced Metering Infrastructure (AMI) Head End System (HES) to communicate the command to the meter. The HES evaluates current conditions and, if suitable (e.g. reconnects are not executed if the system is in a rolling black out state), sends the command to the meter. When the meter receives the command and parameters, the meter evaluates the command as to whether it is permitted. If the command is permitted, the meter executes the command and sends the result to the HES. If the command is not permitted, the meter sends the result to the HES. The HES evaluates the result (whether the action was successful or not and why) and relays that to the MRC. The MRC records the command result and notifies the appropriate actors.
- Configuration request
- Calibration request
- Connect Disconnect request
- Prepaid metering configuration/setup

Smart Grid Characteristics	**Cybersecurity Objectives/Requirements**	**Potential Stakeholder Issues**
• Optimizes asset utilization and operate efficiently • Operates resiliently against attack and natural disasters	• Integrity of control commands to the meter is critical to avoid dangerous/unsafe connections. Availability is not important with the exception of situations such as fire or medical emergency for remote connect/disconnect. • Confidentiality requirements of the meter command is generally not very important	• Customer Safety • Third Party or party acting as an agent of the utility access to energy usage information for market and/or consumer services

2.1	**Data Privacy Recommendations** Utilities collect personal data that includes customer name and address/location to establish an account, and this information is associated with a meter number. This personal data should be restricted to those software applications and resources that require this information to associate meter location and billing information. The security safeguard principle has specific application here. Information about data access that will or may be given to a Contracted Agent should be provided in the initial notice to the customer. The notice may be listed by service (e.g., data formatting, billing) instead of contractor's company name. Separate notice is not necessary for the sharing of CEUD with a Contracted Agent, unless the purpose is materially different than has been previously authorized.
2.2	Any connect or disconnect event should be identified by the meter number and completely disassociated with any personal data (i.e., it is not John Smith's meter that is turned on/off, rather, it is meter number 123456 that is the subject of an action). This avoids the transmission of personal data across the AMI network.

2.3	The data quality principle applies - customers need the ability to review and update their personal data as the parties who are responsible for payments may change over time.
2.4	Special consideration must be given to situations where collection of past due amounts is done by a Contracted Agent. Utilities should provide easy to understand statements as part of the connect/reconnect process that outlines any role of Contracted Agents such as collection agencies. Utilities should ensure that their Contracted Agents, and any Third Parties, are handling personal data with the same levels of privacy safeguards as conducted by utilities themselves.

2.5	To a great extent, the effect of Prepaid AMI on Privacy is dependent on the details of implementation. For example;
	   ○ Were the meter itself capable of performing the "countdown" of the amount of prepaid service remaining, then the utility might not have to collect any usage data. The utility could simply update the meter with the amount of service prepaid, and the meter itself could track remaining service, and shut service off if the prepaid amount were exceeded.
	   ○ On the other hand, if the "countdown" were handled in the utility backend systems, quite granular usage data collection may be required.
	Prepaid metering has the potential to reduce the number of utility/consumer transactions – specifically connect/disconnect transactions that could potentially expose personal data during each transaction as well as utility need to conduct credit checks and/or maintain records on account deposits. As a new practice for almost all utilities, care should be exercised in the definition of new processes and procedures to ensure that data privacy principles are enacted.

2.6	The simple fact of whether a customer was on a Prepaid tariff could be seen as information that a customer would want protected. However, this may be no different in effect from the desire of commercial and industrial customers to keep their operating costs confidential.

	AICPA Principle	**Applies: X**	**Notes**
2.7	**Management Principle**	X	Maintain policies that oversee the implementation and compliance with the related privacy and security policies to protect the data involved with this use case.
2.8	**Notice Principle**	X	Information about data access that will or may be given to a Contracted Agent should be provided in the initial notice to the customer. The notice may be listed by service (e.g., data formatting, billing) instead of contractor's company name. Separate notice is not necessary for the sharing of CEUD with a Contracted Agent, unless the purpose is materially different than has been previously authorized.
2.9	**Choice and Consent Principle**	X	Identify if personal data may be used for billing and collections as part of a connect/disconnect process.
2.10	**Collection Principle**	X	Personal data is required for billing purposes, but should be protected and maintained per management principle.
2.11	**Use and Retention Principle**	X	Data involved should only be retained for as long as necessary to perform the associated business activities.

2.12	**Access Principle**	X	Access to personal data should be limited to only those with a specific job responsibility requiring such access.
2.13	**Disclosure to Third Parties Principle**	X	May be shared with Contracted Agents if these are used for authorized purposes. Disclosure to Third Parties should not occur without consent consistent with the data privacy recommendations (<u>Appendix D: Recommended Privacy Practices for Customer/Consumer Smart Grid Energy Usage Data Obtained Directly by Third Parties</u>).
2.14	**Security for Privacy Principle**	X	Financial information has particular sensitivity, and utility procedures regarding protection of personal data and financial information should limit physical and electronic access on a "need to know" basis by implementing appropriate policies and technical safeguards.
2.15	**Quality Principle**	X	Utilities must ensure that they have correct and accurate contact information if accounts are sent to collections, and to ensure that any disconnects are targeted to the right meters.
2.16	**Monitoring and Enforcement Principle**	X	Access logs should be generated and regular audits of those logs should occur.

Category: AMI	Privacy Use Case #3

Scenario: Utility sends non-operational instruction to meter (peer-to-peer)

Category Description

AMI systems consist of the hardware, software, and associated system and data management applications that create a communications network between end systems at customer premises (including meters, gateways, and other equipment) and diverse business and operational systems of utilities and Third Parties. AMI systems provide the technology to allow the exchange of information between customer end systems and those other utility and Third Party systems. In order to protect this critical infrastructure, end-to-end security must be provided across the AMI systems, encompassing the customer end systems, as well as the utility and Third Party systems which are interfaced to the AMI systems.

Scenario Description

This use case describes the Utility sending a non-operational instruction send to meter as a peer-to-peer transaction. A Utility requires actions from a set of meters which may or may not result in a change to the power state of the grid. These include at least meter reading, and certain configuration changes. The Meter Reading and Control (MRC) determines the need to send instruction(s) to a meter. The MRC looks up the meter associated with the customer and then instructs the Advanced Metering Infrastructure (AMI) Head End System (HES) to queue up and execute the instruction(s). The AMI Head End can determine the instruction needs to be split into packets, schedules the sending of the packets and continues to send the packets to the meter until all instruction packets have been sent. The meter receives the instruction(s) and determines if the instruction is permitted. After execution, the meter sends the instruction result to the HES. The HES will then send the instruction result to the MRC. If the instruction result is energy usage information, the MRC will then forward the energy usage information onto the Meter Data Management System (MDMS). If the MDMS receives energy usage information, then the MDMS forwards the energy usage information onto other actors for other actions.

1. Meter calibration validation
2. Connectivity validation
3. Geolocation of meter
4. Smart meter battery management

Smart Grid Characteristics	**Cybersecurity Objectives/Requirements**	**Potential Stakeholder Issues**
• Optimizes asset utilization and operate efficiently • Operates resiliently against attack and natural disasters • Increases the timeliness, availability, and granularity of information for billing	• Confidentiality may or may not be an issue depending on whether information is public (date, time) or private (password change, Personally Identifiable Information). Some items must be confidential due to laws and regulations; confidentiality of other items, such as firmware or GPS coordinates, may be left up to local policy, • Integrity of meter maintenance repairs and updates is essential to prevent malicious intrusions • Availability is important, but only in terms of hours or maybe days to provide synchronization and coherence of devices on the network, i.e. all devices acting together for entire population	• Customer data privacy and security • Third Party or party acting as an agent of the utility having access to customer & Utility information • Third Party access to electrical distribution system, e.g. separation of duties & authority (regulatory impact) • Vendor product quality

3.1	**Data Privacy Considerations**

	The Customer Information Systems (CIS), Meter Data Management Systems (MDMS) and Outage Management Systems (OMS) may contain multiple types of personal data that may be impacted by meter reading and configuration changes or updates. Utility resources and authorized Third Parties should follow utility privacy policies to safeguard any personal data, including energy usage data. For example, a connectivity ping that is negative may trigger a request to an OMS and/or workforce management system to schedule an onsite repair visit. Personal data in the form of customer name and address would be needed to schedule that repair with utility or authorized Contracted Agents. That connectivity ping may also generate a report identifying unresponsive meters. Care should be exercised to minimize personal data that appears in these reports, and limits on the access to these reports by resources trained in privacy policies and practices.
3.2	Care should be exercised to ensure authorized Third Parties or other service providers do not have unnecessary access to customer information that is not required for completion of their responsibilities.
3.4	The personal data in any report should be kept to a minimum to limit privacy risk, particularly data that could unintentionally provide a potential exploit or expose a vulnerability. Data should be limited to only the minimum necessary to effectively aid the appropriate utility or Contracted Agent workers in completion of their responsibilities.
3.5	Utility repair and maintenance teams may have name/address/location associated with meters. Utility teams may include Contracted Agents that are subcontractors to utilities or even subcontractors to utility subcontractors, so all processes should be evaluated to determine what, if any, personal data is required to complete their responsibilities. When personal data is required, all resources should be trained to safeguard the data from unauthorized exposure, display, or updates to that data.
3.6	Associating meter data with personal data can create privacy risks. Meter number is associated with personal data in one or more systems – CIS being the most likely application. Care must be exercised by field resources who may have printouts, smart device displays, or laptop displays that contain customer personal data. Any reports on these non-operational activities should be assessed from a privacy perspective to ensure that if any personal data is included that appropriate safeguards are taken to limit exposure to authorized utility or Third Party resources.
3.7	Data used to specify location could reveal personal data associated with the location. Determine what data is used in any reports and who has access to these reports in digital or print formats. Location-based information may be considered privacy information itself.
3.8	Access to personal data should be limited to only that necessary to accomplish individual job responsibilities.
3.9	Different applications keep information for differing periods of time. CIS might keep data about outages that impacted a specific customer in that specific customer's file for a long time. Some historical data can be very helpful to identifying future maintenance needs, assess equipment performance, or determine meter upgrade schedules. This data may be indefinitely held, but should be anonymized, i.e. stripped of personal data, so that personal data is associated with a meter number but not personal data or energy usage information.
3.10	Assess how long any reports generated on non-operational activities are retained. Create policy safeguards for any reports that must contain personal data.

	AICPA Principle	Applies: X	Notes
3.11	**Management Principle**	X	Policies and procedures should exist for the data collected, used, shared and stored for non-operational meter reading, configuration, or other activities. A position should exist with assigned accountability for ensuring such policies and procedures exist, are effectively communicated to all personnel, and are followed, including during exception processing such as an outage.
3.12	**Notice Principle**	X	Customers should be given notice about the types of data involved in these meter activities if their personal data is involved, and the policies and procedures that are in place for protecting the information and using it appropriately.
3.13	**Choice and Consent Principle**	X	Customers should be given choices, as feasible, about how communications with them are made regarding any outreach required as part of these non-operational activities. They should also be asked during initial account setup for consent to share their data with any Contracted Agents or Third Parties, and consent to having their data retained to allow for historical statistical analysis.
3.14	**Collection Principle**	X	Only the data necessary to effectively and efficiently support any activity should be collected, used, or reported as part of non-operational meter functions.
3.15	**Use and Retention Principle**	X	The data collected for any non-operational activities should be used only for the purpose set forth in the customer's authorization. Personal data collected or generated that is not necessary to fulfill the purpose set forth in the customer's authorization, should be deleted as soon as possible upon completion of the meter task.
3.16	**Access Principle**	X	Access to personal data should be limited to only those with a specific job responsibility requiring such access.
3.17	**Disclosure to Third Parties Principle**	X	Data collected or created during performance of non-operational meter tasks should not be shared with any Contracted Agents or Third Parties unless there is an authorized processing need for such sharing, and if the customer has given consent for the information to be shared. During planned or unplanned meter activities, select customer data may be shared with Contracted Agents for purposes of maintenance and repair of meters.

3.18	Security for Privacy Principle	X	All personal data collected and created during these activities must be appropriately safeguarded to ensure unauthorized access to the data does not occur, to preserve integrity of the data, and to allow for appropriate availability.
3.19	Quality Principle	X	Controls and processes should be in place to ensure data is kept accurate as it is collected, and as it is updated during performance of meter activities.
3.20	Monitoring and Enforcement Principle	X	Processes should be in place to monitor compliance with the privacy policies and procedures related to collecting, storing, using, sharing and retaining data. Utilities may consider conducting a privacy audit whenever any changes to these non-operational meter activities are enacted. Procedures should exist to address privacy-related inquiries and disputes from customers involved in any non-operational activities involving meters.

Category: AMI	Privacy Use Case #4

Scenario: Field tool sends instruction to the meter

Category Description

AMI systems consist of the hardware, software, and associated system and data management applications that create a communications network between end systems at customer premises (including meters, gateways, and other equipment) and diverse business and operational systems of utilities and Third Parties. AMI systems provide the technology to allow the exchange of information between customer end systems and those other utility and Third Party systems. In order to protect this critical infrastructure, end-to-end security must be provided across the AMI systems, encompassing the customer end systems as well as the utility and Third Party systems that are interfaced to the AMI systems.

Scenario Description

A field tool requires onsite maintenance of an electric smart meter. The Field Tool connects directly to an electric smart meter, then the command flows to the smart meter. When the meter receives the command and parameters, the meter evaluates the command as to whether it is permitted. If the command is permitted, the meter executes the command and sends the result back to the field tool. This use case is a closed loop, as stated in the preconditions.

- Meter calibration update
- Meter configuration update

Smart Grid Characteristics	Cybersecurity Objectives/Requirements	Potential Stakeholder Issues
• Enables new products, services and markets • Optimizes asset utilization and operate efficiently	• Confidentiality is not important unless some maintenance activity involves personal information • Integrity of meter maintenance repairs and updates are essential to prevent malicious intrusions and integrity of billing data to prevent high utility bills • Availability is important, because field tool requires real time interaction with the meter.	• Customer data privacy and security • Third party or party acting as an agent of the utility having access to customer & Utility information

4.1	**Data Privacy Recommendations** Utilities collect personal data that includes customer name and address/location to establish an account, and this information is associated with a meter number. This personal data should be restricted to only authorized purposes. The security safeguard principle has specific application here.
4.2	Utilities should review their policies regarding notifications to customers of planned and unplanned meter maintenance to ensure that any personal data is managed to minimize unnecessary exposure to utility resources, and that any resources that have access to this information have appropriate training to safeguard data privacy. What is "unnecessary exposure" will need to be determined by each utility based upon their organization, location and associated requirements.
4.3	Any maintenance event should be identified by the meter number and completely disassociated with any personal data, so it is not John Smith's meter that is subject to maintenance, but it is Meter number 123456 that is the subject of an action. This avoids the transmission of personal data across any utility network.

	AICPA Principle	**Applies: X**	**Notes**
4.4	**Management Principle**	X	Maintenance policies should exist and be followed as part of the new account setup and outline how

			personally identifiable information is used in maintenance processes.
4.5	**Notice Principle**	X	Notice that a power company employee might need access to physical premises is required.
4.6	**Choice and Consent Principle**	X	Initial set up of a customer account should include utility statements about meter maintenance, as well as other utility assets, and should secure customer acceptance of scheduled and emergency maintenance procedures at that time.
4.7	**Collection Principle**	X	Establish the collection policy during the new account process, or update existing policies to indicate how personally identifiable information may be used in any meter maintenance process.
4.8	**Use and Retention Principle**	X	Meter maintenance may entail direct contact with customers at their homes or work locations. Maintenance resources in the field may have personally identifiable information about customers to establish their validity as authorized representatives of the utility. Utility processes should incorporate practices to minimize exposure of customer information and delete the information from field equipment and related systems as soon as the full maintenance operation is completed.
4.9	**Access Principle**	X	Meter maintenance should not change this general utility policy. It has particular relevance if meter maintenance is triggered by a change in customer account that requires a change in the meter itself. Customers may wish to review their information for accuracy in these situations where a meter has been changed to ensure that all personal data regarding the new meter is correct. Access to personal data should be limited to only those with a specific job responsibility requiring such access.
4.10	**Disclosure to Third Parties Principle**	X	Any Contracted Agents performing maintenance on behalf of the utility must comply with all utility data privacy policies.
4.11	**Security for Privacy Principle**	X	Meter maintenance may impact cybersecurity settings in a meter, so utilities should institute practices that fully test any proposed updates on all relevant models of meters prior to field implementation.
4.12	**Quality Principle**	X	This is relevant to ensure that any changes to a meter (update, upgrade, change to different meter to support net metering, etc.) reflect accurate information.
4.13	**Monitoring and Enforcement Principle**	X	Conduct a test or audit of privacy protections on a random statistically valid sampling of meters after a maintenance procedure such as a meter upgrade or change impacting a statistically significant number of meters.

Category: AMI	Privacy Use Case #5

Scenario: Utility sends batch instruction to meters (group multicast transaction)

Category Description

The AMI category covers the fundamental functions of an advanced metering system. These functions include: meter reading, use of an integrated service switch, theft detection, and improved outage detection and restoration. The high-level technical requirements for these functions are well understood by the industry, but the specific benefit varies from utility to utility.

Advanced functions that are often associated with AMI are demand response program support and communications to in-home devices. These functions are not exclusive to AMI and will be discussed in separate category areas.

Scenario Description

This use case describes a batch instruction send to meters as a multicast transaction in an open loop situation. The open loop situation means that Advanced Metering Infrastructure (AMI) Head End System (HES) does not expect a response for each packet sent to a meter. A Utility requires actions from a set of meters which may or may not result in a change to the power state of the grid. These include at least meter reading, and certain configuration changes. The Meter Reading and Control (MRC) determines the need to send batch instructions to more than one meter. MRC looks up the meter associated with the customer and then instructs the Advanced Metering Infrastructure (AMI) Head End System (HES) to queue up and execute the instructions. The AMI Head End can determine the instruction needs to be split into packets, schedules the sending of the packets and continues to send the packets to the meters until all instruction packets have been sent. The meter(s) receive the instruction(s) and determines if the instruction is permitted. After execution, the meter(s) send the instruction result to the HES. The HES will then send the instruction result to the MRC. If the instruction result is energy usage information, the MRC will then forward the energy usage information onto the Meter Data Management System (MDMS). If the MDMS receives energy usage information, then the MDMS forwards the energy usage information on to other actors for other actions.

- Firmware update
- Key management update

Smart Grid Characteristics	Cybersecurity Objectives/Requirements	Potential Stakeholder Issues
• Optimizes asset utilization and operate efficiently • Enables new products, services and markets • Reduces cost of operations	• Confidentiality is not important unless some maintenance activity involves personal data • Integrity of meter maintenance repairs and updates are essential to prevent malicious intrusions • Availability is important, but only in terms of hours or maybe days	• Confirmation (if required) of update status. • Customer data privacy and security • Third party or party acting as an agent of the utility access to energy usage information for market and/or consumer services

5.1	**Privacy Recommendations** This scenario is similar to Use Case 3, the exception being this case involves batch communications instead of single peer-to-peer communications. The Customer Information System (CIS), Meter Data Management System (MDMS) and Outage Management System (OMS) may contain multiple types of personal data that may be impacted by meter reading and configuration changes or updates. Utility resources and authorized Contracted Agents should follow utility privacy policies to safeguard any personal and energy usage data. For example, a failed update ping may trigger a request to an OMS and/or workforce management system to schedule an onsite repair visit. Personal data in the form of customer name and address would be needed to schedule that repair with utility or authorized Contracted Agent resources. Care should be exercised to minimize personal data that appears in these reports, and limits should be put on the access to these reports by resources trained in privacy policies and practices.
5.2	Care should be exercised to ensure authorized Contracted Agents or other service providers do not have unnecessary access to customer information that is not required for completion of their responsibilities.

5.3	The personal data in any report should be kept to a minimum to limit privacy risk, particularly data that could unintentionally provide a potential exploit or expose a vulnerability. Data should be limited to only the minimum necessary to effectively aid the appropriate utility or Contracted Agent workers in completion of their responsibilities.
5.4	Utility repair teams may have name/address/location associated with meters that are subject to a non-operational activity (remote or onsite). Utility repair teams may include Contracted Agents that are subcontractors to utilities or even subcontractors to utility subcontractors, so all processes should be evaluated to determine what, if any, personal data is required to complete their responsibilities. When personal data is required, all resources should be trained to safeguard the data from unauthorized exposure, display, or updates to that data.
5.5	Associating meter data with personal data can create privacy risks. Meter number is associated with personal data in one or more systems - CIS and TCS being the most likely applications. Care must be exercised by field resources who may have printouts, smart device displays, or laptop displays that contain customer personal data. Any reports on these non-operational activities should be assessed from a privacy perspective to ensure that if any personal data is included that appropriate safeguards are taken to limit exposure to authorized utility or Contracted Agent resources.
5.6	Data used to specify location could reveal personal data associated with the location. Determine what data is used in any reports and who has access to these reports in digital or print formats. Location-based information may be considered privacy information itself.
5.7	Access to personal data should be limited to only that necessary to accomplish job responsibilities.
5.8	Different applications keep information for differing periods of time. CIS might keep data about outages that impacted a specific customer in that specific customer's file for a long time. Some historical data can be very helpful to identifying future maintenance needs, assess equipment performance, or determine meter upgrade schedules. This data may be indefinitely held, but should be anonymized, i.e. stripped of personal data, so that it is associated with a meter number but not personal data or energy usage information.
5.9	Assess how long any reports generated on non-operational activities are retained. Create policy safeguards for any reports that must contain personal data.

	AICPA Principle	Applies: X	Notes
5.10	**Management Principle**	X	Policies and procedures should exist for the data collected, used, shared and stored for non-operational meter reading, configuration, or other activities. A position should exist with assigned accountability for ensuring such policies and procedures exist, are effectively communicated to all personnel, and are followed.
5.11	**Notice Principle**	X	Customers should be given notice about the types of data involved in these meter activities if their personal data is involved, and the policies and procedures that are in place for protecting the information and using it appropriately. Customers should be given notice that their data may be made available to utilities' Contracted Agents in the course of providing electrical services.

5.12	Choice and Consent Principle	X	Customers should be given choices, as feasible, about how communications with them are made regarding any outreach required as part of these non-operational activities.
5.13	Collection Principle	X	Only the data necessary to effectively and efficiently support any activity should be collected, used, or reported as part of non-operational meter functions.
5.14	Use and Retention Principle	X	The data collected for any non-operational activities should be used only for the purposes authorized by the consumer. Personal data collected or generated that is not needed for statistical or analytical purposes, should be deleted as soon as possible upon completion of the meter task.
5.15	Access Principle	X	Access to personal data should be limited to only those with a specific job responsibility requiring such access.
5.16	Disclosure to Third Parties Principle	X	Data collected or created during performance of non-operational meter tasks should not be shared with any Contracted Agents or Third Parties unless there is an authorized need for such sharing, and if the customer has given consent for the information to be shared. During planned or unplanned meter activities, select customer data may be shared with Contracted Agents for purposes of maintenance and repair of meters.
5.17	Security for Privacy Principle	X	All personal data collected and created during these activities must be appropriately safeguarded to ensure unauthorized access to the data does not occur, to preserve integrity of the data, and to allow for appropriate availability.
5.18	Quality Principle	X	Controls and processes should be in place to ensure data is kept accurate as it is collected, and as it is updated during performance of meter activities.
5.19	Monitoring and Enforcement Principle	X	Processes should be in place to monitor compliance with the privacy policies and procedures related to collecting, storing, using, sharing and retaining data. Utilities may consider conducting a privacy audit whenever any changes to these activities are enacted that relate to personal or energy usage information. Procedures should exist to address privacy-related inquiries and disputes from customers involved in any non-operational activities involving meters.

Category: AMI	Privacy Use Case #6

Scenario: Meter sends alarm or unsolicited and unscheduled request to the utility

Category Description

The AMI category covers the fundamental functions of an advanced metering system. These functions include: meter reading, use of an integrated service switch, theft detection, and improved outage detection and restoration. The high-level technical requirements for these functions are well understood by the industry, but the specific benefit varies from utility to utility.

Advanced functions that are often associated with AMI are demand response program support and communications to in-home devices. These functions are not exclusive to AMI and will be discussed in separate category areas.

Scenario Description

A meter sends an alarm or unsolicited and unscheduled request to the Utility (e.g. Physical tamper detection, Network join request, or HAN device / direct load control device enrollment request (proxy for customer). The message is initiated by the meter and sends the messages to the Advanced Metering Infrastructure (AMI) Head End System (HES). The HES message flows to the Meter Reading and Control (MRC). The MRC evaluates the message. The MRC records the command result and notifies the appropriate actors.

Smart Grid Characteristics	Cybersecurity Objectives/Requirements	Potential Stakeholder Issues
• Optimizes asset utilization and operate efficiently • Operates resiliently against attack and natural disasters	• Confidentiality is not important unless alarm contains private information or exposes an attempt to obtain security information stored in the meter • Integrity - Protect against energy theft Protect integrity of meter configuration Protect integrity of reporting To protect the integrity of the network (authorized devices) • Availability is important to capture last gasp detecting, join detection, and reporting	• Network Service Providers • Customer may receive outage notification through Third Party • Billing service provider • Transmission & Distribution service provider

6.1	**Data Privacy Recommendations** Utilities collect personal data that includes customer name and address to establish an account, and this information is associated with a meter number. This personal data should be restricted to those software applications and resources that require this information in processes that identify and schedule meter maintenance for the purposes authorized by the customer. The security safeguard principle has specific application here.
6.2	Utilities should develop policies regarding meter tampering/removal detection that ensure that any personally identifiable information is managed to minimize its exposure to utility resources, and that any resources that have access to this information have appropriate training to safeguard data privacy. Utilities should understand the capabilities and any security vulnerabilities of the meters that are installed to develop appropriate policies to minimize exposure of personal data at the meter itself.
6.3	Any meter message event should be identified by the meter number and address, so it is not John Smith's meter that is sending an unsolicited message, but it is meter number 123456 at a specific location that is the subject of an action.
6.4	Utilities should review their account setup policies to ensure that notice is given up front that attempts to interfere with the operations of a meter may result in civil or criminal actions, and that information may be shared with law enforcement in such situations.

	AICPA Principle	Applies: X	Notes
6.5	Management Principle	X	Defining the management of issues of power theft accusation and ultimate adjudication and disposition are critical. Policies and procedures should exist for the data collected, used, shared and stored. A position should exist with assigned accountability for ensuring such policies and procedures exist, are effectively communicated to all personnel, and are followed.
6.6	Notice Principle	X	Utility should provide a statement in the notice that meter tampering could lead to access to meter data, including personal data, which could then result in investigation and legal actions that could have impacts on the future disposition of the account.
6.7	Choice and Consent Principle	X	See discussion under Recommendations, above.
6.8	Collection Principle	X	See discussion under Recommendations, above.
6.9	Use and Retention Principle	X	Use and retention of smart meter data, including data related to energy theft, should be subject to sunset and expungement requirements as set by the appropriate regulatory or legal authority. In the absence of regulatory or legal requirements, a utility may wish to consider setting requirements that are congruent with other expungement laws regarding personal data.
6.10	Access Principle	X	Data regarding energy theft might be requested by legal authorities, credit agencies and other utilities and vendors. Utility policies should include education and training for utility and contracted personnel regarding consistent treatment of these requests in compliance with applicable laws and regulations, as well as the AICPA principles. Access should be limited to only those with a specific job responsibility requiring such access.
6.11	Disclosure to Third Parties Principle	X	Organizations should have procedures in place to provide data access to law enforcement or other organizations with a legal need when presented with legal obligations to do so. These procedures should include validation that the necessary legal requirements have been met (e.g., subpoena, court order, etc.).
6.12	Security for Privacy Principle	X	Protection of data related to criminal theft records would need to be as securely guarded against unauthorized disclosure as personal data.

6.13	**Quality Principle**	X	The harm from inaccurate data sent by a meter - such as an incorrect tamper alarm - could be considerable. Utilities should develop policies that expunge "false positive" meter messages from customer personal data and any records that may be used for establishing financial credit or new customer deposits.
6.14	**Monitoring and Enforcement Principle**	X	Failure to monitor and enforce could result in harm to the perpetrator, the falsely accused, the energy provider and Third Parties who are inaccurately informed.

Category: Demand Response (DR)	Privacy Use Case #7

Scenario: Real-Time Pricing (RTP) for Customer Load and DER/PEV

Category Description

Demand response is a general capability that could be implemented in many different ways. The primary focus is to provide the customer with pricing information for current or future time periods so they may respond by modifying their demand. This may entail just decreasing load or may involve shifting load by increasing demand during lower priced time periods so that they can decrease demand during higher priced time periods. The pricing periods may be real-time based or may be tariff based, while the prices may also be operationally based or fixed or some combination. RTP inherently requires computer-based responses, while the fixed time-of-use pricing may be manually handled once the customer is aware of the time periods and the pricing.

Scenario Description

Use of RTP for electricity is common for very large customers, affording them an ability to determine when to use power and minimize the costs of energy for their business. The extension of RTP to smaller industrial and commercial customers and even residential customers is possible with smart metering and in-home displays. Aggregators or customer energy management systems must be used for these smaller consumers due to the complexity and 24□7 nature of managing power consumption. Pricing signals may be sent via an AMI system, the Internet, or other data channels.

Smart Grid Characteristics	Cybersecurity Objectives/Requirements	Potential Stakeholder Issues
• Enables active participation by consumers • Accommodates all generation and storage options • Enables new products, services and markets	• Integrity, including nonrepudiation, of pricing information is critical, since there could be large financial and possibly legal implications • Availability, including nonrepudiation, for pricing signals is critical because of the large financial and possibly legal implications • Confidentiality is important mostly for the responses that any customer might make to the pricing signals	• Customer data privacy and security • Retail Electric Supplier access • Customer data access

7.1	**Data Privacy Recommendations** Utilities have personal consumer information such as name, phone number and address for billing. If customer has opted for an electronic payment arrangement, the utility would also have sensitive financial data in cases of payments from consumers. The security safeguard principle has specific application here.
7.2	The use and retention principle applies - utilities should provide notification of why personal data is needed for enrollment in RTP pricing programs and how this data is managed.
7.3	The data quality principle applies - customers need the ability to review and update this information as residences or businesses change hands and new occupants may want to revise the RTP pricing arrangement if that option is available to them. While the utility is presumed to have the direct relationship with the consumer, there may be intermediated situations where a Third Party Energy Services Provider manages the consumer relationship as a DR or EE aggregator, or manages Direct Load Control (DLC) on behalf of the consumer. The consumer may not be aware of all the entities involved in their participation in RTP pricing programs. The utility should consider clear, simple identification of all entities or some formal statement of the data management principle to help educate consumers as to the "data chain" that may be in place based on their relationships with utility, utility-authorized Third Parties, and/or ESPs that are not affiliated with a utility.

		AICPA Principle	Applies: X	Notes
7.4		**Management Principle**	X	Policies and procedures should exist for the data collected, used, shared and stored.
				A position should exist with assigned accountability for ensuring such policies and procedures exist, are effectively communicated to all personnel, and are followed.
7.5		**Notice Principle**	X	Customers should be given notice for the types of data collected, how it will be used, shared and retained.
7.6		**Choice and Consent Principle**	X	Consumers may be given a choice regarding this pricing option, but it is not a privacy concern if all utility consumers are enrolled in this pricing scenario.
7.7		**Collection Principle**	X	Consumer data is collected as part of any enrollment process in TOU pricing – whether done directly as a pricing switch or as part of a DR program. Provide adequate information about the data that is collected
7.8		**Use and Retention Principle**	X	Any data that is used or retained for analytics purposes should be anonymized and its treatment disclosed to consumers.
7.9		**Access Principle**	X	All consumers have access to their data. Access should be limited to only those with a specific job responsibility requiring such access.
7.10		**Disclosure to Third Parties Principle**	X	Energy Service Providers (ESPs) may have the direct relationship with consumers enrolled in TOU programs and have personal data as well. Consumers should be aware if this principle and all others are equally applicable with any ESP.
7.11		**Security for Privacy Principle**	X	As utilities will house their operations in their own or authorized Contracted Agent facilities, physical and logical security should be in place. If there is equipment that is not under the utility's physical control which contains personal data, physical security will be dependent on the customer or an ESP. All personal data collected and created during these activities must be appropriately safeguarded to ensure unauthorized access to the data does not occur, to preserve integrity of the data, and to allow for appropriate availability.
7.12		**Quality Principle**	X	As is the case for security, quality will be critical for operational purposes.
7.13		**Monitoring and Enforcement Principle**	X	Develop and maintain audit policies to ensure that procedures are consistently applied with regards to personal data.

Category: Demand Response	Privacy Use Case #8

Scenario: Time of Use (TOU) Pricing

Category Description

Demand response is a general capability that could be implemented in many different ways. The primary focus is to provide the customer with pricing information for current or future time periods so they may respond by modifying their demand. This may entail just decreasing load or may involve shifting load by increasing demand during lower priced time periods so that they can decrease demand during higher priced time periods. The pricing periods may be real-time based or may be tariff based, while the prices may also be operationally based or fixed or some combination. Real-time pricing inherently requires computer-based responses, while the fixed TOU pricing may be manually handled once the customer is aware of the time periods and the pricing.

Scenario Description

TOU creates blocks of time and seasonal differences that allow smaller customers with less time to manage power consumption to gain some of the benefits of real-time pricing. This is the favored regulatory method in most of the world for dealing with global warming.

Although RTP is more flexible than TOU, it is likely that TOU will still provide many customers with all of the benefits that they can profitably use or manage.

Smart Grid Characteristics	Cybersecurity Objectives/Requirements	Potential Stakeholder Issues
• Enables active participation by consumers • Accommodates all generation and storage options • Enables new products, services and markets	• Integrity is not critical since TOU pricing is fixed for long periods and is not generally transmitted electronically • Availability is not an issue • Confidentiality is not an issue, except with respect to meter reading	• Customer data privacy and security • Retail Electric Supplier access • Customer data access

8.1	**Data Privacy Recommendations** Utilities have personal consumer information such as name, phone number and address for billing. If customer has opted for an electronic payment arrangement, the utility would also have sensitive financial data in cases of payments from consumers. The security safeguard principle has specific application here.
8.2	The use and retention principle applies - utilities should provide notification of why personal data is needed for enrollment in TOU pricing programs and how this data is managed.
8.3	The data quality principle applies - customers need the ability to review and update this information as residences or businesses change hands and new occupants may want to revise the TOU pricing arrangement if that option is available to them.
8.4	While the utility is presumed to have the direct relationship with the consumer, there may be intermediated situations where a Third Party Energy Services Provider manages the consumer relationship as a DR or EE aggregator, or manages Direct Load Control (DLC) on behalf of the consumer. The consumer may not be aware of all the entities involved in their participation in TOU pricing programs. The utility should consider clear, simple identification of all entities or some formal statement of the data management principle to help educate consumers as to the "data chain" that may be in place based on their relationships with utility, utility-authorized Third Parties, and/or ESPs that are not affiliated with a utility.

	AICPA Principle	Applies: X	**Notes**
8.5	**Management Principle**	X	Establish and maintain policies that oversee the implementation and compliance with the related

			privacy and security policies to protect the data involved with this use case.
8.6	**Notice Principle**	X	Utilities should provide notice to customers participating in TOU pricing programs of the personal data that will be collected related to this activity, and the related purposes for the collection. Information about data access that will or may be given to a Contracted Agent should be provided in the initial notice to the customer. The notice may be listed by service (e.g., data formatting, billing) instead of contractor's company name. Separate notice is not necessary for the sharing of personal data with a Contracted Agent, unless the purpose is materially different than has been previously authorized.
8.7	**Choice and Consent Principle**	X	Consumers may be given a choice regarding this pricing option, but it is not a privacy concern if all utility consumers are enrolled in this same pricing scenario.
8.8	**Collection Principle**	X	Consumer data is collected as part of any enrollment process in TOU pricing – whether done directly as a pricing switch or as part of a DR program. Collect only the data necessary to support the enrollment process and provide adequate information about the data that is collected within the notice.
8.9	**Use and Retention Principle**	X	Any data that is used or retained for TOU, analytics, or other purposes should be anonymized and its treatment disclosed to consumers.
8.10	**Access Principle**	X	All consumers should be provided with a process to have access to their data. Access should be limited to only those with a specific job responsibility requiring such access.
8.11	**Disclosure to Third Parties Principle**	X	Energy Service Providers (ESPs) may have the direct relationship with consumers enrolled in TOU programs and have personal data as well. Consumers should be aware if this principle and all others are equally applicable with any ESP.
8.12	**Security for Privacy Principle**	X	As Utilities will house their operations in their own or authorized Contracted Agent facilities, physical, administrative, and technical security should be in place under their existing information security program. If there is equipment that is not under the utility's physical control that contains personal data, physical, administrative and technical security will be dependent on the customer or an ESP. All personal data collected and created during these activities must be appropriately safeguarded to ensure unauthorized access to the data does not occur, to preserve integrity of the data, and to allow for appropriate availability.

| 8.13 | Quality Principle | X | As is the case for security, quality (data accuracy) will be critical for operational purposes. |
| 8.14 | Monitoring and Enforcement Principle | X | Access logs for TOU related files should be generated and regular audits of those logs should occur. |

Category: Demand Response	Privacy Use Case #9
Scenario: Net Metering for DER and PEV	

Category Description

Demand response is a general capability that could be implemented in many different ways. The primary focus is to provide the customer with pricing information for current or future time periods so they may respond by modifying their demand. This may entail just decreasing load or may involve shifting load by increasing demand during lower priced time periods so that they can decrease demand during higher priced time periods. The pricing periods may be real-time based or may be tariff based, while the prices may also be operationally based or fixed or some combination. Real-time pricing inherently requires computer-based responses, while the fixed time-of-use pricing may be manually handled once the customer is aware of the time periods and the pricing.

Scenario Description

When customers have the ability to generate or store power as well as consume power, net metering is installed to measure not only the flow of power in each direction, but also when the net power flows occurred. Often TOU tariffs are employed.

Today larger commercial and industrial (C&I) customers and an increasing number of residential and smaller C&I customers have net metering installed for their photovoltaic systems, wind turbines, combined heat and power (CHP), and other DER devices. As PEVs become available, net metering may increasingly be implemented in homes and small businesses, even parking lots.

Smart Grid Characteristics	Cybersecurity Objectives/Requirements	Potential Stakeholder Issues
• Enables active participation by consumers • Accommodates all generation and storage options • Enables new products, services and markets	• Integrity is not very critical since net metering pricing is fixed for long periods and is not generally transmitted electronically • Availability is not an issue • Confidentiality is not an issue, except with respect to meter reading	• Customer data privacy and security • Retail Electric Supplier access • Customer data access

9.1	**Data Privacy Recommendations** Utilities have personal consumer information such as name, phone number and address for billing. If customer has opted for an electronic payment arrangement, the utility would also have sensitive financial data and perhaps authorized access to deposit funds in cases of payments to consumers. The security safeguard principle has specific application here.
9.2	The use and retention principle applies - utilities should provide notification of why personal data is needed for billing and how this data is managed.
9.3	The data quality principle applies - customers need the ability to review and update this information as residences or business change hands and new occupants may want to revise the DR or net metering arrangement.
9.4	While the utility is presumed to have the direct relationship with the consumer, there may be intermediated situations where an Energy Services Provider manages the DR relationship as an aggregator, or manages generation on behalf of the consumer. While the utility is presumed to have the direct relationship with the consumer, there may be intermediated situations where an Energy Services Provider manages generation on behalf of the consumer. The consumer may not be aware of all the entities involved in their participation in a DR program. The utility should consider clear, simple identification of all entities or some formal statement of the data management principle to help educate consumers as to the "data chain" that may be in place based on their relationships with utility, authorized Third Parties, and/or ESPs.

	AICPA Principle	Applies: X	Notes
9.5	Management Principle	X	Maintain policies and supporting procedures that govern compliance with the related privacy and security policies to protect the data involved with this use case.
9.6	Notice Principle	X	Given that net metering situations will be a result of specific customer choice to enter into the tariff / arrangement, it seems that these two principles will likely be addressed in the process of signing up for net metering.
9.7	Choice and Consent Principle	X	
9.8	Collection Principle	X	Only the information necessary to support net monitoring for DERs and PEVs should be collected.
9.9	Use and Retention Principle	X	Particular emphasis should be placed on this in situations where a Third Party is involved so that consumer data is not misused by that Third Party.
9.10	Access Principle	X	Access to the data related to DER and PEV use should be limited to only those with a need for access to support the related business purposes.
9.11	Disclosure to Third Parties Principle	X	Energy Service Providers (ESPs) may have the direct relationship with DR or net metering customers and may have personal data as well. Consumers should be aware if this principle and all others are equally applicable with any ESP.
9.12	Security for Privacy Principle	X	As utilities will house their operations in their own or authorized Contracted Agent facilities, physical and logical security should be in place. If there is equipment that is not under the utility's physical control which contains personal data, physical security will be dependent on the customer or an ESP. All personal data collected and created during these activities must be appropriately safeguarded to ensure unauthorized access to the data does not occur, to preserve integrity of the data, and to allow for appropriate availability.
9.13	Quality Principle	X	As is the case for security, quality (data accuracy and integrity) will be critical for operational purposes.
9.14	Monitoring and Enforcement Principle	X	Access logs for TOU related files should be generated and regular audits of those logs should occur.

Category: Demand Response	Privacy Use Case #10

Scenario: Feed-In Tariff Pricing for DER and PEV

Category Description

Demand response is a general capability that could be implemented in many different ways. The primary focus is to provide the customer with pricing information for current or future time periods so they may respond by modifying their demand. This may entail just decreasing load or may involve shifting load by increasing demand during lower priced time periods so that they can decrease demand during higher priced time periods. The pricing periods may be real-time based or may be tariff based, while the prices may also be operationally based or fixed or some combination. Real-time pricing inherently requires computer-based responses, while the fixed time-of-use pricing may be manually handled once the customer is aware of the time periods and the pricing.

Scenario Description

Feed-in tariff (FiT) pricing is similar to net metering except that generation from customer DER/PEV has a different tariff rate than the customer load tariff rate during specific time periods.

Smart Grid Characteristics	Cybersecurity Objectives/Requirements	Potential Stakeholder Issues
• Enables active participation by consumers • Accommodates all generation and storage options • Enables new products, services and markets	• Integrity is not critical, since feed-in tariff pricing is fixed for long periods and is generally not transmitted electronically • Availability is not an issue • Confidentiality is not an issue, except with respect to meter reading	• Customer data privacy and security • Retail Electric Supplier access • Customer data access

10.1	**Data Privacy Recommendations** Utilities have personal consumer information such as name, phone number and address for billing. If customer has opted for an electronic payment arrangement, the utility would also have sensitive financial data and perhaps authorized access to deposit funds in cases of payments to consumers. The security safeguard principle has specific application here.
10.2	The use and retention principle applies - utilities should provide notification of why personal data is needed for billing and how this data is managed.
10.3	The data quality principle applies - customers need the ability to review and update this information as residences or businesses change hands and new occupants may want to revise the DR or net metering arrangement.
10.4	While the utility is presumed to have the direct relationship with the consumer, there may be intermediated situations where an Energy Services Provider manages generation on behalf of the consumer. The consumer may not be aware of all the entities involved in their participation in a FiT program. The utility should consider clear, simple identification of all entities or some formal statement of the data management principle to help educate consumers as to the "data chain" that may be in place based on their relationships with utility, authorized Third Parties, and/or ESPs.

		AICPA Principle	Applies: X	Notes
10.4		Management Principle	X	Responsibility for privacy and information security management must be assigned, and policies and supporting procedures created to apply to the data within this use case. As the only difference here is in the actual pricing of the service, the privacy principles and comments for the net metering for DER and PEV use case 11 apply here.
				Maintain policies and supporting procedures that govern compliance with the related privacy and security policies to protect the data involved with this use case.
10.5		Notice Principle	X	Customer should be provided with notice of the types of personal data that will be collected as part of the use case. Given that FiT situations will be a result of specific customer choice to enter into the tariff / arrangement, this principle will be best addressed in the process of signing up for an FiT.
10.6		Choice and Consent Principle	X	Given that FiT situations will be a result of specific customer choice to enter into the tariff / arrangement, this principle will be best addressed in the process of signing up for an FiT.
10.7		Collection Principle	X	Only the additional data, beyond that already in possession for energy service, necessary for FiT should be collected.
10.8		Use and Retention Principle	X	As with any type of personal data, FiT data should only be retained as long as possible to support business purposes, and as required by applicable legal requirements. Particular emphasis should be placed on this in situations where a Third Party is involved so that consumer data is not misused by that Third Party.
10.9		Access Principle	X	Access to personal data should be limited to only those with a specific job responsibility requiring such access.
10.10		Disclosure to Third Parties Principle	X	Energy Service Providers (ESPs) may have the direct relationship with FiT customers and have personal data as well. Consumers should be aware if this principle and all others are equally applicable with any ESP.

10.11	Security for Privacy Principle	X	As utilities will house their operations in their own or authorized Contracted Agent facilities, physical and logical security should be in place. If there is equipment that is not under the utility's physical control which contains personal data, physical security will be dependent on the customer or an ESP. All personal data collected and created during these activities must be appropriately safeguarded to ensure unauthorized access to the data does not occur, to preserve integrity of the data, and to allow for appropriate availability.
10.12	Quality Principle	X	The quality (accuracy) of the personal data used for FiT will be critical for operational purposes. NOTE: Accuracy of personal data is both a privacy and security issue.
10.13	Monitoring and Enforcement Principle	X	Access to FiT data should be logged, and regularly audited, to ensure it is being used appropriately. This helps to address the insider threat that so often causes privacy breaches.

Category: Demand Response	**Privacy Use Case #11**
Scenario: Critical Peak Pricing	

Category Description

Demand response is a general capability that could be implemented in many different ways. The primary focus is to provide the customer with pricing information for current or future time periods so they may respond by modifying their demand. This may entail just decreasing load or may involve shifting load by increasing demand during lower priced time periods so that they can decrease demand during higher priced time periods. The pricing periods may be real-time based or may be tariff based, while the prices may also be operationally based or fixed or some combination. Real-time pricing inherently requires computer-based responses, while the fixed time-of-use pricing may be manually handled once the customer is aware of the time periods and the pricing.

Scenario Description

Critical Peak Pricing (CPP) builds on TOU pricing by selecting a small number of days each year where the electric delivery system will be heavily stressed and increasing the peak (and sometime shoulder peak) prices by up to 10 times the normal peak price. This is intended to reduce the stress on the system during these days.

Smart Grid Characteristics	Cybersecurity Objectives/Requirements	Potential Stakeholder Issues
• Enables active participation by consumers • Accommodates all generation and storage options • Enables new products, services and markets	• Integrity is not critical, since FiT pricing is fixed for long periods and is generally not transmitted electronically • Availability is not an issue • Confidentiality is not an issue, except with respect to meter reading	• Customer data privacy and security • Retail Electric Supplier access • Customer data access

11.1	**Data Privacy Recommendations** Utilities may have personal consumer data such as name, phone number and address for billing. If customer has opted for an electronic payment arrangement, the utility would also have sensitive financial data and perhaps authorized access to deposit funds in cases of payments to consumers. The security safeguard principle has specific application here.
11.2	The use and retention principle applies - utilities should provide notification of why personal data is needed for billing and how this data is managed.
11.3	The data quality principle applies - customers need the ability to review and update this information as residences or business change hands and new occupants may want to revise the CPP arrangement.
11.4	ESPs or other Contracted Agents who act as utility agents may have access to personal data. The consumer may not be aware of all the entities involved in their participation in a CPP program. The utility should consider clear, simple identification of all entities or some formal statement of the data management principle to help educate consumers as to the "data chain" that may be in place based on their relationships with utility, authorized Contracted Agents, and/or ESPs.

		AICPA Principle	Applies: X	Notes
11.5		Management Principle	X	As the only difference here is in the actual pricing of the service, the privacy principles and comments for the net metering for DER and PEV (Privacy Use Case 12) apply here. Maintain policies and supporting procedures that govern compliance with the related privacy and security policies to protect the data involved with this use case.
11.6		Notice Principle	X	Given that CPP situations will be a result of specific customer choice to enter into the tariff / arrangement, it seems that this principle should be addressed in the process of signing up for CPP.
11.7		Choice and Consent Principle	X	Given that CPP situations will be a result of specific customer choice to enter into the tariff / arrangement, it seems that this principle will likely be addressed in the process of signing up for CPP.
11.8		Collection Principle	X	If additional data is collected to support this use case scenario, it should be limited to only that necessary to support the actions within the scenario.
11.9		Use and Retention Principle	X	Particular emphasis should be placed on this in situations where a Third Party is involved so that consumer data is not misused by that Third Party.
11.10		Access Principle	X	Access should be limited to only those with a specific job responsibility requiring such access.
11.11		Disclosure to Third Parties Principle	X	Energy Service Providers (ESPs) may have the direct relationship with CPP customers and have personal data as well. Consumers should be aware if this principle and all others are equally applicable with any ESP.
11.12		Security for Privacy Principle	X	As utilities will house their operations in their own or authorized Contracted Agent facilities, physical and logical security should be in place. If there is equipment that is not under the utility's physical control which contains personal data, physical security will be dependent on the customer or an ESP. All personal data collected and created during these activities must be appropriately safeguarded to ensure unauthorized access to the data does not occur, to preserve integrity of the data, and to allow for appropriate availability.
11.13		Quality Principle	X	Data needs to be as accurate as possible and applicable for the purposes for which it is used.

11.14	Monitoring and Enforcement Principle	X	Access to pricing data should be logged, and regularly audited, to ensure it is being used appropriately. This helps to address the insider threat (from mistakes, doing things unwittingly, and from malicious intent) that so often causes privacy breaches.

Category: Demand Response	**Privacy Use Case #12**
Scenario: Mobile Plug-In Electric Vehicle Functions	

Category Description

Demand response is a general capability that could be implemented in many different ways. The primary focus is to provide the customer with pricing information for current or future time periods so they may respond by modifying their demand. This may entail just decreasing load or may involve shifting load by increasing demand during lower priced time periods so that they can decrease demand during higher priced time periods. The pricing periods may be real-time based or may be tariff based, while the prices may also be operationally based or fixed or some combination. Real-time pricing inherently requires computer-based responses, while the fixed time-of-use pricing may be manually handled once the customer is aware of the time periods and the pricing.

Scenario Description

In addition to customers with PEVs participating in their home-based Demand Response functions, they will have additional requirements for managing the charging and discharging of their mobile PEVs in other locations:
Customer connects PEV at another home
Customer connects PEV outside home territory
Customer connects PEV at public location
Customer charges the PEV

Smart Grid Characteristics	**Cybersecurity Objectives/Requirements**	**Potential Stakeholder Issues**
• Enables active participation by consumers • Accommodates all generation and storage options • Enables new products, services and markets	• Integrity is not critical, since feed-in tariff pricing is fixed for long periods and is generally not transmitted electronically • Availability is not an issue • Confidentiality is not an issue, except with respect to meter reading	• Customer data privacy and security • Retail Electric Supplier access • Customer data access

12.1	**Data Privacy Recommendations** This use case presumes residential (one owner/car) situations, but DR may also be used with EV fleets that are common to governmental entities and other businesses. These recommendations address residential situations only. There are three possible grid interfaces considered here: basic 120 V or 240 V plug for electricity downloads connected to a dumb or smart meter; a meter that is capable of running backwards for download and upload of electricity (net metering); and charging stations that can charge/discharge electricity to and from the grid. From the perspective of customer relationship - utilities are involved in the first two interfaces in terms of owning the meter, but the third scenario may involve Third Parties that intermediate the utility/consumer relationship with ownership of charging stations. This would be similar to the situation in which old pay telephones were owned by a number of different vendors, not just the phone company. Consumers may not always be aware of the "ownership" of the charging point and may assume that the privacy policies and practices the utility adopts apply in all scenarios. Utilities may wish to add a statement in their general privacy policies that serves to educate consumers that there are select situations where EV energy consumption data (or other data) could be handled by Third Parties that are not required to abide by utility privacy policies.
12.2	Roaming models for AC charge billing purposes are developing around the world. DC charging appears to be settled into the familiar gas station analogy of credit/debit/cash payments, although affluent customers may opt for similar charging stations. Industry speculation is that credit cards or mobile phones will be the common payment mechanism for roaming AC charging, and may entirely bypass utility operations. However, here are some other scenarios to consider: Utilities may have personal consumer data such as name, credit card/debit card, phone number and address for billing for any roaming charge programs that they manage. In addition, customers may

have opted for an electronic payment arrangement, so the utility would also have sensitive financial data and perhaps authorized access to deposit funds in cases of payments to consumers. For instance, in California the IOUs are not allowed to provide charging stations, so all charging stations will be owned by Third Party energy service providers, property owners, or businesses. However, these utilities may still have smart charging agreements in place with specific cars or charging stations and will require this information. The security safeguard principle has specific application here.

For charging or discharging that occurs away from the consumer's home address but is billed back to a utility account, utilities will need to determine what non-home address location information is necessary to collect for billing/payment purposes, and what should be displayed on paper or electronic bills. Consider the amount of identification that appears on a bank statement if a consumer uses an ATM, or the level of detail on credit card statements for gas purchases to develop policies. Consider the minimum necessary information about charge time, date, and location on electric bills. The purpose specification and accountability principles apply here.

Charging Service Providers (CSPs) or other Contracted Agents who act as utility agents may have access to personal data for billing purposes. The consumer may not be aware of all the entities involved when they plug into a charging station. The utility should consider clear, simple identification of all entities or some formal statement of the data management principle to help educate consumers as to the "data chain" that may be in place based on their relationships with utility, authorized Contracted Agents, and/or CSPs. The notice principle applies here.

The potential for the collection of location information creates special privacy concerns regarding PEVs. It actually creates special safety and security concerns as well. This is pertinent for charging information that occurs at the consumer's home, not just away from home. This is because PEV charging at home can inform of habits and motoring range for any given date and time. This information is of special interest to law enforcement. Further, it allows individuals to be tracked and stalked, endangering their safety.

	AICPA Principle	Applies: X	Notes
12.3	Management Principle	X	This use case covers mobile or roaming charge/discharge.

At home, charging/discharging information related to PEVs provides motoring range and habit information that can endanger a person's safety and freedom. This requires special privacy protection.

When using a Third Party charging station, there is a need to determine how all principles apply, and how consumers are educated is important. It may not be appropriate for a utility to address this issue, but it could still be a smart grid issue. Consumers will appreciate education from a trusted source to understand what personal data may be collected, used, and retained by various entities in mobile charging scenarios.

Utilities will need to determine and assign responsibility for how EVs are incorporated into DR programs, and then develop appropriate privacy policies regarding any personal data that would accompany the reporting, billing, and management of these DR programs. |

12.4	Notice Principle	X	Notice may be challenging when it is a charging station owned by a Third Party as discussed above in 12.1. Special efforts must be required of Third Parties through the contracts between the Third Parties, utility authorized Contracted Agents, and utilities. Utilities should ensure that authorized Contracted Agents adhere to the privacy policies and practices enacted by the utility to protect PII and energy consumption data. For unrelated Third Parties, utilities lack immediate and/or ongoing opportunities to inform consumers that different privacy policies may be in effect. Utilities may wish to add a statement to their general privacy policies that addresses EV charging devices that are "in their control" or "out of their control." and the consumers must be made aware of the risk of disclosure of this information.
12.5	Choice and Consent Principle	X	There may be choices available at the charging stations/points. If not, then the charging station should clearly indicate the data being collected, how it will be used, shared and retained, and then obtain consent to use the data as a consequence of charging at that location.
12.6	Collection Principle	X	This principle applies for any entity that is delivering power or maintaining a financial transaction. Only the data necessary for the customer to obtain the electricity charge, and then for the charging company to be financially reimbursed, should be collected.
12.7	Use and Retention Principle	X	Data collected from PEV charging stations should be used only for the purposes of supporting the associated payments, and then irreversibly deleted after they are no longer needed for business purposes. If data is intended for planning, balancing, or operational purposes, the utility should adopt Privacy enhancing technologies and practice to anonymize this data and de-identify it.
12.8	Access Principle	X	Since charging stations may be owned by a number of entities, it may be difficult for individuals to know who to contact to gain access to their personal data. PEV charging stations need to ensure customers can get access to their associated PEV charging data, and access to that data within related businesses should be limited to only those with a business need to know.
12.9	Disclosure to Third Parties Principle	X	Since charging stations may be owned by a number of entities, it may be challenging to obtain implicit or explicit consent before sharing data. Even if consent is not feasible, consumers should be told the ways in which the data is used.

12.10	Security for Privacy Principle	X	Applies with special regard to any financial transactions. Applies with special regard to location-based information. All personal data collected and created during these activities must be appropriately safeguarded to ensure unauthorized access to the data does not occur, to preserve integrity of the data, and to allow for appropriate availability.
12.11	Quality Principle	X	PEV charging data must be accurate, and controls need to be incorporated to ensure this.
12.12	Monitoring and Enforcement Principle	X	Develop and maintain audit policies to ensure that procedures are consistently applied with regards to personal data.

Category: Customer Interfaces	Privacy Use Case #13

Scenario: Customer's In-Home Device is Provisioned to Communicate With the Utility

Category Description

Customers want to understand how their energy consumption habits affect their monthly energy bills and to find ways to reduce their monthly energy costs. Customers should have the ability to receive information on their usage and the price of energy on a variety of devices (in-home displays, computers, and mobile devices). In addition to real-time and historical energy data, customers should be able to receive messages from the utility notifying them about outages.

Scenario Description

This scenario describes the process to configure a customer's in-home device to receive and send data to utility systems. The device could be an information display, communicating thermostat, load control device, or smart appliance.

Smart Grid Characteristics	Cybersecurity Objectives/Requirements	Potential Stakeholder Issues
• Enables active participation by consumers • Accommodates all generation and storage options • Enables new products, services and markets	• To protect passwords • To protect key material • To authenticate with other devices on the AMI system	• Customer device standards • Customer data privacy and security

13.1	Data Privacy Recommendations The information for in-home displays (IHDs) or computers may be richer than the information transmitted by a load control device or communicating thermostat. However, with the possible exception of web portals viewed on computer screens, these devices do not transmit personal data about consumers. The devices are associated with a meter and are simply seen as additional loads to be met in a building. Utility practices regarding personal data handled in billing processes needs to be assessed with regards to new energy consumption data that may be communicated in bills, on IHD devices, on mobile devices, or via computer screens.
13.2	Security practices come into play to protect these devices from unauthorized access – specifically for the communications processes that could transmit control signals to communicating thermostat, load control device, or smart appliance appliances.
13.3	Communications to IHDs need to be considered from a security perspective – are the signals originating from a device in the home – like a WiFi router, and is that router password-protected or not? It is most likely that communications networks for computers and mobile devices have some level of security offered by the communications service provider, but end users should be aware before configuring the device that energy consumption data may be transmitted over these networks and they should avail themselves of all the protections offered by these providers.
13.4	Utilities that collect energy consumption data will need to develop policies for all AICPA principles, and pay particular attention to use and retention. Any use of data by Third Parties will mean that utilities must obtain consent to make that data available to Third Parties.
13.5	Due to the evolution of energy consumption/provision measurement devices into communication devices, special care must be exercised regarding their implementation. They open up the risk of interpretation of communications information laws to apply to energy consumption, and thus increase the risk of inadvertent disclosure through data breaches.

	AICPA Principle	Applies: X	Notes
13.6	**Management Principle**	X	Insofar as programmable communicating thermostats, in home displays, load control and smart appliances that are simply devices "beyond the meter", their energy use is just additional kWh in a utility bill. All principles apply to utility management of personal data in billing processes. This principle is relevant for energy consumption data as a form of personal data. Policies, procedures, and oversight must be established covering these issues. Policies and procedures should exist for the data collected, used, shared and stored.
			A position should exist with assigned accountability for ensuring such policies and procedures exist, are effectively communicated to all personnel, and are followed.
13.7	**Notice Principle**	X	This principle is relevant. Customers need to be provided notice regarding the data being collected, generated, accessed, and how it is used prior to establishing the service.
13.8	**Choice and Consent Principle**	X	Individuals should be provided with an "opt in" or "opt out" choice for utilities to use energy consumption data for any purpose other than billing or other authorized purposes, and for specific features of the devices' services.
13.9	**Collection Principle**	X	Applies to energy consumption data, and utilities should address their interests in analyses of data to deliver better quality of service and/or additional services that will be of value to individuals. Only the data necessary to achieve these services should be collected.
13.10	**Use and Retention Principle**	X	Specific application with regards to energy consumption data and analytics. Utilities should provide a statement that describes why analytics optimize reliability, quality or cost of electricity services. Information should indicate how long the data will be retained, and for what purposes.
13.11	**Access Principle**	X	Access to personal data should be limited to only those with a specific job responsibility requiring such access. Similarly, procedures should be created that will allow customers to have access to the information/data involved with this use case. Utilities may wish to advise customers that Third Parties, unlike Contracted Agents, may not have the same privacy guidelines and practices regarding personal data.
13.12	**Disclosure to Third Parties Principle**	X	Applies, with emphasis on the analyses of energy consumption data – whether anonymized or not.

				Controls need to be applied, using contractual requirements as well as data protection best practices for data sharing (see the NISTIR 7628. Volume 2). Customers should know the entities that have their data.
13.13	**Security for Privacy Principle**		X	Consumers will need assurances that any devices that may be authorized for limited control by utilities, such as setting AC temperatures higher on peak days, are managed via secure communications to prevent unauthorized access by entities inside utilities or external entities. Policies and procedures need to be implemented establishing the safeguards required for the data associated with this use case. All personal data collected and created during these activities must be appropriately safeguarded to ensure unauthorized access to the data does not occur, to preserve integrity of the data, and to allow for appropriate availability.
13.14	**Quality Principle**		X	Insofar as programmable communicating thermostats, in home displays, load control and smart appliances that are simply devices "beyond the meter", their energy use is just additional kWh in a utility bill. All principles apply to utility management of personal data in billing processes if the provisioning of these devices or their ongoing operation incur fees that appear in utility bills or bills created by Contracted Agents. Procedures need to be followed to ensure data is as accurate as required for the purposes for which it is used.
13.15	**Monitoring and Enforcement Principle**		X	Given sensitivities around privacy and smart meters, strong policies and practices of monitoring and consistent enforcement must be implemented to help allay consumer concerns about energy consumption data.

Category: Customer Interfaces	Privacy Use Case #14

Scenario: Customer Views Pricing or Energy Data on Their In-Home Device

Category Description

Customers want to understand how their energy consumption habits affect their monthly energy bills and to find ways to reduce their monthly energy costs. Customers should have the ability to receive information on their usage and the price of energy on a variety of devices (in-home displays, computers, and mobile devices). In addition to real-time and historical energy data, customers should be able to receive messages from the utility notifying them about outages.

Scenario Description

This scenario describes the information that should be available to customers on their in-home devices. Multiple communication paths and device functions will be considered.

Smart Grid Characteristics	Cybersecurity Objectives/Requirements	Potential Stakeholder Issues
• Enables active participation by consumers • Accommodates all generation and storage options • Enables new products, services and markets	• To validate that information is trustworthy (integrity)	• Customer device standards • Customer data privacy and security

14.1	**Data Privacy Recommendations** This scenario identifies pricing information or energy data on an In-Home-Device (IHD) via a variety of communication paths. We will discuss two – communications path to a smart meter, and communications path to a Third Party that uses WiFi. We will also consider IHDs to be dedicated, single purpose devices for this scenario, and exclude web portals, tablets, and smart phones. We will also exclude any scenario where electricity is flowing back to the utility, so no net metering information would be displayed on these IHDs.
14.2	In the case where the communications path is from an IHD to a smart meter, the utility should ensure that data that is transmitted to IHDs should not include any personal data – specifically granular energy consumption data - without exercising the choice and consent principle to educate consumers that they consent to display this data.
14.3	In the case where the IHD is receiving information via some other source than a smart meter, it is important to establish where the utility's custody of information such as energy consumption terminates. If an authorized Contracted Agent is reading a meter and communicating that information to an application that wirelessly updates an IHD display, the utility has control over that data because that agent is working in an official capacity with the utility. In these cases, the utility must ensure that all principles, particularly choice and consent, collection, access, notice, use and retention, and disclosure are addressed with consumers.
14.4	IHDs may be selected by consumers independent of utility actions. In this case, utilities have no control over how any data that is extracted from a meter or added by a consumer is displayed. In this case, IHD manufacturers should inform consumers about the types of information that may be collected, retained, and/or displayed.
14.5	Security for privacy principles should come into play to protect IHDs from unauthorized access – specifically for the communications processes that could transmit personal data.

	AICPA Principle	Applies: X	Notes
14.6	Management Principle	X	The information that a utility provides to a customer should be based on successful password-protected login to an account. Such practices must be followed and managed using established and consistently applied procedures. Policies and procedures should exist for the data collected, used, shared and stored. A position should exist with assigned accountability for ensuring such policies and procedures exist, are effectively communicated to all personnel, and are followed.
14.7	Notice Principle	X	This applies for utility and Third Party situations. Customers should be given notice for the types of data collected, how it will be used, shared and retained.
14.8	Choice and Consent Principle	X	This is important to educate consumers about what information is displayed in an IHD. Customers should be given choices with regard to the data collected and used to the extent possible for each associated purpose.
14.9	Collection Principle	X	This applies for any enrollment process that a utility uses to receive information from an IHD, as well as the actual display of information itself. Only data needed to fulfill the business purposes of this use case should be collected, and no more than necessary.
14.10	Use and Retention Principle	X	Since the information is being pushed from a utility smart meter or by a Third Party means to an IHD, the data should be used only for the purposes for which it was collected, and retained only for as long as necessary for those purposes.
14.11	Access Principle	X	The ability to view information about a customer account reinforces this principle, but many IHDs may not support this capability. Therefore, procedures need to be established to provide customers access to their associated information. Access to personal data should be limited to only those with a specific job responsibility requiring such access.
14.12	Disclosure to Third Parties Principle	X	This applies in scenarios where utilities have selected Third Parties to provision and/or manage deployment of IHDs. Controls need to be applied, using contractual requirements as well as data protection best practices for data sharing (Consider using the DoE Voluntary Code of Conduct or the NAESB REQ.22 standard.). Customers should know the entities that have their data.
14.13	Security for Privacy Principle	X	Information transmission security is important. Risk based information security policies and supporting

			procedures should be implemented and consistently followed. All personal data collected and created during these activities must be appropriately safeguarded to ensure unauthorized access to the data does not occur, to preserve integrity of the data, and to allow for appropriate availability.
14.14	**Quality Principle**	X	Procedures and technical controls should be implemented to ensure data stays as accurate as necessary to support the business purposes for which it was collected.
14.15	**Monitoring and Enforcement Principle**	X	Contracted Agents operate under the same privacy guidelines as the utilities that contract them, so utilities have a responsibility to have some sort of processes in place to monitor and enforce their policies on Contracted Agents. Third parties are not necessarily subject to utility privacy policies, so utilities may wish to make note of that in their privacy notice to customers.

Category: Customer Interfaces	Privacy Use Case #15

Scenario: In-Home Device Troubleshooting

Category Description

Customers want to understand how their energy consumption habits affect their monthly energy bills and to find ways to reduce their monthly energy costs. Customers should have the ability to receive information on their usage and the price of energy on a variety of devices (in-home displays, computers, and mobile devices). In addition to real-time and historical energy data, customers should be able to receive messages from the utility notifying them about outages.

Scenario Description

This alternate scenario describes the resolution of communication or other types of errors that could occur with in-home devices. Roles of the customer, device vendor, and utility will be discussed.

Smart Grid Characteristics	Cybersecurity Objectives/Requirements	Potential Stakeholder Issues
• Enables active participation by consumers • Accommodates all generation and storage options • Enables new products, services and markets	• To avoid disclosing customer information • To avoid disclosing key material and/or passwords	• Customer device standards • Customer data privacy and security

15.1	**Data Privacy Recommendations** Customer: A communication error on the part of a programmable communicating thermostat, in home display, load control and/or smart appliance may result in a dearth of data, not a display or sharing of personal data if it shows energy usage and/or specific times, dates, appliances, etc. A performance error on the part of a programmable communicating thermostat, in home display, load control and/or smart appliance may cause consumer frustration, but will not necessarily result in a display or sharing of personal data. A loss of power to a programmable communicating thermostat, in home display, load control and/or smart appliance may cause consumer reprogramming, but will not necessarily result in a display or sharing of personal data.
15.2	Device vendor: A communication or performance error on the part of a programmable communicating thermostat, in home display, load control and/or smart appliance will likely result in a support call from either the consumer to the device manufacturer or vice versa. The personal details that may be shared could possibly include consumer name to initiate a support call if the consumer is the caller. If it is a distributor, personal data is unlikely to be shared. A loss of power to a programmable communicating thermostat, in home display, load control and/or smart appliance may cause consumer reprogramming, but will not necessarily result in a display or sharing of personal data. It is unlikely that a support call will be initiated for a power loss. Vendors that take support calls should examine the policies and practices for handling customer data by support operations that typically see or take control (it should be with customer permission) of computer screens to conduct troubleshooting and resolution functions. Similar practices could be enacted that conform to the AICPA principles, particularly with regard to notice, choice and consent, and use and retention.

| | 15.3 | Utility: A communication error on the part of a programmable communicating thermostat, in home display, load control and/or smart appliance will likely result in a support call from either the consumer or the entity that sold or provided the device to the consumer or the utility.

A performance error on the part of a programmable communicating thermostat, in home display, load control and/or smart appliance may cause consumer frustration, but will not necessarily result in a display or sharing of personal data.

In both cases above, if the utility does not provide support for devices, then there is no need to collect any personal data. If the utility offers support or arranges support via an authorized Contracted Agent, any consumer personal data must be safeguarded as outlined by the principles below.

A loss of power to a programmable communicating thermostat, in home display, load control and/or smart appliance may trigger a call from the consumer to the utility, but the trouble ticket will be for an outage, not a device malfunction.

Utilities that take support calls should have policies and practices that cover handling customer data by support operations that typically see or take control, with customer permission, of computer screens to conduct troubleshooting and resolution functions. Similar practices could be enacted that conform to the AICPA principles particularly with regard to notice, choice and consent, and use and retention.

[Outage notifications sent to any display outside the premise should be designed to not include address information to protect consumers from inadvertent displays or announcements of this personal data.] |

		AICPA Principle	Applies: X	Notes
15.4		**Management Principle**	X	Policies and supporting procedures need to be established and consistently followed based upon the specific data items involved, as implemented by the utility.

A position should exist with assigned accountability for ensuring such policies and procedures exist, are effectively communicated to all personnel, and are followed. |
15.5		**Notice Principle**	X	Notice needs to be given depending upon whether personal data, or data that can reveal personal activities, locations, etc., are involved. Customers should be given notice for the types of data collected, how it will be used, shared and retained.
15.6		**Choice and Consent Principle**	X	Customers need to be given notice for the data involved, why it is necessary and then, as feasible, be given a choice for which data items to provide consent for use.
15.7		**Collection Principle**	X	Only the data necessary for the associated purpose should be collected.
15.8		**Use and Retention Principle**	X	How is data that is personal data, or that can reveal personal activities, or other associated personal data such as appliances, used? The uses should only be for the purposes for which it was collected, and then retained for only the amount of time necessary to fulfill the business reasons for the collection.

15.9	Access Principle	X	Procedures should be created to provide customers with access to the data, or to a description of the data, involved with this use case. Access to personal data should be limited to only those with a specific job responsibility requiring such access.
15.10	**Disclosure to Third Parties Principle**	X	This principle should be applied in scenarios where a Third Party or Contracted Agent is are involved in support or troubleshooting. Controls need to be applied, using contractual requirements, where appropriate, as well as data protection best practices for data sharing (see <u>Appendix D: Recommended Privacy Practices for Customer/Consumer Smart Grid Energy Usage Data Obtained Directly by Third Parties</u>).
15.11	**Security for Privacy Principle**	X	In a troubleshooting scenario, this principle should be taken into account. Security and safeguard controls must be applied as appropriate to mitigate risks and protect personal data and other information that reveals personal activities and characteristics. All personal data collected and created during these activities must be appropriately safeguarded to ensure unauthorized access to the data does not occur, to preserve integrity of the data, and to allow for appropriate availability.
15.12	**Quality Principle**	X	Procedures and technical controls should be implemented to ensure data stays as accurate as necessary to support the business purposes for which it was collected.
15.13	**Monitoring and Enforcement Principle**	X	Utilities should establish policies, procedures, and possibly even a dedicated position, to ensure requirements are monitored and compliance enforced.

Category: Customer Interfaces	Privacy Use Case #16
Scenario: Customer Views Pricing or Energy Data via the Internet	

Category Description

Customers want to understand how their energy consumption habits affect their monthly energy bills and to find ways to reduce their monthly energy costs. Customers should have the ability to receive information on their usage and the price of energy on a variety of devices (in-home displays, computers, and mobile devices). In addition to real-time and historical energy data, customers should be able to receive messages from the utility notifying them about outages.

Scenario Description

In addition to a utility operated communications network (i.e., AMI), the Internet can be used to communicate to customers and their devices. Personal computers and mobile devices may be more suitable for displaying some types of energy data than low cost specialized in-home display devices. This scenario describes the information that should be available to the customer using the Internet and some possible uses for the data.

Smart Grid Characteristics	Cybersecurity Objectives/Requirements	Potential Stakeholder Issues
• Enables active participation by consumers • Accommodates all generation and storage options • Enables new products, services and markets	• To protect customer's information (privacy) • To provide accurate information	• Customer device standards • Customer data privacy and security

16.1	**Data Privacy Recommendations** These devices almost certainly contain personal data about consumers that was placed there by consumers. However, utility practices should be designed to not push any personal data to these devices unless a successful login with password has been completed.
16.2	Utility outage notifications pushed to smart phones and computers should not identify personal information on the first screen, but should be designed to offer the consumer an option to receive that additional information.
16.3	Security practices around authorized access need to be in place to ensure that each consumer is only able to access their account information via web portals for computer or smart phone displays. All privacy practices that utilities apply for standard computer-based viewing would apply to the management of the data displayed for consumers.
16.4	Because the evolution of energy consumption/provision measurement devices into communication devices, special care must be exercised regarding their implementation. They open up the risk of interpretation of communications information laws to apply to energy consumption, and thus increase the risk of inadvertent disclosure through data breaches.

	AICPA Principle	**Applies: X**	**Notes**
16.5	**Management Principle**	X	Policies and supporting procedures need to be established and consistently followed based upon the specific data items involved, as implemented by the utility. A position should exist with assigned accountability for ensuring such policies and procedures exist, are effectively communicated to all personnel, and are followed.

16.6	Notice Principle	X	Notice needs to be given depending upon whether personal data, or data that can reveal personal activities, locations, etc., are involved.
16.7	Choice and Consent Principle	X	Customers need to be given notice for the data involved, why it is necessary and then, as feasible, be given a choice for which data items to provide consent for use.
16.8	Collection Principle	X	Only the data necessary for the associated purpose should be collected.
16.9	Use and Retention Principle	X	How is data that is personal data, or that can reveal personal activities, or other associated personal data such as appliances, used? The uses should only be for the purposes for which it was collected, and then retained for only the amount of time necessary to fulfill the business reasons for the collection.
16.10	Access Principle	X	Applicability of (and compliance with) the Access principle must be established in the service offering. Procedures should be established to provide customers access to their associated data. Access to others should be given only to those with a specific job responsibility requiring such access.
16.11	Disclosure to Third Parties Principle	X	This principle should be applied in scenarios where a Third Party or Contracted Agent is involved in support or troubleshooting. Controls need to be applied, using contractual requirements, where appropriate, as well as data protection best practices for data sharing (see Appendix D: Recommended Privacy Practices for Customer/Consumer Smart Grid Energy Usage Data Obtained Directly by Third Parties).
16.12	Security for Privacy Principle	X	The price paid for electric service may be considered as information impacting personal privacy. Internet access to prices for specific consumers need to be secured appropriately. All personal data collected and created during these activities must be appropriately safeguarded to ensure unauthorized access to the data does not occur, to preserve integrity of the data, and to allow for appropriate availability.
16.13	Quality Principle	X	Procedures and technical controls should be implemented to ensure data stays as accurate as necessary to support the business purposes for which it was collected.
16.14	Monitoring and Enforcement Principle	X	Utilities should establish policies, procedures, and possibly even a dedicated position, to ensure requirements are monitored and compliance enforced.

Category: Customer Interfaces	Privacy Use Case #17

Scenario: Utility Notifies Customers of Outage

Category Description

Customers want to understand how their energy consumption habits affect their monthly energy bills and to find ways to reduce their monthly energy costs. Customers should have the ability to receive information on their usage and the price of energy on a variety of devices (in-home displays, computers, and mobile devices). In addition to real-time and historical energy data, customers should be able to receive messages from the utility notifying them about outages.

Scenario Description

When an outage occurs the utility can notify affected customers and provide estimated restoration times and report when power has been restored. Smart grid technologies can improve the utility's accuracy for determination of affected area and restoration progress.

Smart Grid Characteristics	Cybersecurity Objectives/Requirements	Potential Stakeholder Issues
• Enables active participation by consumers • Accommodates all generation and storage options • Enables new products, services and markets	• To validate that the notification is legitimate • Customer's information is kept private	• Customer device standards • Customer data privacy and security

17.1	**Data Privacy Recommendations** Utilities would need personal data such as phone number or email address to provide notification, and would need to retain this information for access by outage management systems for automated or manually updated notification. The security safeguard principle has specific application here.
17.2	The purpose specification principle applies - utilities should provide notification of why this data is needed and how this data is managed.
17.3	The data quality principle applies - customers need the ability to review and update this contact information as channel contact preferences may change over time.
17.4	If outage management notification is provided to a contracted Third Party, all utility policies regarding privacy of information apply.
17.5	If outage management notification is provided to a non-contracted Third Party, utilities may wish to provide information to consumers to build awareness about risks to any personally identifiable information delivered by this notification.

	AICPA Principle	**Applies: X**	**Notes**
17.6	**Management Principle**	X	Policies and procedures for providing customer access to update their information, answering their questions, etc. need to exist and periodically be reviewed and updated as necessary to ensure customers' privacy is addressed. A position should exist with assigned accountability for ensuring such policies and procedures exist, are effectively communicated to all personnel, and are followed.
17.7	**Notice Principle**	X	Must be provided to identify outage management contact purpose. Also to communicate how the data

				will be used. Customers should be given notice for the types of data collected, how it will be used, shared and retained.
17.8	**Choice and Consent Principle**	X		Choice for how to notify. Also to provide consent for the method used to notify, if there are limits on the communication methods.
17.9	**Collection Principle**	X		Collect only the information necessary to allow for these communications.
17.10	**Use and Retention Principle**	X		Retain the communications
17.11	**Access Principle**	X		Customers must have ability to access and update contact data. Access to personal data should be limited to only those with a specific job responsibility requiring such access.
17.12	**Disclosure to Third Parties Principle**	X		May be shared with Third Parties if these are used for outage notification. Customers should be given notice in this case.
17.13	**Security for Privacy Principle**	X		Associated data needs to have appropriate safeguards to ensure minimum access based upon job responsibilities. All personal data collected and created during these activities must be appropriately safeguarded to ensure unauthorized access to the data does not occur, to preserve integrity of the data, and to allow for appropriate availability.
17.14	**Quality Principle**	X		Important to have accurate data, which should be accomplished by providing the customer with access and establishing appropriate procedures and associated technical controls.
17.15	**Monitoring and Enforcement Principle**	X		Important to have accurate data, which should be accomplished by providing the customer with access and establishing appropriate procedures and associated technical controls.

Category: Customer Interfaces	Privacy Use Case #18

Scenario: Customer Access to Energy-Related Information

Category Description

Customers with home area networks (HANs) and/or building energy management (BEM) systems will be able to interact with the electric utilities as well as Third Party energy services providers to access information on their own energy profiles, usage, pricing, etc.

Scenario Description

Customers with HANs and/or BEM systems will be able to interact with the electric utilities as well as Third Party energy services providers. Some of these interactions include:

Access to real-time (or near-real-time) energy and demand usage and billing information

Requesting energy services such as move-in/move-out requests, prepaying for electricity, changing energy plans (if such tariffs become available), etc.

Access to energy pricing information

Access to their own DER generation/storage status

Access to their own PEV charging/discharging status

Establishing thermostat settings for demand response pricing levels

Although different types of energy related information access is involved, the security requirements are similar.

Smart Grid Characteristics	Cybersecurity Objectives/Requirements	Potential Stakeholder Issues
• Enables active participation by consumers • Accommodates all generation and storage options • Enables new products, services and markets	• Integrity, including non-repudiation, is critical since energy and pricing data will have financial impacts • Availability is important to the individual customer, but will not have wide-spread impacts • Confidentiality is critical because of customer privacy issues	• Customer data privacy and security • Retail Electric Supplier access • Customer data access

18.1	**Data Privacy Recommendations** Provide secure access according to utility cybersecurity policies to real-time or near real-time energy, demand usage, billing information, pricing information, and utility-supplied applications that control in-home appliances for demand response (DR) purposes.
18.2	Customers may authorize Third Party access to energy use data, and utilities will have to accommodate multiple Third Parties that may be competitors and ensure that practices similar to telecom "slamming" and "cramming" are prevented through strong authorization procedures, particularly based on choice and consent principles.
18.3	For Third Parties, limit the access to only the data needed to accomplish their activities as authorized by utility or customer.
18.4	Protect all pricing information and contact information through use of the principles. To the extent that pricing information is considered personal energy information, it may include payment information for electricity purchased from DER assets owned by customers.
18.5	All recommendations for pre-paid metering (Use case 2) apply to address that energy services scenario above.
18.6	Public EV charging stations have unique challenges in securing any personal data for purposes of payment transactions. If supplied by a utility or the utility has a Third Party contractual relationship with a charging station vendor, ensure that all personal data is handled according to the principles, particularly use and retention and security.

	AICPA Principle	Applies: X	Notes
18.7	**Management Principle**	X	Policies and procedures should exist for the data collected, used, shared and stored. A position should exist with assigned accountability for ensuring such policies and procedures exist, are effectively communicated to all personnel, and are followed.
18.8	**Notice Principle**	X	Customers should be given notice for the types of data collected, how it will be used, shared and retained.
18.9	**Choice and Consent Principle**	X	Initial or HAN-related set up of a customer account should include utility statements about any personal data that may be available to utilities or their authorized agents. Account setup or modification should secure customer acceptance of this use of personal data. If Third Party providers may also handle personal data, utilities may wish to consider inclusion of a statement that defines boundaries of utility responsibilities for protecting the privacy of their customers' personal data.
18.10	**Collection Principle**	X	Limit personal data collection to only what is necessary to support these activities.
18.11	**Use and Retention Principle**	X	Retain only as long as the customer is in the program.
18.12	**Access Principle**	X	Access to personal data should be limited to only those with a specific job responsibility requiring such access.
18.13	**Disclosure to Third Parties Principle**	X	Policies must accommodate multiple Third Parties that may be authorized to access customer data at customer's request.
18.14	**Security for Privacy Principle**	X	Strong safeguards for the data need to be in place. All personal data collected and created during these activities must be appropriately safeguarded to ensure unauthorized access to the data does not occur, to preserve integrity of the data, and to allow for appropriate availability.
18.15	**Quality Principle**	X	Ensure that collected personal data is accurate data, which may be accomplished by providing the customer with access and establishing appropriate procedures to correct any incorrect data.
18.16	**Monitoring and Enforcement Principle**	X	Develop and maintain audit policies to ensure that procedures are consistently applied with regards to customer data

Category: Electricity Market	Privacy Use Case #19

Scenario: Bulk Power Electricity Market

Category Description

The electricity market varies significantly from state to state, region to region, and at local levels. The market is still evolving after some initial setbacks and is expected to expand from bulk power to retail power and eventually to individual customer power as tariffs are developed to provide incentives. Demand response, previously addressed, is a part of the electricity market.

Scenario Description

The bulk power market varies from region to region, and is conducted primarily through RTOs and ISOs. The market is handled independently from actual operations, although the bids into the market obviously affect which generators are used for what time periods and which functions (base load, regulation, reserve, etc.). Therefore there are no direct operational security impacts, but there are definitely financial security impacts.

Smart Grid Characteristics	Cybersecurity Objectives/Requirements	Potential Stakeholder Issues
• Enables active participation by consumers • Accommodates all generation and storage options • Enables new products, services and markets	• Integrity for pricing and generation information is critical • Availability for pricing and generation information is important within minutes to hours • Confidentiality for pricing and generation information is critical	• Customer data privacy and security • Retail Electric Supplier access • Customer data access

19.1	**Data Privacy Recommendations** Certain pieces of information must become public information to meet federal regulatory requirements. However, if there is any personal information involved in a transaction that is not required to be disclosed, it should be managed appropriately to preserve privacy.

	AICPA Principle	**Applies: X**	**Notes**
19.2	**Management Principle**	X	Entities may include ISO/RTOs or other market clearinghouse agencies. These entities should have someone with assigned responsibility for preserving the privacy of any personal information involved in the transaction that is not required to be disclosed for regulatory purposes.
19.3	**Notice Principle**	X	If there is any personal information involved in a transaction, the customer must be given notice about it. Customers should be given notice for the types of data collected, how it will be used, shared and retained.
19.4	**Choice and Consent Principle**	X	Set up of a customer account as a participant in the bulk electricity market should include utility statements about any personal data that may be available to other organizations or entities. Account setup should secure customer acceptance of this use of personal data.
19.5	**Collection Principle**	X	Limit personal data collection to only what is necessary to support bulk power market activities.

19.6	Use and Retention Principle	X	Data on bids may need to be retained for market review.
19.7	Access Principle	X	Access to personal data should be limited to only those with a specific job responsibility requiring such access.
19.8	Disclosure to Third Parties Principle	X	Need policies to manage multiple Third Parties that may be authorized to request information about bidders or bids.
19.9	Security for Privacy Principle	X	May have heightened importance in competitive generation scenarios. All personal data collected and created during these activities must be appropriately safeguarded to ensure unauthorized access to the data does not occur, to preserve integrity of the data, and to allow for appropriate availability.
19.10	Quality Principle	X	Accurate information may be required by regulatory agencies and tax agencies. Ensure that collected personal data is accurate data, which may be accomplished by providing the customer with access and establishing appropriate procedures to correct any incorrect data
19.11	Monitoring and Enforcement Principle	X	Develop and maintain audit policies to ensure that procedures are consistently applied with regards to personal data.

Category: Electricity Market	Privacy Use Case #20

Scenario: Retail Power Electricity Market

Category Description
The electricity market varies significantly from state to state, region to region, and at local levels. The market is still evolving after some initial setbacks and is expected to expand from bulk power to retail power and eventually to individual customer power as tariffs are developed to provide incentives. Demand response, previously addressed, is a part of the electricity market.

Scenario Description
The retail power electricity market is still minor, but growing, compared to the bulk power market but typically involves aggregators and energy service providers bidding customer-owned generation or load control into both energy and ancillary services. Again it is handled independently from actual power system operations. Therefore there are no direct operational security impacts, but there are definitely financial security impacts. (The aggregator's management of the customer-owned generation and load is addressed in the Demand Response scenarios.)

Smart Grid Characteristics	Cybersecurity Objectives/Requirements	Potential Stakeholder Issues
• Enables active participation by consumers • Accommodates all generation and storage options • Enables new products, services and markets	• Integrity for pricing and generation information is critical • Availability for pricing and generation information is important within minutes to hours • Confidentiality for pricing and generation information is critical	• Customer data privacy and security • Retail Electric Supplier access • Customer data access

20.1	**Data Privacy Recommendations** All pricing information must be managed to remain private unless required for disclosure by some governmental or regulatory request, or as consented to or requested by the customer. If there is any personal information involved in a transaction that is not required to be disclosed, it should be managed appropriately to preserve privacy. Utilities may be required by tariffs to allow greater participation by retail customers into the retail energy market. Those tariffs may have requirements for disclosure of information about market participants that could include personal information. Utilities' privacy notice policies should be reviewed to ensure that customers are informed that personal data may be publicly disclosed as required by state or local tariffs.

	AICPA Principle	Applies: X	**Notes**
20.2	**Management Principle**	X	Entities may include ISO/RTOs or other market clearinghouse agencies. These entities should have someone with assigned responsibility for preserving the privacy of any personal information involved in the transaction that is not required to be disclosed for regulatory purposes.
20.3	**Notice Principle**	X	If there is any personal information involved in a transaction, the customer must be given notice about it. Customers should be given notice for the types of data collected, how it will be used, shared and retained.

20.4	**Choice and Consent Principle**	X	Set up of a customer account as a participant in the bulk electricity market should include utility statements about any personal data that may be available to other organizations or entities. Account setup should secure customer acceptance of this use of personal data.
20.5	**Collection Principle**	X	Limit personal data collection to only what is necessary to support bulk power market activities.
20.6	**Use and Retention Principle**	X	Data on bids may need to be retained for market review.
20.7	**Access Principle**	X	Access to personal data should be limited to only those with a specific job responsibility requiring such access.
20.8	**Disclosure to Third Parties Principle**	X	Need policies to manage multiple Third Parties that may be authorized to request information about bidders or bids.
20.9	**Security for Privacy Principle**	X	May have heightened importance in competitive generation scenarios. All personal data collected and created during these activities should be appropriately safeguarded to ensure unauthorized access to or use of the data does not occur, to preserve integrity of the data, and to allow for appropriate availability.
20.10	**Quality Principle**	X	Accurate information may be required by regulatory agencies and tax agencies. Ensure that collected personal data is accurate data, which may be accomplished by procedural or technical methods.
20.11	**Monitoring and Enforcement Principle**	X	Develop and maintain audit policies to ensure that procedures are consistently applied with regards to personal data.

Category: Electricity Market	Privacy Use Case #21
Scenario: Carbon Trading Market	

Category Description

The electricity market varies significantly from state to state, region to region, and at local levels. The market is still evolving after some initial setbacks and is expected to expand from bulk power to retail power and eventually to individual customer power as tariffs are developed to provide incentives. Demand response, previously addressed, is a part of the electricity market.

Scenario Description

The carbon trading market does not exist yet, but the security requirements will probably be similar to the retail electricity market.

Smart Grid Characteristics	Cybersecurity Objectives/Requirements	Potential Stakeholder Issues
• Enables active participation by consumers • Accommodates all generation and storage options • Enables new products, services and markets	• Integrity for pricing and generation information is critical • Availability for pricing and generation information is important within minutes to hours • Confidentiality for pricing and generation information is critical	• Customer data privacy and security • Retail Electric Supplier access • Customer data access

21.1	**Data Privacy Recommendations** The carbon trading market is extremely nascent. We considered the bulk electricity market to be a use case that has some similarities and modeled our recommendations based on that. All personal information must be managed to remain private, however, personal data may become public information to meet regulatory requirements of federal or state agencies involved in carbon markets. However, if there is any personal data involved in a transaction that is not required to be disclosed, it should be managed appropriately to preserve privacy.

	AICPA Principle	**Applies: X**	**Notes**
21.2	**Management Principle**	X	Entities may include ISO/RTOs or other market clearinghouse agencies. These entities should have someone with assigned responsibility for preserving the privacy of any personal information involved in the transaction that is not required to be disclosed for regulatory purposes.
21.3	**Notice Principle**	X	If there is any personal information involved in a transaction, the customer must be given notice about it.
21.4	**Choice and Consent Principle**	X	Set up of a customer account as a participant in the bulk electricity market should include utility statements about any personal data that may be available to other organizations or entities. Account setup should secure customer acceptance of this use of personal data.
21.5	**Collection Principle**	X	Limit personal data collection to only what is necessary to support bulk power market activities.

21.6	**Use and Retention Principle**	X	Data on bids may need to be retained for market review.
21.7	**Access Principle**	X	Access to personal data should be limited to only those with a specific job responsibility requiring such access.
21.8	**Disclosure to Third Parties Principle**	X	Need policies to manage multiple Third Parties that may be authorized to request information about bidders or bids.
21.9	**Security for Privacy Principle**	X	May have heightened importance in competitive generation scenarios.
21.10	**Quality Principle**	X	Accurate information may be required by regulatory agencies and tax agencies.
21.11	**Monitoring and Enforcement Principle**	X	Develop and maintain audit policies to ensure that procedures are consistently applied with regards to personal data.

Category: Distribution Automation (DA)	Privacy Use Case #22

Scenario: DA within Substations

Category Description

A broad definition of "distribution automation" includes any automation that is used in the planning, engineering, construction, operation, and maintenance of the distribution power system, including interactions with the transmission system, interconnected distributed energy resources, and automated interfaces with end-users.

No one approach is optimal for a utility or its customers. Certain DA functions, such as optimal volt/VAR control, can be more beneficial to one utility or even a few feeders in one utility, while other DA functions, such as fault detection, isolation, and service restoration, could be far more beneficial in other utilities.

Increasingly, distribution automation will entail closed-loop control, where distribution algorithms, applied to real-time models of the distribution system, will increase reliability and/or efficiency of the distribution system without direct operator involvement.

Scenario Description

Distribution automation within substations involves monitoring and controlling equipment in distribution substations to enhance power system reliability and efficiency. Different types of equipment are monitored and controlled:

Distribution supervisory control and data acquisition (SCADA) system monitors distribution equipment in substations

Supervisory control on substation distribution equipment

Substation protection equipment performs system protection actions

Reclosers in substations

Smart Grid Characteristics	Cybersecurity Objectives/Requirements	Potential Stakeholder Issues
• Provides power quality for the range of needs in a digital economy • Optimizes asset utilization and operating efficiency • Anticipates and responds to system disturbances in a self-correcting manner	• Integrity of distribution control commands is critical for distribution operations, avoiding outages, and providing power to customers reliably and efficiently • Availability for control is critical, while monitoring individual equipment is less critical • Confidentiality is not very important	• Customer safety • Device standards • Cybersecurity

Data Privacy Recommendations

No personal data, or information that could point to an individual or specific account, is involved within this use case.

Category: Distribution Automation	Privacy Use Case #23
Scenario: DA Using Local Automation	

Category Description

A broad definition of "distribution automation" includes any automation that is used in the planning, engineering, construction, operation, and maintenance of the distribution power system, including interactions with the transmission system, interconnected distributed energy resources, and automated interfaces with end-users.

No one approach is optimal for a utility or its customers. Certain distribution automation functions, such as optimal volt/VAR control, can be more beneficial to one utility or even a few feeders in one utility, while other distribution automation functions, such as fault detection, isolation, and service restoration, could be far more beneficial in other utilities.

Increasingly, distribution automation will entail closed-loop control, where distribution algorithms, applied to real-time models of the distribution system, will increase reliability and/or efficiency of the distribution system without direct operator involvement.

Scenario Description

Local automation of feeder equipment consists of power equipment that is managed locally by computer-based controllers that are preset with various parameters to issue control actions. These controllers may just monitor power system measurements locally, or may include some short range communications to other controllers and/or local field crews. However, in these scenarios, no communications exist between the feeder equipment and the control center.

Local automated switch management

Local volt/VAR control

Local Field crew communications to underground network equipment

Smart Grid Characteristics	Cybersecurity Objectives/Requirements	Potential Stakeholder Issues
• Provides power quality • Optimizes asset utilization • Anticipates and responds to system disturbances	• Integrity of distribution control commands is critical for distribution operations, avoiding outages, and providing power to customers reliably and efficiently • Availability for control is critical, while monitoring individual equipment is less critical • Confidentiality is not very important	• Customer safety • Customer device standards • Demand response acceptance by customers

Data Privacy Recommendations

No personal data, or information that could point to an individual or specific account, is involved within this use case.

Category: Distribution Automation	Privacy Use Case #24

Scenario: DA Monitoring and Controlling Feeder Equipment

Category Description

A broad definition of "distribution automation" includes any automation that is used in the planning, engineering, construction, operation, and maintenance of the distribution power system, including interactions with the transmission system, interconnected distributed energy resources, and automated interfaces with end-users.

No one approach is optimal for a utility or its customers. Certain distribution automation functions, such as optimal volt/VAR control, can be more beneficial to one utility or even a few feeders in one utility, while other distribution automation functions, such as fault detection, isolation, and service restoration, could be far more beneficial in other utilities.

Increasingly, distribution automation will entail closed-loop control, where distribution algorithms, applied to real-time models of the distribution system, will increase reliability and/or efficiency of the distribution system without direct operator involvement.

Scenario Description

Operators and distribution applications can monitor the equipment on the feeders and determine whether any actions should be taken to increase reliability, improve efficiency, or respond to emergencies. For instance, they can—

Remotely open or close automated switches

Remotely switch capacitor banks in and out

Remotely raise or lower voltage regulators

Block local automated actions

Send updated parameters to feeder equipment

Interact with equipment in underground distribution vaults

Retrieve power system information from smart meters

Automate emergency response

Provide dynamic rating of feeders

Smart Grid Characteristics	Cybersecurity Objectives/Requirements	Potential Stakeholder Issues
• Provides power quality • Optimizes asset utilization • Anticipates and responds to system disturbances	• Integrity of distribution control commands is critical for distribution operations, avoiding outages, and providing power to customers reliably and efficiently • Availability for control is critical, while monitoring individual equipment is less critical • Confidentiality is not very important	• Customer safety • Customer device standards • Demand response acceptance by customers

Data Privacy Recommendations
No personal data, or information that could point to an individual or specific account, is involved within this use case.

Category: Distribution Automation	Privacy Use Case #25

Scenario: Fault Detection, Isolation, and Restoration

Category Description

A broad definition of "distribution automation" includes any automation that is used in the planning, engineering, construction, operation, and maintenance of the distribution power system, including interactions with the transmission system, interconnected distributed energy resources, and automated interfaces with end-users.

No one approach is optimal for a utility or its customers. Certain distribution automation functions, such as optimal volt/VAR control, can be more beneficial to one utility or even a few feeders in one utility, while other distribution automation functions, such as fault detection, isolation, and service restoration, could be far more beneficial in other utilities.

Increasingly, distribution automation will entail closed-loop control, where distribution algorithms, applied to real-time models of the distribution system, will increase reliability and/or efficiency of the distribution system without direct operator involvement.

Scenario Description

AMI smart meters and distribution automated devices can detect power outages that affect individual customers and larger groups of customers. As customers rely more fundamentally on power (e.g., PEV) and become used to not having to call in outages, outage detection, and restoration will become increasingly critical.

The automated fault location, isolation, and restoration (FLIR) function uses the combination of the power system model with the SCADA data from the field on real-time conditions to determine where a fault is probably located by undertaking the following steps:

Determines the faults cleared by controllable protective devices:

Determines the faulted sections based on SCADA fault indications and protection lockout signals

Estimates the probable fault locations based on SCADA fault current measurements and real-time fault analysis

Determines the fault-clearing non-monitored protective device

Uses closed-loop or advisory methods to isolate the faulted segment

Once the fault is isolated, it determines how best to restore service to unfaulted segments through feeder reconfiguration.

Smart Grid Characteristics	Cybersecurity Objectives/Requirements	Potential Stakeholder Issues
• Provides power quality • Optimizes asset utilization • Anticipates and responds to system disturbances	• Integrity of outage information is critical • Availability to detect large-scale outages usually involve multiple sources of information • Confidentiality is not very important	• Customer safety • Customer device standards • Demand response acceptance by customers

Data Privacy Recommendations
No personal data, or information that could point to an individual or specific account, is involved within this use case.

Category: Distribution Automation	Privacy Use Case #26
Scenario: Load Management	

Category Description

A broad definition of "distribution automation" includes any automation that is used in the planning, engineering, construction, operation, and maintenance of the distribution power system, including interactions with the transmission system, interconnected distributed energy resources, and automated interfaces with end-users.

No one approach is optimal for a utility or its customers. Certain distribution automation functions, such as optimal volt/VAR control, can be more beneficial to one utility or even a few feeders in one utility, while other distribution automation functions, such as fault detection, isolation, and service restoration, could be far more beneficial in other utilities.

Increasingly, distribution automation will entail closed-loop control, where distribution algorithms, applied to real-time models of the distribution system, will increase reliability and/or efficiency of the distribution system without direct operator involvement.

Scenario Description

Load management provides active and passive control by the utility of customer appliances (e.g. cycling of air conditioner, water heaters, and pool pumps) and certain C&I customer systems (e.g., plenum precooling, heat storage management).

Direct load control and load shedding

Demand side management

Load shift scheduling

Curtailment planning

Selective load management through HANs

Smart Grid Characteristics	Cybersecurity Objectives/Requirements	Potential Stakeholder Issues
• Provides power quality • Optimizes asset utilization • Anticipates and responds to system disturbances	• Integrity of load control commands is critical to avoid unwarranted outages • Availability for load control is important – in aggregate (e.g. > 300 MW), it can be critical • Confidentiality is not very important	• Customer safety • Customer device standards • Demand response acceptance by customers

Data Privacy Recommendations

No personal data, or information that could point to an individual or specific account, is involved within this use case.

Category: Distribution Automation	Privacy Use Case #27

Scenario: Distribution Analysis using Distribution Power Flow Models

Category Description

A broad definition of "distribution automation" includes any automation which is used in the planning, engineering, construction, operation, and maintenance of the distribution power system, including interactions with the transmission system, interconnected distributed energy resources, and automated interfaces with end-users.

No one approach is optimal for a utility or its customers. Certain distribution automation functions, such as optimal volt/VAR control, can be more beneficial to one utility or even a few feeders in one utility, while other distribution automation functions, such as fault detection, isolation, and service restoration, could be far more beneficial in other utilities.

Increasingly, distribution automation will entail closed-loop control, where distribution algorithms, applied to real-time models of the distribution system, will increase reliability and/or efficiency of the distribution system without direct operator involvement.

Scenario Description

The brains behind the monitoring and controlling of field devices are the DA analysis software applications. These applications generally use models of the power system to validate the raw data, assess real-time and future conditions, and issue the appropriate actions. The applications may be distributed and located in the field equipment for local assessments and control, and/or may be centralized in a distribution management system (DMS) for global assessment and control.

Local peer-to-peer interactions between equipment

Normal distribution operations using the Distribution System Power Flow (DSPF) model

Emergency distribution operations using the DSPF model

Study-Mode DSPF model

DSPF/DER model of distribution operations with significant DER generation/storage

Smart Grid Characteristics	Cybersecurity Objectives/Requirements	Potential Stakeholder Issues
• Provides power quality • Optimizes asset utilization • Anticipates and responds to system disturbances	• Integrity is critical to operate the distribution power system reliably, efficiently, and safely • Availability is critical to operate the distribution power system reliably, efficiently, and safely • Confidentiality is not important	• Customer safety • Customer device standards • Demand response acceptance by customers

Data Privacy Recommendations
No personal data, or information that could point to an individual or specific account, is involved within this use case.

137

Category: Distribution Automation	Privacy Use Case #28

Scenario: Distributed Energy Resources Management

Category Description

A broad definition of "distribution automation" includes any automation which is used in the planning, engineering, construction, operation, and maintenance of the distribution power system, including interactions with the transmission system, interconnected DER, and automated interfaces with end-users.

No one approach is optimal for a utility or its customers. Certain distribution automation functions, such as optimal volt/VAR control, can be more beneficial to one utility or even a few feeders in one utility, while other distribution automation functions, such as fault detection, isolation, and service restoration, could be far more beneficial in other utilities.

Increasingly, distribution automation will entail closed-loop control, where distribution algorithms, applied to real-time models of the distribution system, will increase reliability and/or efficiency of the distribution system without direct operator involvement.

Scenario Description

In the future, more and more of generation and storage resources will be connected to the distribution network and will significantly increase the complexity and sensitivity of distribution operations. Therefore, the management of DER generation will become increasingly important in the overall management of the distribution system, including load forecasts, real-time monitoring, feeder reconfiguration, virtual and logical microgrids, and distribution planning.

Direct monitoring and control of DER

Shut-down or islanding verification for DER

PEV management as load, storage, and generation resource

Electric storage fill/draw management

Renewable energy DER with variable generation

Small fossil resource management, such as backup generators to be used for peak shifting

Smart Grid Characteristics	Cybersecurity Objectives/Requirements	Potential Stakeholder Issues
• Provides power quality • Optimizes asset utilization • Anticipates and responds to system disturbances	• Integrity is critical for any management/ control of generation and storage • Availability requirements may vary depending on the size (individual or aggregate) of the DER plant • Confidentiality may involve some privacy issues with customer-owned DER	• Customer safety • Customer device standards • Demand response acceptance by customers

Data Privacy Recommendations

No personal data, or information that could point to an individual or specific account, is involved within this use case.

Category: Distribution Automation	Privacy Use Case #29

Scenario: Distributed Energy Resource Management

Category Description

A broad definition of "distribution automation" includes any automation which is used in the planning, engineering, construction, operation, and maintenance of the distribution power system, including interactions with the transmission system, interconnected distributed energy resources, and automated interfaces with end-users.

No one approach is optimal for a utility or its customers. Certain distribution automation functions, such as optimal volt/VAR control, can be more beneficial to one utility or even a few feeders in one utility, while other distribution automation functions, such as fault detection, isolation, and service restoration, could be far more beneficial in other utilities.

Increasingly, distribution automation will entail closed-loop control, where distribution algorithms, applied to real-time models of the distribution system, will increase reliability and/or efficiency of the distribution system without direct operator involvement.

Scenario Description

Distribution planning typically uses engineering systems with access only to processed power system data that is available from the control center. It is therefore relatively self-contained.

Operational planning

Assessing planned outages

Storm condition planning

Short-term distribution planning

Short term load forecast

Short term DER generation and storage impact studies

Long term distribution planning

Long term load forecasts by area

Optimal placements of switches, capacitors, regulators, and DER

Distribution system upgrades and extensions

Distribution financial planners

Smart Grid Characteristics	Cybersecurity Objectives/Requirements	Potential Stakeholder Issues
• Provides power quality • Optimizes asset utilization • Anticipates and responds to system disturbances	• Integrity not critical due to multiple sources of data • Availability is not important • Confidentiality is not important	• Cybersecurity

Data Privacy Recommendations

No personal data, or information that could point to an individual or specific account, is involved within this use case.

Category: Plug In Hybrid Electric Vehicles (PHEV)	Privacy Use Case #30

Scenario: Customer Connects PHEV to Energy Portal

Category Description

Plug in electric vehicles will have a significant impact on the future electric system and challenge the utility and customer to manage vehicle connection and charging. As adoption rates of electric vehicles increase, the utility will have to handle the new load imposed on the electrical system. Scenarios will consider customer payment issues regarding mobility, load shifting vehicle charging, and the use of electric vehicles as a distributed resource.

Scenario Description

This scenario discusses the simple case of a customer plugging in an electric vehicle at their premise to charge its battery. Variations of this scenario will be considered that add complexity: a customer charging their vehicle at another location and providing payment or charging at another location where the premise owner pays.

Smart Grid Characteristics	**Cybersecurity Objectives/Requirements**	**Potential Stakeholder Issues**
• Enables active participation by consumers • Accommodates all generation and storage options • Enables new products, services and markets • Provides power quality for the digital economy • Optimizes asset utilization and operate efficiently	• The customer's information is kept private • Billing information is accurate	• Vehicle standards • Customer safety • Customer device standards • Demand response acceptance by customers

30.1	**Data Privacy Recommendations** Provide secure access to customer billing and related account information during payments at public location.
30.2	Allow only those authorized individuals, with a business need, access to the information within customer accounts related to PHEV charging and discharging information.
30.3	Utility policy for tracking EV charges should determine if date/time/location/duration of charging will be presented as part of bill. This may be particularly relevant to "roaming" charges. Many consumers may appreciate this detail, similar to a credit card monthly statement showing date/ time/location of fueling stops for gas-fueled vehicles. All this data, whether displayed in a bill presentment (printed or online) or not must be protected.
30.4	Fees for charging and payments for discharging are financially sensitive data and should be protected by utility policies already established for this type of information.

	AICPA Principle	**Applies: X**	**Notes**
30.5	**Management Principle**	X	Policies and procedures should exist for the data collected, used, shared and stored. A position should exist with assigned accountability for ensuring such policies and procedures exist, are effectively communicated to all personnel, and are followed.

140

30.6	Notice Principle	X	Policies and procedures to give notice whenever a Third Party requests, or obtain access to, PHEV charging information. This may arise in the case of EV fleet vehicles, which may be assigned to employees who are responsible for charging, but the EV is actually owned by the employer.
30.7	Choice and Consent Principle	X	Policies and procedures to obtain consent from customer to give Third Parties access to PHEV data. As noted above, EV driver (customer) and EV owner may be different in select situations. Review utility policies regarding landlords (owners) and tenants (customers) to structure consistent application of practices for what is essentially a rolling, not stationary, specialized charging and discharging asset.
30.8	Collection Principle	X	Limit personal data collection to only what is necessary to support business activities.
30.9	Use and Retention Principle	X	Policies and procedures to retain customer identifiable data only while the customer is participating in the program.
30.10	Access Principle	X	Access to personal data should be limited to only those with a specific job responsibility requiring such access.
30.11	Disclosure to Third Parties Principle	X	Policies and procedures for disclosing PHEV charging information access to Third Parties. See discussion about EV drivers as customers and EV owners as Third Parties.
30.12	Security for Privacy Principle	X	All personal data collected and created during these activities must be appropriately safeguarded to ensure unauthorized access to the data does not occur, to preserve integrity of the data, and to allow for appropriate availability.
30.13	Quality Principle	X	Ensure that collected personal data is accurate data, which may be accomplished by providing the customer with access and establishing appropriate procedures to correct any incorrect data.
30.14	Monitoring and Enforcement Principle	X	Develop and maintain audit and sanction policies to ensure that procedures are consistently applied with regards to personal data.

Category: Plug In Hybrid Electric Vehicles	Privacy Use Case #31

Scenario: Customer Connects PHEV to Energy Portal and Participates in "Smart" (Optimized) Charging

Category Description

Plug in electric vehicles will have a significant impact on the future electric system and challenge the utility and customer to manage vehicle connection and charging. As adoption rates of electric vehicles increase, the utility will have to handle the new load imposed on the electrical system. Scenarios will consider customer payment issues regarding mobility, load shifting vehicle charging, and the use of electric vehicles as a distributed resource.

Scenario Description

In addition to simply plugging in an electric vehicle for charging, in this scenario the electric vehicle charging is optimized to take advantage of lower rates or help prevent excessive load peaks on the electrical system.

Smart Grid Characteristics	Objectives/Requirements	Potential Stakeholder Issues
• Enables active participation by consumers • Accommodates all generation and storage options • Enables new products, services and markets • Provides power quality for the digital economy • Optimizes asset utilization and operate efficiently	• Customer information is kept private	• Vehicle standards • Customer safety • Customer device standards • Demand response acceptance by customers

31.1	**Data Privacy Recommendations**
	Safeguard customer information related to the PHEVs, energy usage and billing rates.
31.2	Customers should be able to authorize Third Party access to the PHEV charging program data.

	AICPA Principle	Applies: X	Notes
31.3	**Management Principle**	X	Policies and procedures should exist for the data collected, used, shared and stored. A position should exist with assigned accountability for ensuring such policies and procedures exist, are effectively communicated to all personnel, and are followed.
31.4	**Notice Principle**	X	Policies and procedures to give notice to customers for how PHEV program data is used and shared. This may arise in the case of EV fleet vehicles, which may be assigned to employees who are responsible for charging, but the EV is actually owned by the employer.
31.5	**Choice and Consent Principle**	X	Policies and procedures to obtain consent prior to allowing access to additional Third Parties. As noted above, EV driver (customer) and EV owner

			may be different in select situations. Review utility policies regarding landlords (owners) and tenants (customers) to structure consistent application of practices for what is essentially a rolling, not stationary, specialized charging and discharging asset.
31.6	**Collection Principle**	X	Limit personal data collection to only what is necessary to support business activities.
31.7	**Use and Retention Principle**	X	Policies and procedures to retain customer identifiable data only while the customer is participating in the program.
31.8	**Access Principle**	X	Policies/procedures should be in place to allow customers access to their PHEV program account data. Access to personal data should be limited to only those with a specific job responsibility requiring such access.
31.9	**Disclosure to Third Parties Principle**	X	Policies must accommodate multiple Third Parties that may be authorized to access customer data at customer's request.
31.10	**Security for Privacy Principle**	X	All personal data collected and created during these activities must be appropriately safeguarded to ensure unauthorized access to or use of the data does not occur, to preserve integrity of the data, and to allow for appropriate availability.
31.11	**Quality Principle**	X	Ensure that collected personal data is accurate data, which may be accomplished by procedural or technical methods.
31.12	**Monitoring and Enforcement Principle**	X	Develop and maintain audit and sanctions policies to ensure that procedures are consistently applied with regards to personal data.

Category: Plug In Hybrid Electric Vehicles	Privacy Use Case #32

Scenario: PHEV or Customer Receives and Responds to Discrete Demand Response Events

Category Description

Plug in electric vehicles will have a significant impact on the future electric system and challenge the utility and customer to manage vehicle connection and charging. As adoption rates of electric vehicles increase, the utility will have to handle the new load imposed on the electrical system. Scenarios will consider customer payment issues regarding mobility, load shifting vehicle charging, and the use of electric vehicles as a distributed resource.

Scenario Description

An advanced scenario for electric vehicles is the use of the vehicle to provide energy stored in its battery back to the electrical system. Customers could participate in demand response programs where they are provided an incentive to allow the utility to request power from the vehicle at times of high system load.

Smart Grid Characteristics	Objectives/Requirements	Potential Stakeholder Issues
• Enables active participation by consumers • Accommodates all generation and storage options • Enables new products, services and markets • Provides power quality for the digital economy • Optimizes asset utilization and operate efficiently	• Improved system stability and availability • To keep customer information private • To insure DR messages are accurate and trustworthy	• Vehicle standards • Customer safety • Customer device standards • Demand response acceptance by customers

32.1	**Data Privacy Recommendations** Safeguard customer information related to the PHEVs, energy usage, distributed energy provision, and billing and discharging rates.
32.2	Customers should be able to authorize Third Party access to the PHEV charging and provisioning program data.
32.3	Consider vehicle discharging as grid stabilization activity, which presumes a financial transaction between vehicle owner and utility or an aggregator of EVs and a utility. All customer information required for these transactions must be protected.

	AICPA Principle	Applies: X	Notes
32.4	**Management Principle**	X	Policies and procedures should exist for the data collected, used, shared and stored. A position should exist with assigned accountability for ensuring such policies and procedures exist, are effectively communicated to all personnel, and are followed.
32.5	**Notice Principle**	X	Policies and procedures to give notice to customers for how PHEV program and provisioning data is used and shared.

32.6	**Choice and Consent Principle**	X	Policies and procedures to obtain consent prior to allowing access to additional Third Parties.
32.7	**Collection Principle**	X	Limit personal data collection to only what is necessary to support business activities.
32.8	**Use and Retention Principle**	X	Policies and procedures to retain customer identifiable data only while the customer is participating in the program.
32.9	**Access Principle**	X	Policies/procedures should be in place to allow customers access to their PHEV program account data. Access to personal data should be limited to only those with a specific job responsibility requiring such access.
32.10	**Disclosure to Third Parties Principle**	X	Policies must accommodate multiple Third Parties that may be authorized to access customer data at customer's request.
32.11	**Security for Privacy Principle**	X	All personal data collected and created during these activities must be appropriately safeguarded to ensure unauthorized access to or use of the data does not occur, to preserve integrity of the data, and to allow for appropriate availability.
32.12	**Quality Principle**	X	Ensure that collected personal data is accurate data, which may be accomplished by procedural or technical methods.
32.13	**Monitoring and Enforcement Principle**	X	Develop and maintain audit and sanctions policies to ensure that procedures are consistently applied with regards to personal data.

Category: Plug In Hybrid Electric Vehicles	Privacy Use Case #33

Scenario: PHEV or Customer Receives and Responds to Utility Price Signals

Category Description

Plug in electric vehicles will have a significant impact on the future electric system and challenge the utility and customer to manage vehicle connection and charging. As adoption rates of electric vehicles increase, the utility will have to handle the new load imposed on the electrical system. Scenarios will consider customer payment issues regarding mobility, load shifting vehicle charging, and the use of electric vehicles as a distributed resource.

Scenario Description

In this scenario, the electric vehicle is able to receive and act on electricity pricing data sent from the utility. The use of pricing data for charging is primarily covered in another scenario. The pricing data can also be used in support of a distributed resource program where the customer allows the vehicle to provide power to the electric grid based on market conditions.

Smart Grid Characteristics	Objectives/Requirements	Potential Stakeholder Issues
• Enables active participation by consumers • Accommodates all generation and storage options • Enables new products, services and markets • Provides power quality for the digital economy • Optimizes asset utilization and operate efficiently	• Improved system stability and availability • Pricing signals are accurate and trustworthy • Customer information is kept private	• Vehicle standards • Customer safety • Customer device standards • Demand response acceptance by customers

33.1	**Data Privacy Recommendations** Safeguard customer information related to the PHEVs, energy usage, pricing data, and billing and discharging rates.
33.2	Customers should be able to authorize Third Party access to the PHEV pricing data.
33.3	Consider vehicle discharging as grid stabilization activity, which presumes a financial transaction between vehicle owner and utility or an aggregator of EVs and a utility. All customer information required for these transactions must be protected.

	AICPA Principle	Applies: X	Notes
33.4	**Management Principle**	X	Policies and procedures should exist for the data collected, used, shared and stored. A position should exist with assigned accountability for ensuring such policies and procedures exist, are effectively communicated to all personnel, and are followed.
33.5	**Notice Principle**	X	Policies and procedures to give notice to customers for how PHEV program and pricing data is used and shared.

33.6	**Choice and Consent Principle**	X	Policies and procedures to obtain consent prior to allowing access to additional Third Parties.
33.7	**Collection Principle**	X	Limit personal data collection to only what is necessary to support business activities.
33.8	**Use and Retention Principle**	X	Policies and procedures to retain customer identifiable data and related pricing data only while the customer is participating in the program.
33.9	**Access Principle**	X	Policies/procedures should be in place to allow customers access to their PHEV pricing program account data. Access to personal data should be limited to only those with a specific job responsibility requiring such access.
33.10	**Disclosure to Third Parties Principle**	X	Policies must accommodate multiple Third Parties that may be authorized to access customer data at customer's request.
33.11	**Security for Privacy Principle**	X	All personal data collected and created during these activities must be appropriately safeguarded to ensure unauthorized access to or use of the data does not occur, to preserve integrity of the data, and to allow for appropriate availability.
33.12	**Quality Principle**	X	Ensure that collected personal data is accurate data, which may be accomplished by procedural or technical methods.
33.13	**Monitoring and Enforcement Principle**	X	Develop and maintain audit and sanctions policies to ensure that procedures are consistently applied with regards to personal data.

Category: Distributed Resources	Privacy Use Case #34

Scenario: Customer Provides Distributed Resource

Category Description

Traditionally, distributed resources have served as a primary or emergency backup energy source for customers that place a premium on reliability and power quality. Distributed resources include generation and storage devices that can provide power back to the electric power system. Societal, policy, and technological changes are increasing the adoption rate of distributed resources, and smart grid technologies can enhance the value of these systems.

Scenario Description

This scenario describes the process of connecting a distributed resource to the electric power system and the requirements of net metering.

Smart Grid Characteristics	Cybersecurity Objectives/Requirements	Potential Stakeholder Issues
• Enables active participation by consumers • Accommodates all generation and storage options • Enables new products, services and markets • Provides power quality for the digital economy • Optimizes asset utilization and operate efficiently	• Customer information is kept private • Net metering is accurate and timely	• Safety • Customer data privacy and security

34.1	**Data Privacy Recommendations** This use case is similar to Use Case 9 (Net Metering of DER and PEV)
34.2	Utilities have personal consumer information such as name, phone number and address for billing. If customer has opted for any payment arrangement to sell electricity back to the utility, the utility would also have sensitive financial data and perhaps authorized access to deposit funds in cases of payments to consumers. The security safeguard principle has specific application here.
34.3	The use and retention principle applies - utilities should provide notification of why personal data is needed for billing and/or payments, and how this data is managed.
34.4	The data quality principle applies - customers need the ability to review and update this information as residences or business change hands and new occupants may want to revise a DER arrangement made on assets that are affixed to property.
34.5	While the utility is presumed to have the direct relationship with the consumer, there may be intermediated situations where an Energy Services Provider (ESP) manages the DER asset on behalf of the consumer. The utility should consider clear, simple identification of all entities or some formal statement of the data management principle to help educate consumers as to the "data chain" that may be in place based on their relationships with utility, authorized Third Parties, and/or ESPs.

	AICPA Principle	**Applies: X**	**Notes**
34.6	**Management Principle**	X	Maintain policies and supporting procedures that govern compliance with the related privacy and security policies to protect the data involved with this use case.

34.7	Notice Principle	X	Account setups for DER scenarios should include information that describes any personal data that is collected and how it is used, shared and retained.
34.8	Choice and Consent Principle	X	Account setup procedures should provide customers with the ability to consent to the described uses of their personal data.
34.9	Collection Principle	X	Only the data necessary to support DER accounts should be collected.
34.10	Use and Retention Principle	X	Particular emphasis should be placed on this in situations where a Third Party is involved so that consumer data is not misused by that Third Party.
34.11	Access Principle	X	Access to the data related to DER use should be limited to only those with a need for access to support the related business purposes.
34.12	Disclosure to Third Parties Principle	X	ESPs may have the direct relationship with DER customers and have personal data as well. Consumers should be aware if this principle and all others are equally applicable with any ESP.
34.13	Security for Privacy Principle	X	If there is equipment that is not under the utility's physical control which contains personal data, physical security will be dependent on the customer or an ESP. All personal data collected and created during these activities should be appropriately safeguarded to ensure unauthorized access to or use of the data does not occur, to preserve integrity of the data, and to allow for appropriate availability.
34.14	Quality Principle	X	As is the case for security, quality will be critical for operational purposes. Ensure that collected personal data is accurate data, which may be accomplished by procedural or technical methods.
34.15	Monitoring and Enforcement Principle	X	Access to personal data should be logged, and regularly audited, to ensure it is being used appropriately.

Category: Distributed Resources	Privacy Use Case 35

Scenario: Utility Controls Customer's Distributed Resource

Category Description
Traditionally, distributed resources have served as a primary or emergency backup energy source for customers that place a premium on reliability and power quality. Distributed resources include generation and storage devices that can provide power back to the electric power system. Societal, policy, and technological changes are increasing the adoption rate of distributed resources, and smart grid technologies can enhance the value of these systems.

Scenario Description
Distributed generation and storage can be used as a demand response resource where the utility can request or control devices to provide energy back to the electrical system. Customers enroll in utility programs that allow their distributed resource to be used for load support or to assist in maintaining power quality. The utility programs can be based on direct control signals or pricing information.

Smart Grid Characteristics	Cybersecurity Objectives/Requirements	Potential Stakeholder Issues
• Enables active participation by consumers • Accommodates all generation and storage options • Enables new products, services and markets • Provides power quality for the digital economy • Optimizes asset utilization and operate efficiently	• Commands are trustworthy and accurate • Customer's data is kept private • DR messages are received timely	• Safety • Customer data privacy and security

35.1	**Data Privacy Recommendations** This use case is similar to Use Cases 9 and 34.
35.2	Utilities have personal consumer information such as name, phone number and address for billing. If customer has opted for any payment arrangement with the utility, the utility would also have sensitive financial data and perhaps authorized access to deposit funds in cases of payments to consumers. The security safeguard principle has specific application here.
35.3	The use and retention principle applies - utilities should provide notification of why personal data is needed for billing and/or payments, and how this data is managed.
35.4	The data quality principle applies - customers need the ability to review and update this information as residences or businesses change hands and new occupants may want to revise the DER arrangement.
35.5	While the utility is presumed to have the direct relationship with the consumer, there may be intermediated situations where an Energy Services Provider (ESP) manages the DER asset on behalf of the utility (or the customer). The utility should consider clear, simple identification of all entities or some formal statement of the data management principle to help educate consumers as to the "data chain" that may be in place based on their relationships with utility, authorized Third Parties, and/or ESPs.

	AICPA Principle	Applies: X	Notes
35.6	Management Principle	X	Policies and procedures should exist for the data collected, used, shared and stored. A position should exist with assigned accountability for ensuring such policies and procedures exist, are

			effectively communicated to all personnel, and are followed.
35.7	Notice Principle	X	Customers should be given notice for the types of data collected, how it will be used, shared and retained.
35.8	Choice and Consent Principle	X	Since utilities or their agents are given control of a DER asset by the customer, choice and consent write-ups should be clearly and concisely written to identify options for opt outs and opt ins.
35.9	Collection Principle	X	Only the data necessary to support DER accounts should be collected.
35.10	Use and Retention Principle	X	Particular emphasis should be placed on this in situations where a Third Party is involved so that consumer data is not misused by that Third Party.
35.11	Access Principle	X	Access to the data related to DER use should be limited to only those with a need for access to support the related business purposes.
35.12	Disclosure to Third Parties Principle	X	Energy Service Providers (ESPs) may have the direct relationship with DER customers and have personal data as well. Consumers should be aware if this principle and all others are equally applicable with any ESP.
35.13	Security for Privacy Principle	X	As utilities will house their operations in their own or authorized Contracted Agent facilities, physical and logical security should be in place. If there is equipment that is not under the utility's physical control which contains personal data, physical security will be dependent on the customer or an ESP. All personal data collected and created during these activities should be appropriately safeguarded to ensure unauthorized access to the data does not occur, to preserve integrity of the data, and to allow for appropriate availability.
35.14	Quality Principle	X	As is the case for security, quality will be critical for operational purposes. Ensure that collected personal data is accurate data, which may be accomplished by providing the customer with access and establishing appropriate procedures to correct any incorrect data.
35.15	Monitoring and Enforcement Principle	X	Develop and maintain audit policies to ensure that procedures are consistently applied with regards to personal data.

Category: Transmission Operations	Privacy Use Case #36

Scenario: Real-Time Normal Transmission Operations Using Energy Management System (EMS) Applications and SCADA Data

Category Description

Transmission operations involve monitoring and controlling the transmission system using the SCADA system to monitor and control equipment in transmission substations. The EMS assesses the state of the transmission system using applications typically based on transmission power flow models. The SCADA/EMS is located in the utility's control center, while the key equipment is located in the transmission substations. Protective relaying equipment monitors the health of the transmission system and takes corrective action within a few milliseconds, such as tripping circuit breakers if power system anomalies are detected.

Scenario Description

Transmission normal real-time operations involve monitoring and controlling the transmission system using the SCADA and EMS. The types of information exchanged include—
Monitored equipment states (open/close), alarms (overheat, overload, battery level, capacity), and measurements (current, voltage, frequency, energy).
Operator command and control actions, such as supervisory control of switching operations, setup/options of EMS functions, and preparation for storm conditions.
Closed-loop actions, such as protective relaying tripping circuit breakers upon power system anomalies.
Automation system controls voltage, VAR, and power flow based on algorithms, real-time data, and network linked capacitive and reactive components.

Smart Grid Characteristics	Cybersecurity Objectives/Requirements	Potential Stakeholder Issues
• Provides power quality • Optimizes asset utilization • Anticipates and responds to system disturbances	• Integrity is vital to the safety and reliability of the transmission system • Availability is critical to protective relaying (e.g. < 4 ms) and operator commands (e.g., 1 s) • Confidentiality is not important	• Customer safety • Customer device standards • Demand response acceptance by customers

Data Privacy Recommendations

No personal data, or information that could point to an individual or specific account, is involved within this use case.

Category: Transmission Operations	**Privacy Use Case #37**

Scenario: EMS Network Analysis Based on Transmission Power Flow Models

Category Description

Transmission operations involve monitoring and controlling the transmission system using the SCADA system to monitor and control equipment in transmission substations. The EMS assesses the state of the transmission system using applications typically based on transmission power flow models. The SCADA/EMS is located in the utility's control center, while the key equipment is located in the transmission substations. Protective relaying equipment monitors the health of the transmission system and takes corrective action within a few milliseconds, such as tripping circuit breakers if power system anomalies are detected.

Scenario Description

EMS assesses the state of the transmission power system using the transmission power system analysis models and the SCADA data from the transmission substations
EMS performs model update, state estimation, bus load forecast
EMS performs contingency analysis, recommends preventive and corrective actions
EMS performs optimal power flow analysis, recommends optimization actions
EMS or planners perform stability study of network
Exchange power system model information with RTOs/ISOs and/or other utilities

Smart Grid Characteristics	**Cybersecurity Objectives/Requirements**	**Potential Stakeholder Issues**
• Provides power quality • Optimizes asset utilization • Anticipates and responds to system disturbances	• Integrity is vital to the reliability of the transmission system • Availability is critical to react to contingency situations via operator commands (e.g. one second) • Confidentiality is not important	• Cybersecurity

Data Privacy Recommendations

No personal data, or information that could point to an individual or specific account, is involved within this use case.

Category: Transmission Operations	**Privacy Use Case #38**

Scenario: Real-Time Emergency Transmission Operations

Category Description

Transmission operations involve monitoring and controlling the transmission system using the SCADA system to monitor and control equipment in transmission substations. The EMS assesses the state of the transmission system using applications typically based on transmission power flow models. The SCADA/EMS is located in the utility's control center, while the key equipment is located in the transmission substations. Protective relaying equipment monitors the health of the transmission system and takes corrective action within a few milliseconds, such as tripping circuit breakers if power system anomalies are detected.

Scenario Description

During emergencies, the power system takes some automated actions and the operators can also take actions:

Power System Protection: Emergency operations handles under-frequency load/generation shedding, under-voltage load shedding, load tap changer (LTC) control/blocking, shunt control, series compensation control, system separation detection, and wide area real-time instability recovery

Operators manage emergency alarms

SCADA system responds to emergencies by running key applications such as disturbance monitoring analysis (including fault location), dynamic limit calculations for transformers and breakers based on real-time data from equipment monitors, and pre-arming of fast acting emergency automation

SCADA/EMS generates signals for emergency support by distribution utilities (according to the T&D contracts):

Operators perform system restorations based on system restoration plans prepared (authorized) by operation management

Smart Grid Characteristics	**Cybersecurity Objectives/Requirements**	**Potential Stakeholder Issues**
• Provides power quality • Optimizes asset utilization • Anticipates and responds to system disturbances	• Integrity is vital to the safety and reliability of the transmission system • Availability is critical to protective relaying (e.g. < 4 ms) and operator commands (e.g., 1 s) • Confidentiality is not important	• Customer safety • Customer device standards • Demand response acceptance by customers

Data Privacy Recommendations

No personal data, or information that could point to an individual or specific account, is involved within this use case.

Category: Transmission Operations	Privacy Use Case #39
Scenario: Wide Area Synchro-Phasor System	

Category Description

Transmission operations involve monitoring and controlling the transmission system using the SCADA system to monitor and control equipment in transmission substations. The EMS assesses the state of the transmission system using applications typically based on transmission power flow models. The SCADA/EMS is located in the utility's control center, while the key equipment is located in the transmission substations. Protective relaying equipment monitors the health of the transmission system and takes corrective action within a few milliseconds, such as tripping circuit breakers if power system anomalies are detected.

Scenario Description

The wide area synchro-phasor system provides synchronized and time-tagged voltage and current phasor measurements to any protection, control, or monitoring function that requires measurements taken from several locations, whose phase angles are measured against a common, system-wide reference. Present day implementation of many protection, control, or monitoring functions is hobbled by not having access to the phase angles between local and remote measurements. With system-wide phase angle information, they can be improved and extended. The essential concept behind this system is the system-wide synchronization of measurement sampling clocks to a common time reference.

Smart Grid Characteristics	Cybersecurity Objectives/Requirements	Potential Stakeholder Issues
• Provides power quality • Optimizes asset utilization • Anticipates and responds to system disturbances	• Integrity is vital to the safety and reliability of the transmission system • Availability is critical to protective relaying (e.g. < 4 ms) and operator commands (e.g., 1 s) • Confidentiality is not important	• Cybersecurity • Customer data privacy and security

Data Privacy Recommendations

No personal data, or information that could point to an individual or specific account, is involved within this use case.

Category: RTO/ISO Operations	Privacy Use Case #40

Scenario: RTO/ISO Management of Central and DER Generators and Storage

Category Description

An ISO/RTO control center that participates in the market and does not operate the market.

Scenario Description

RTOs and ISOs manage the scheduling and dispatch of central and distributed generation and storage. These functions include—

Real-time scheduling with the RTO/ISO (for nonmarket generation/storage)

Real-time commitment to RTO/ISO

Real-time dispatching by RTO/ISO for energy and ancillary services

Real-time plant operations in response to RTO/ISO dispatch commands

Real-time contingency and emergency operations

Black start (system restoration after blackout)

Emissions monitoring and control

Smart Grid Characteristics	Cybersecurity Objectives/Requirements	Potential Stakeholder Issues
• Provides power quality • Optimizes asset utilization • Anticipates and responds to system disturbances	• Integrity is vital to the safety and reliability of the transmission system • Availability is critical to operator commands (e.g. one second) • Confidentiality is not important	• Cybersecurity • Customer data privacy and security

40.1	**Data Privacy Recommendations** If an RTO/ISO has personal customer data associated with a DER asset, these entities would need to exercise the same security and privacy policies that utilities would follow as outlined in Use Case 28 (Distributed Energy Resources Management). However, if only aggregate and not individual data is available to RTO/ISOs, utilities or Third Parties, no privacy impacts would be applicable.

40.2	Analytics applications may be used to assess performance of various programs that engage customer DER assets. These programs may be managed by utilities, RTO/ISOs, or by Contracted Agents or authorized (by utility, RTO/ISO, or customer) Third Parties.
	   • Utilities should exercise their existing policies and practices for personal data when managing DER assets on behalf of customers. To the extent that customers may directly share personal data with Third Parties, the data is then outside of the control of the utilities.
	   • It will be important to ensure through ongoing audits that the Contracted Agents comply with all utility policies regarding any customer data for both privacy and security reasons.
	   • If the Third Party arrangement is between the customer (DER asset owner) and RTO/ISO, the RTO/ISO should emphasize that any consumer data that is shared directly by the consumer with that Third Party is outside of the control of the RTO/ISO.

	AICPA Principle	Applies: X	Notes
40.3	Management Principle	X	Policies and procedures for providing customer access to update their information, answering their questions, etc. should exist and be updated as

			appropriate whenever business and/or technology changes occur. Particularly for: 1) Direct monitoring and control of DER; 2) Shut-down or islanding verification for DER; and 3) Electric storage fill/draw management.
40.4	Notice Principle	X	Customers should be given notice for the types of data collected, how it will be used, shared and retained.
40.5	Choice and Consent Principle	X	Choice for how to notify. Also to provide consent for the method used to notify, if there are limits on the communication methods.
40.6	Collection Principle	X	Collect only the information necessary to allow for these communications.
40.7	Use and Retention Principle	X	Retain the data and associated communications only as long as necessary, and use the data only for the purposes for which it was collected.
40.8	Access Principle	X	Procedures should be established to allow customers to access and correct appropriate data.
40.9	Disclosure to Third Parties Principle	X	Customers should be given notice in cases where Third Parties have access to personal data, and understand the differences in how data may be handled by RTO/ISO-contracted Third Parties or by independent Third Parties.
40.10	Security for Privacy Principle	X	Associated data needs to have appropriate safeguards to ensure minimum access based upon job responsibilities, and also to protect against other types of unauthorized access. All personal data collected and created during these activities should be appropriately safeguarded to ensure unauthorized access to the data does not occur, to preserve integrity of the data, and to allow for appropriate availability.
40.11	Quality Principle	X	Ensure that collected personal data is accurate data, which may be accomplished by providing the customer with access and establishing appropriate procedures to correct any incorrect data.
40.12	Monitoring and Enforcement Principle	X	Applies for all types of entities (business or individual) that own assets that are connected as DER assets that can transact sale of electricity to RTO/ISOs.

Category: Asset Management	Privacy Use Case #41

Scenario: Utility Gathers Circuit and/or Transformer Load Profiles

Category Description

At a high level, asset management seeks a balance between asset performance, cost, and risk to achieve the utility's business objectives. A wide range of conventional functions, models, applications, devices, methodologies, and tools may be deployed to effectively plan, select, track, utilize, control, monitor, maintain, and protect utility assets.

For our purposes we will establish the scope for the asset management category to be the use of specific applications and devices by utility staff, such as condition monitoring equipment, protection equipment, event recorders, computer-based maintenance management systems (CMMS), display applications, ratings databases, analysis applications, and data marts (historians).

Scenario Description

Load profile data is important for the utility planning staff and is also used by the asset management team that is monitoring the utilization of the assets and by the SCADA/EMS and system operations team. This scenario involves the use of field devices that measure loading, the communications network that delivers the data, the historian database, and the load profile application and display capability that is either separate or an integrated part of the SCADA/EMS.

Load profile data may also be used by automatic switching applications that use load data to ensure new system configurations do not cause overloads.

Smart Grid Characteristics	Cybersecurity Objectives/Requirements	Potential Stakeholder Issues
• Provides power quality for the range of needs in a digital economy	• Data is accurate (integrity)	• Customer data privacy and security
• Optimizes asset utilization and operating efficiency	• Data is provided timely	• Cybersecurity
• Anticipates and responds to system disturbances in a self-correcting manner	• Customer data is kept private (confidentiality)	

41.1	**Data Privacy Recommendations** The potential exists for abuse of privacy of individual consumer data collected by field devices including event recorders, if, for example the event recorder was associated with an individual meter. This may be a situation that occurs in rural areas where one residential customer may be on a transformer or circuit; for agricultural operations; or for some C&I customers that have dedicated transformers or circuits. However, in general, this is not more or less than the same potential that exists regarding normal equipment that is used to deliver power and perform other functions such as billing. Possibly data stored locally in consumer's on-site equipment that is not available online could pose an additional threat. However, it is not clear that this is the case.
41.2	Generally, the collection of aggregate load data does not seem to pose a privacy risk to individual consumers. Thus, in general, this use case pertains less to the point that field equipment may be used than to the fact that load data is aggregated. From this point of view, AICPA principles would not seem to apply.
41.3	From the point of view of tools and activities related to assessing and maintaining equipment assets, again the privacy threat seems no more or less than that posed by normal energy delivery and data collection activities, again, such as billing.
41.4	The monitoring, collection and storage of information regarding equipment, networks or any other component of the technical service delivery environment would affect consumer privacy to no greater or lesser extent than applies to other data collected.

| | 41.5 | However, as noted above, if a transformer or circuit is associated with a single customer, the data collected here would have privacy impacts as there is no aggregation to be had. In these cases of single customer association to a transformer or circuit, privacy policies that govern meter data collection should be followed (Use Case 1). |

	AICPA Principle	Applies: X	Notes
41.6	Management Principle	X	For aggregate load data, this recommendation would not apply. For monitored equipment that is associated with a single customer, follow the recommendations for Use Case 1 to ensure data privacy.
41.7	Notice Principle	X	For aggregate load data, this recommendation would not apply. For monitored equipment that is associated with a single customer, follow the recommendations for Use Case 1 to ensure data privacy.
41.8	Choice and Consent Principle	X	For monitored equipment that is associated with a single customer, follow the recommendations for Use Case 1 to ensure data privacy.
41.9	Collection Principle	X	For monitored equipment that is associated with a single customer, follow the recommendations for Use Case 1 to ensure data privacy.
41.10	Use and Retention Principle	X	For aggregate load data, this recommendation would not apply. For monitored equipment that is associated with a single customer, follow the recommendations for Use Case 1 to ensure data privacy.
41.11	Access Principle	X	For aggregate load data, this recommendation would not apply. For monitored equipment that is associated with a single customer, follow the recommendations for Use Case 1 to ensure data privacy.
41.12	Disclosure to Third Parties Principle	X	For aggregate load data, this recommendation would not apply. For monitored equipment that is associated with a single customer, follow the recommendations for Use Case 1 to ensure data privacy.
41.13	Security for Privacy Principle	X	For aggregate load data, this recommendation would not apply. For monitored equipment that is associated with a single customer, follow the recommendations for Use Case 1 to ensure data privacy. All personal data collected and created during these activities must be appropriately safeguarded to ensure unauthorized access to the data does not occur, to preserve integrity of the data, and to allow for appropriate availability.

41.14	Quality Principle	X	For aggregate load data, this recommendation would not apply. For monitored equipment that is associated with a single customer, follow the recommendations for Use Case 1 to ensure data privacy.
41.15	Monitoring and Enforcement Principle	X	For aggregate load data, this recommendation would not apply. For monitored equipment that is associated with a single customer, follow the recommendations for Use Case 1 to ensure data privacy.

Category: Asset Management	Privacy Use Case #42

Scenario: Utility Makes Decisions on Asset Replacement Based on a Range of Inputs Including Comprehensive Offline and Online Condition Data and Analysis Applications

Category Description

At a high level, asset management seeks a balance between asset performance, cost, and risk to achieve the utilities business objectives. A wide range of conventional functions, models, applications, devices, methodologies, and tools may be deployed to effectively plan, select, track, utilize, control, monitor, maintain, and protect utility assets.

For our purposes we will establish the scope for the asset management category to be the use of specific applications and devices by utility staff such as condition monitoring equipment, protection equipment, event recorders, CMMS, display applications, ratings databases, analysis applications and data marts (historians).

Scenario Description

When decisions on asset replacement become necessary, the system operator, asset management, apparatus engineering, and maintenance engineering staff work closely together with the objective of maximizing the life and utilization of the asset while avoiding an unplanned outage and damage to the equipment.

This scenario involves the use of online condition monitoring devices for the range of assets monitored, offline test results, mobile work force technologies, the communications equipment used to collect the online data, data marts (historian databases) to store and trend data as well as condition analysis applications, CMMS applications, display applications, and SCADA/EMS.

Smart Grid Characteristics	Cybersecurity Objectives/Requirements	Potential Stakeholder Issues
• Provides power quality for the range of needs in a digital economy • Optimizes asset utilization and operating efficiency • Anticipates and responds to system disturbances in a self-correcting manner	• Data provided is accurate and trustworthy • Data is provided timely	• Cybersecurity • Customer data privacy and security

42.1	**Data Privacy Recommendations** Most scenarios would adhere to the recommendations outlined in Use Case 43. However, the same exceptions apply as noted in that use case. If an asset is associated with a single customer, the data collected here would have privacy impacts as there is no aggregation to be had. In these cases of single customer association to an asset, privacy policies that govern meter data collection should be followed (Use Case 1). Please follow the recommendations for the AICPA principles outlined in Use Case 1 when equipment is associated with a single customer.

Category: Asset Management	Privacy Use Case #43

Scenario: Utility Performs Localized Load Reduction to Relieve Circuit and/or Transformer Overloads

Category Description

At a high level, asset management seeks a balance between asset performance, cost, and risk to achieve the utilities business objectives. A wide range of conventional functions, models, applications, devices, methodologies, and tools may be deployed to effectively plan, select, track, utilize, control, monitor, maintain, and protect utility assets.

For our purposes we will establish the scope for the asset management category to be the use of specific applications and devices by utility staff, such as condition monitoring equipment, protection equipment, event recorders, CMMS, display applications, ratings databases, analysis applications, and data marts (historians). Advanced functions that are associated with asset management include dynamic rating and end of life estimation.

Scenario Description

Transmission capacity can become constrained due to a number of system-level scenarios and result in an overload situation on lines and substation equipment. Circuit and/or transformer overloads at the distribution level can occur when higher than anticipated customer loads are placed on a circuit or when operator or automatic switching actions are implemented to change the network configuration.

Traditional load reduction systems are used to address generation shortfalls and other system-wide issues. Localized load reduction can be a key tool enabling the operator to temporarily curtail the load in a specific area to reduce the impact on specific equipment. This scenario describes the integrated use of the AMI system, the demand response system, other load reduction systems, and the SCADA/EMS to achieve this goal.

Smart Grid Characteristics	Cybersecurity Objectives/Requirements	Potential Stakeholder Issues
• Provides power quality for the range of needs in a digital economy • Optimizes asset utilization and operating efficiency • Anticipates and responds to system disturbances in a self-correcting manner	• Load reduction messages are accurate and trustworthy • Customer's data is kept private • Demand Response (DR) messages are received and processed timely	• Demand response acceptance by customers • Customer data privacy and security • Retail Electric Supplier access • Customer data access

43.1	**Data Privacy Recommendations** Overall the recommendations are similar to those for Use Case #42. However, DR programs are associated with individual customers. There could be other load reduction programs such as AC or pool pump cycling that also apply to specific customers. Therefore, personal data including energy data consumption needs protection as outlined in these recommendations for DR programs.
43.2	Demand Response behaviors are customer-specific and participation in these programs may be directly managed by a utility; by a Contracted Agent on behalf of the utility; or by a DR aggregator (Third Party) acting independently from a utility.
43.3	DR participation typically involves a financial transaction, so accuracy of meter read data is extremely important.
43.4	Meter read data is protected information regardless of type of DR program, or if the participant is working with a utility, a Contracted Agent of a utility, or a DR aggregator not affiliated with a utility. Similarly, choice and consent information requires that any DR participant has been notified and consented to Third Party access to the data identified as necessary for that activity.
43.5	Meter reading for DR is an ongoing activity, so it is important that utilities create a monitoring and enforcement process that ensures compliance with privacy protections on an ongoing basis.

			Applies: X	Notes
43.6		Contracted Agents may be given access to meter reading data for DR program purposes. These agents should also conform and comply with utility privacy policies, and customers must be notified about the disclosure of their information to these Contracted Agents. Notification may occur when the customer enters into a contract with a utility.		

		AICPA Principle	Applies: X	Notes
43.7		Management Principle	X	Policies and procedures should exist for the data collected, used, shared and stored. A position should exist with assigned accountability for ensuring such policies and procedures exist, are effectively communicated to all personnel, and are followed. For aggregate load data, this recommendation would not apply.
43.8		Notice Principle	X	Would have to be provided for all meter reading in DR scenarios. Customers should be given notice for the types of data collected, how it will be used, shared and retained. For aggregate load data, this recommendation would not apply.
43.9		Choice and Consent Principle	X	Ensure that when customers sign up for DR service that this choice and consent requirement is met.
43.10		Collection Principle	X	Data collection may change as new applications, technologies, or programs are made available. Utility policy should indicate that collection purposes may change over time and that utilities will notify customers of any proposed changes that may impact collection in order to secure an updated choice and consent.
43.11		Use and Retention Principle	X	Retention may be impacted by time frames to record and compensate for DR scenarios. For aggregate load data, this recommendation would not apply.
43.12		Access Principle	X	For aggregate load data, this recommendation would not apply.
43.13		Disclosure to Third Parties Principle	X	DR payments to customers may be considered revenue or income and thus subject to tax laws, or garnishments for child support, legal claims, etc. Some of the legal implications may not require implicit or explicit consent. For aggregate load data, this recommendation would not apply.
43.14		Security for Privacy Principle	X	All personal data collected and created during these

			activities must be appropriately safeguarded to ensure unauthorized access to the data does not occur, to preserve integrity of the data, and to allow for appropriate availability.	
			For aggregate load data, this recommendation would not apply.	
43.15	**Quality Principle**	X	Data quality is important for DR program participation. Ensure that collected personal data is accurate data, which may be accomplished by providing the customer with access and establishing appropriate procedures to correct any incorrect data.	
			For aggregate load data, this recommendation would not apply.	
43.16	**Monitoring and Enforcement Principle**	X	DR participation may be an ongoing activity. Utilities should create a practice of regular monitoring and provide audits of Contracted Agents. Utilities should also advise that customers may have authorized DR aggregators to have access to meter data. Policy guidance should be defined for where utility responsibility for meter data ends and what rights customers have regarding their data once they have given authorization for a Third Party to access that info.	
			For aggregate load data, this recommendation would not apply.	

Category: Asset Management	Privacy Use Case #44

Scenario: Utility System Operator Determines Level of Severity for an Impending Asset Failure and Takes Corrective Action

Category Description

At a high level, asset management seeks a balance between asset performance, cost, and risk to achieve the utilities business objectives. A wide range of conventional functions, models, applications, devices, methodologies, and tools may be deployed to effectively plan, select, track, utilize, control, monitor, maintain, and protect utility assets.

For our purposes we will establish the scope for the asset management category to be the use of specific applications and devices by utility staff, such as condition monitoring equipment, protection equipment, event recorders, CMMS, display applications, ratings databases, analysis applications, and data marts (historians).

Scenario Description

When pending asset failure can be anticipated, the system operator, asset management, apparatus engineering, and maintenance engineering staff work closely together with the objective of avoiding an unplanned outage while avoiding further damage to the equipment.

This scenario involves the use of online condition monitoring devices for the range of assets monitored, offline test results, mobile workforce technologies, the communications equipment used to collect the online data, data marts (historian databases) to store, and trend data, as well as condition analysis applications, CMMS applications, display applications, and SCADA/EMS.

Smart Grid Characteristics	**Objectives/Requirements**	**Potential Stakeholder Issues**
• Provides power quality for the range of needs in a digital economy • Optimizes asset utilization and operating efficiency • Anticipates and responds to system disturbances in a self-correcting manner	• Asset information provided is accurate and trustworthy • Asset information is provided timely	• Cybersecurity • Customer data privacy and security

44.1	**Data Privacy Recommendations** Many aspects of this use case are the same as Use case #43. If notification is given to customers about pending corrective actions, utility practices regarding protection of personal data should be exercised.
44.2	Utility resources will consider critical needs flags for residential, commercial, or industrial customers such as home health equipment that requires electricity, health care facilities, etc in determining corrective actions for pending asset failures. Certain customers may be the last to lose electricity as part of any corrective action, or others may be identified as first for restoration of services because of their special circumstances. Utilities already have life-safety policies in place for planned and unplanned outage recovery. These policies should be reviewed to identify any exposure of Personally Identifiable Information. Except as necessary to implement the life-safety policy to preserve the health of the customer, personal data should be removed from records.
44.3	Utility resources will also need to know if there are any customer assets that produce or store energy for two purposes: a) for inclusion in outage recovery plans, and b) for worker safety. Again, information should be limited to identification of asset at customer address and enabled connections to the distribution grid, but limit exposure of personal data.

	AICPA Principle	Applies: X	Notes
44.4	Management Principle	X	Customer records may include information about life-safety that may be accessed by utility resources in this scenario. Utility resources will need to be trained to comply with all data privacy policies, and existing utility policies regarding policies for corrective actions must be reviewed for compliance with data privacy policies. For aggregate load data, this recommendation would not apply.
44.5	Notice Principle	X	When corrective action is about to be taken, the utility would be required to give notice. However, this does not trigger specific privacy or security issues. Utilities should provide an explanation regarding need to know about life-safety situations that require constant electricity for equipment. For aggregate load data, this recommendation would not apply.
44.6	Choice and Consent Principle	X	Utilities should indicate that customers who do not provide consent to collection of information regarding healthcare needs may not receive any special consideration in outage and restoration scheduling.
44.7	Collection Principle	X	Utilities should indicate to customers that collection of information regarding healthcare needs is necessary for planned and unplanned outage restoration plans.
44.8	Use and Retention Principle	X	For aggregate load data, this recommendation would not apply.
44.9	Access Principle	X	For aggregate load data, this recommendation would not apply.
44.10	Disclosure to Third Parties Principle	X	If Third Parties are involved in outage or restoration services, care must be taken that personal data is not disclosed. For aggregate load data, this recommendation would not apply.

44.11	**Security for Privacy Principle**	X	Since information about health may be involved, this principle must be emphasized in all processes. All personal data collected and created during these activities must be appropriately safeguarded to ensure unauthorized access to the data does not occur, to preserve integrity of the data, and to allow for appropriate availability. For aggregate load data, this recommendation would not apply.
44.12	**Quality Principle**	X	Customers move, conditions change, so any flags about health conditions must be tied to the customer, not to the meter. Ensure that collected personal data is accurate data, which may be accomplished by providing the customer with access and establishing appropriate procedures to correct any incorrect data. For aggregate load data, this recommendation would not apply.
44.13	**Monitoring and Enforcement Principle**	X	For aggregate load data, this recommendation would not apply.

APPENDIX F: SUMMARY OF THE SMART GRID HIGH-LEVEL CONSUMER-TO-UTILITY PRIVACY IMPACT ASSESSMENT

The following points summarize the PIA findings and recommendations as presented in the draft *NIST Smart Grid High Level Consumer-to-Utility Privacy Impact Assessment (draft v3.0)*[157] in relation to the privacy principles used as the basis for the PIA. Each privacy principle statement is followed by the related findings from the PIA and the suggested privacy practices that may serve to mitigate the privacy risks associated with each principle:

1. **Management and Accountability**: Organizations that access or provide data to the smart grid should appoint personnel to a position responsible for ensuring that documented information security and privacy policies and practices exist and are followed. Information security and personal information privacy practices should include requirements for regular training and ongoing awareness activities. Audit functions should also be present to monitor the smart grid data access activities.

   Findings:

   Some organizations that participate within the smart grid (1) do not have documented information security and privacy responsibilities and authority within the organization; (2) do not have information security and privacy training and awareness programs; and (3) do not monitor access to smart grid data.

   Privacy Practices Recommendations:

   - **Assign privacy responsibility**. Each organization collecting or using smart grid data from or about consumer locations should assign responsibility to a position or person to ensure that privacy policies and practices exist and are followed. Responsibilities should include documenting, ensuring the implementation of, and managing requirements for regular training and ongoing awareness activities.

   - **Establish privacy audits**. Audit functions should be modified to monitor all energy data access.

   - **Establish law enforcement request policies and procedures**. Organizations accessing, storing, or processing energy data should include specific documented incident response procedures for incidents involving energy data.

2. **Notice and Purpose:** A clearly specified notice should exist and be shared with the customer in advance of the collection, use, retention, and sharing of energy data and personal information.

   Findings:

   The data obtained from systems and devices that are part of the smart grid and accompanying potential and actual uses for that data create the need for organizations to

---

[157] R. Herold, C. Veltsos, and W. Pyles, *NIST Smart Grid High Level Consumer-to-Utility Privacy Impact Assessment DRAFT v3.0*, September 9, 2009, http://collaborate.nist.gov/twiki-sggrid/pub/SmartGrid/CSCTGPrivacy/NIST_High_Level_PIA_Report_-_Herold_09_09_09_w-edits.doc [accessed 8/11/2014].

be more transparent and clearly provide notice to the customer documenting the types of information items collected and the purposes for collecting the data.

Privacy Practices Recommendations:

- **Provide notification for the personal information collected.** Any organization collecting energy data from or about consumers should establish a process to notify consumer account inhabitants and person(s) paying the bills (which may be different entities), when appropriate, of the data being collected, why it is necessary to collect the data, and the intended use, retention, and sharing of the data. This notification should include information about when and how information may or may not be shared with law enforcement officials. Individuals should be notified before the time of collection.

- **Provide notification for new information use purposes and collection.** Organizations should update consumer notifications whenever they want to start using existing collected data for materially different purposes other than those the consumer has previously authorized. Also, organizations should notify the recipients of services whenever they want to start collecting additional data beyond that already being collected, along with providing a clear explanation for why the additional data is necessary and what it will be used for.

3. **Choice and Consent**: The organization should describe the choices available to consumers with regard to the use of their associated energy data that could be used to reveal personal information and obtain explicit consent, if possible, or implied consent when this is not feasible, with respect to the collection, use, and disclosure of this information.

Findings:

Currently it is not apparent that utilities or other entities within the smart grid obtain consent to use the personal information generated and collected for purposes other than billing. As smart meters and other smart devices increase capabilities and expand sharing of the data throughout the smart grid, organizations should establish processes to give consumers a choice, where possible and feasible, about the types of data collected and how it is used.

Privacy Practices Recommendation:

- **Provide notification about choices.** The consumer notification should include a clearly worded description to the recipients of services notifying them of (1) any choices available to them about information being collected and obtaining explicit consent when possible; and (2) explaining when and why data items are or may be collected and used without obtaining consent, such as when certain pieces of information are needed to restore service in a timely fashion.

4. **Collection and Scope**: Only personal information that is required to fulfill the stated purpose should be collected from consumers. This information should be obtained by lawful and fair means and, where appropriate and possible, with the knowledge or consent of the consumer.

Findings:

In the current operation of the electric utilities, data taken from traditional meters consists of basic data usage readings required to create bills. In the future, smart meters may be enabled to collect other types of data.[158] Home power generation services will also likely increase the amount of information created and shared. Some of this additional data may constitute personal information or may be used to determine personal activities. Because of the associated privacy risks, only the minimum amount of data necessary for services, provisioning, and billing should be collected.

Privacy Practices Recommendations:

- **Limit the collection** of data to only that necessary for the provision of electric service to the customer and operations, including planning and management, improving energy use and efficiency, account management, and billing.

- **Obtain the data** by lawful and fair means and, where appropriate and possible, with the knowledge or consent of the consumer.

5. **Use and Retention**: Information within the smart grid should be used or disclosed only for the purposes for which it was collected. smart grid data should be aggregated in such a way that personal information or activities cannot be determined, or anonymized wherever possible to limit the potential for computer matching of records. Personal information should be kept only as long as is necessary to fulfill the purposes for which it was collected.

Findings:

In the current operation of the electric utilities, data taken from traditional meters is used to create consumer bills and determine energy use trends. The smart grid will provide data that allows customers to take greater control of their usage or consumption by enabling them to make more informed decisions and actions..

Privacy Practices Recommendations:

- **Review privacy policies and procedures**. Every organization with access to smart grid data should review existing information security and privacy policies to determine how they may need to be modified. This review should include privacy policies already in place in other industries, such as financial and healthcare, which could provide a model for the smart grid.

- **Limit information retention**. Data, and subsequently created information that reveals personal information or activities from and about a specific consumer location, should be retained only for as long as necessary to fulfill the purposes that have been communicated to the energy consumers. When no longer necessary, consistent with data retention and destruction requirements, the data and information, in all forms, should be irreversibly destroyed. This becomes more important as energy data becomes more granular, more refined, and has more potential for commercial uses.

---

[158] For more discussion on smart meter collection capabilities, see §5.3.1.

6. **Individual Access**: Organizations should provide a process to allow for individuals to request access to see their corresponding personal information and energy data, and to request the correction of real or perceived inaccuracies. Individuals should also be informed about parties with whom their associated personal information and energy data has been shared.

Findings:

In the current operation of the electric utilities, data may be manually read from the meters. Consumers also have the capability to read the meters through physical access to the meters. Under a smart grid implementation, smart meter data may be stored in multiple locations to which the consumer may not have ready access.

Privacy Practices Recommendations:

- **Consumer access.** Any organization possessing energy data about consumers should provide a process to allow consumers access to the corresponding energy data for their utilities account.

- **Dispute resolution.** Smart grid entities should establish documented dispute resolution procedures for energy consumers to follow.

7. **Disclosure and Limiting Use**: Personal information should not be disclosed to any other parties except those identified in the notice and only for the purposes originally specified or with the explicit informed consent of the service recipient.

Findings:

As smart grid implementations collect more granular and detailed information, this information is capable of revealing activities and equipment usage in a given location. As this information may reveal business activities, manufacturing procedures, and personal activities, significant privacy concerns and risks arise when the information is disclosed without the knowledge, consent, and authority of the individuals or organizations to which the information applies.

Privacy Practices Recommendation:

- **Limit information use.** Data on energy or other smart grid service activities should be used or disclosed only for the authorized purposes for which it was collected.

- **Disclosure.** Data should be divulged to or shared only with those parties authorized to receive it and with whom the organizations have told the recipients of services it would be shared.

8. **Security and Safeguards**: Smart grid energy data and personal information, in all forms, should be protected from loss and theft, and from unauthorized access, disclosure, copying, use, or modification.

Findings:

Smart grid data may be transmitted to and stored in multiple locations throughout the smart grid. Establishing strong security safeguards is necessary to protect energy data from loss and theft, and from unauthorized access, disclosure, copying, use, or modification.

Privacy Practices Recommendations:

- **Associate energy data with individuals only when and where required**. For example only link equipment data with a location or consumer account when needed for billing, service restoration, or other operational needs. This practice is already common in the utility industry and should be maintained and applied to all entities obtaining or using this data as the smart grid is further deployed.

- **De-identify information**. Energy data and any resulting information, such as monthly charges for service, collected as a result of smart grid operations should be aggregated and anonymized by removing personal information elements wherever possible to ensure that energy data from specific consumer locations is limited appropriately. This may not be possible for some business activities, such as for billing.

- **Safeguard personal information**. All organizations collecting, processing, or handling energy data and other personal information from or about consumer locations should ensure that all information collected and subsequently created about the recipients of smart grid services is appropriately protected in all forms from loss, theft, unauthorized access, disclosure, copying, use, or modification. While this practice is commonly in effect in the utility industry, as other entities recognize commercial uses for this information, they are responsible for adopting appropriate requirements and controls. In addition, given the growing granularity of information from smart grid operations, the responsibility for these existing policies should be reviewed and updated as necessary.

- **Do not use personal information for research purposes**. Any organization collecting energy data and other personal information from or about consumer locations should refrain from using actual consumer data for research until it has been anonymized and/or sufficiently aggregated to assure to a reasonable degree the inability to link detailed data to individuals. Current and planned research is being conducted both inside and outside the utility industry on the smart grid, its effects upon demand response, and other topics. The use of actual information that can be linked to a consumer in this research increases the risk of inadvertent exposure via traditional information sharing that occurs within the research community.

9. **Accuracy and Quality**: Processes should be implemented by all businesses participating within the smart grid to ensure as much as possible that energy data and personal information are accurate, complete, and relevant for the purposes identified in the notice, and that it remains accurate throughout the life of the energy data and personal information while within the control of the organization.

Findings:

The data collected from smart meters and related equipment will potentially be stored in multiple locations throughout the smart grid. Smart grid data may be automatically collected in a variety of ways. Establishing strong security safeguards will be necessary to protect the information and the information's accuracy. Since smart grid data may be stored in many locations, and therefore be accessed by many different individuals/entities and used for a wide variety of purposes, personal information may be inappropriately modified. Automated decisions about energy use could be detrimental for consumers (e.g., restricted power, thermostats turned to dangerous levels, etc.) if it happens that decisions about energy usage are based upon inaccurate information.

Privacy Practices Recommendation:

- **Keep information accurate and complete**. Any organization collecting energy data from or about consumer locations should establish policies and procedures to ensure that the smart grid data collected from and subsequently created about recipients of services is accurate, complete, and relevant for the identified purposes for which they were obtained, and that it remains accurate throughout the life of the smart grid data within the control of the organization.

10. **Openness, Monitoring, and Challenging Compliance**: Privacy policies should be made available to service recipients. These service recipients should be given the ability to review and a process by which to challenge an organization's compliance with the applicable privacy protection legal requirements, along with the associated organizational privacy policies and the organizations' actual privacy practices.[159]

Findings:

Currently electric utilities follow a wide variety of methods and policies for communicating to energy consumers how energy data and personal information is used. The data collected from smart meters and related smart grid equipment will potentially be stored in multiple locations throughout the smart grid, possibly within multiple states and outside the United States. This complicates the openness of organizational privacy compliance and of a consumer being able to challenge the organization's compliance with privacy policies, practices, and applicable legal requirements.

---

[159] Using its authority under Section 5 of the FTC Act, which prohibits unfair or deceptive practices, the Federal Trade Commission has brought a number of cases to enforce the promises in privacy statements, including promises about the security of consumers' personal information.

APPENDIX G: PRIVACY RELATED DEFINITIONS

Because "privacy" and associated terms mean many different things to different audiences, it is important to establish some definitions for the terms used within this volume to create a common base of understanding for their use. The energy-specific terms are defined within Appendix J. The following definitions of the terms related to privacy as they are used within this volume.

Confidential Information

"Confidential information" is information for which access should be limited to only those with a business need to know, and that could result in compromise to a system, data file, application, or other business function if inappropriately shared. Confidential information is a common term used by businesses as one of their data classification labels. For example, the formula for Coca-Cola is confidential. The plans for a new type of wind turbine, that have not yet been publicized, may be confidential.

Market data that does not include customer specific details may be confidential. Many types of personal information can also fall within the "Confidential Information" data classification label. Information can be confidential at one point in the information lifecycle, and then become public at another point in the lifecycle. Information that an organization does not want shared outside of their organization, which they consider to be proprietary, is considered to be confidential information. Confidential information must have appropriate safeguards applied to ensure only those with a business need to fulfill their job responsibilities can access the information.

Contracted Agent

An entity under contract with the Third Party to perform services or provide products using CEUD. In some industries, Contracted Agents are referred to as Business Partners or Business Associates.

Customer

Any entity that takes electric service for its own consumption.

Customer/Consumer[160] Energy Usage Data (CEUD)

Energy usage information and data identifiable to a premise or an individual customer obtained without the involvement of the utility.

Individual

Any specific person.

Personal Information

"Personal information" is a broad term that includes personally identifiable information (PII) and addition to other types of information. Personal information may reveal information about, or describe, an individual, or group of individuals, such as a family, household, or residence. This

---

[160] There may be a legal issue in terms of who has access to this data. There may be situations in which the Customer and the consumer are not the same and that one might want to restrict access to the CEUD. These recommended practices are not designed to determine legal issues.

information includes, but is not limited to, such information as name, Social Security number, physical description, home address, home telephone number, education, financial matters, medical or employment history, statements made by or attributed to the individual, and utility usage information, all of which could be used to impact privacy.

Personal information includes not only PII, as defined below, but also information that may not be specifically covered within existing laws, regulations or industry standards, but does have recognized needs for privacy protections. For example, a social networking site may reveal information about energy usage or creation.

Personal information within the smart grid includes, but is not be limited to, information that reveals details, either explicitly or implicitly, about a specific individual's or specific group's type of premises and energy use activities. This is expanded beyond the normal "individual" component because there could be negative privacy impacts for all individuals within one dwelling or building structure. This can include items such as energy use patterns, characteristics related to energy consumption through smart appliances, and other types of activities. The energy use pattern could be considered unique to a household or premises similar to how a fingerprint or DNA is unique to an individual.

Personal information also includes energy use patterns that might identify specific appliances or devices that may indicate a medical problem of a household member or visitor; the inappropriate use of an employer issued device to an employee that is a household member or visitor; or the use of a forbidden appliance in a rented household. Smart appliances and devices will create additional information that may reveal a significant amount of additional personal information about an individual, such as what food they eat, how much they exercise, and detailed physical information. This could potentially become a privacy issue in a university, office setting, healthcare facility, and so on.

Personally Identifiable Information (PII)

"PII" is information that has been defined within existing laws, regulations, and industry standards, as those specific types of information items that can be tied to a unique individual in certain situations and has some current form of legal protection as a result. For example, the U.S. Health Insurance Portability and Accountability Act (HIPAA) of 1996 requires the following types of protected health information[161] to be safeguarded:

- Names

- All geographic subdivisions smaller than a State, including street address, city, county, precinct, zip code, and their equivalent geo-codes

- All elements of dates (except year) for dates directly related to an individual, including birth date, admission date, discharge date, date of death;

- Telephone numbers

---

[161]Per the current (with Omnibus Final Rule provisions implemented) HIPAA requirements located at 45 CFR § 164.514 (b), these specific items must all be removed to be considered as de-identified; and no longer considered to be protected health information. See the full text in U.S. Department of Health and Human Services, Office for Civil Rights, *HIPAA Administrative Simplification*, March 2013, http://www.hhs.gov/ocr/privacy/hipaa/administrative/combined/hipaa-simplification-201303.pdf [accessed 8/11/2014].

- Fax numbers
- Electronic mail addresses
- Social security numbers
- Medical record numbers
- Health plan beneficiary numbers
- Account numbers (including energy bill account numbers, credit card numbers, and so on)
- Certificate and license numbers
- Vehicle identifiers and serial numbers, including license plate numbers
- Device Identifiers and serial numbers
- Web Universal Resource Locators (URLs)
- Internet Protocol (IP) address numbers
- Biometric identifiers, including finger and voice prints;
- Full face photographic images and any comparable images;
- Any genetic information that is unique to an individual;
- Any other unique identifying number, characteristic, or code.

With the exception of those terms specifically naming energy, the above are the items defined within HIPAA, which arguably has the widest definition of PII within the existing U.S. federal regulations. More identifiers may be considered to be PII as the smart grid evolves and as regulations change.

Privacy Impact Assessment

A privacy impact assessment (PIA) is a structured, repeatable, type of analysis of how information relating to or about individuals or groups of individuals is handled. A report, similar to that of an audit report, is generated to describe the types of privacy risks discovered based upon each privacy category, to document the findings, and then to provide recommendations for mitigating the privacy risk findings. Common goals of a PIA include:

1. Determining if the information handling and use within the identified scope complies with legal, regulatory, and policy requirements regarding privacy;

2. Determining the risks and effects of collecting, maintaining, and disseminating information in identifiable or clear text form in an electronic information system or groups of systems; and

3. Examining and evaluating the protections and alternative processes for handling information to mitigate the identified potential privacy risks.

Privacy Use Case

A method of looking at data flows that will help Third Parties to rigorously track data flows and the privacy implications of collecting and using data, and will help the organization to address and mitigate the associated privacy risks within common technical design and business practices. Use cases can help smart grid architects and engineers build privacy protections into the smart grid.

Private Information

"Private information" is information that is associated with individuals or groups of individuals, which could reveal details of their lives or other characteristics that could impact them. Private information is not necessarily information that, on its own, is linked to individuals directly. "Private information" is a term used by individuals that indicates information they have determined they do not want others to know, and is not a term used as a data classification type by business organizations.

Private information is a broad and general term that is more ambiguously used than other privacy terms. For example, the combination to a bank safety deposit lock is private, but the combination number itself does not point to any specific individual. As another example, some individuals consider how they voted in presidential elections to be private information that they do not want any others to know. Other individuals, however, communicate how they voted on campaign buttons or t-shirts for the world to see because they have determined that, for them, it is not private information.

Individuals often consider PII to be a type of private information, and personal information could also be private information. For utilities, market data that includes information about a negotiated price for a customer is likely considered by the customer to be private information; they may not want their friends, neighbors or the general public to see this information. Smart device data from within consumer dwellings could also be a type of private information. Private information could cause harm to the associated individuals or groups if misused or accessed by those who do not have a business need.

Third Party

An entity — other than the electric utility or other electricity provider for a given premise, the applicable regulatory authority, an independent system operator (ISO) or another regional entity— that performs services or provides products using CEUD. This definition does not include Contracted Agents of an electric utility or electricity provider.

Smart Grid Entity

An entity that participates within the smart grid and that collects, stores, uses, shares, transfers across borders, or retains smart grid data.

www.ingramcontent.com/pod-product-compliance
Lightning Source LLC
Chambersburg PA
CBHW080414060326
40689CB00019B/4236